Verse by Verse Commentary on

GALATIANS

AND

EPHESIANS

Enduring Word Commentary Series

By David Guzik

The grass withers, the flower fades,
but the word of our God stands forever.
Isaiah 40:8

Commentary on Galatians and Ephesians

Copyright ©2019 by David Guzik

Printed in the United States of America
or in the United Kingdom

Print Edition ISBN: 1-56599-034-X

Enduring Word

5662 Calle Real #184

Goleta, CA 93117

Electronic Mail: ewm@enduringword.com

Internet Home Page: www.enduringword.com

Scripture references, unless noted, are from the New King James Version of the Bible, copyright ©1979, 1980, 1982, Thomas Nelson, Inc., Publisher.

Contents

Dedicated to
Randy Guzik

Galatians 1 – Challenging a Different Gospel

A. Introduction to the Apostle Paul's letter to the Galatians.

1. (1-2) The writer and the readers.

Paul, an apostle (not from men nor through man, but through Jesus Christ and God the Father who raised Him from the dead), and all the brethren who are with me, To the churches of Galatia.

a. **Paul**: The apostolic authorship of this magnificent letter is virtually unquestioned, even by more skeptical scholars.

i. Galatians has been called the "Declaration of Independence of Christian liberty." The great reformer Martin Luther especially loved this letter; he called Galatians his "Catherine von Bora" after his wife; because, he said, "I am married to it." Leon Morris wrote, "Galatians is a passionate letter, the outpouring of the soul of a preacher on fire for his Lord and deeply committed to bringing his hearers to an understanding of what saving faith is."

ii. Many scholars believe that Galatians was written in the late 40's or the early 50's. An approximate date of A.D. 50 is often given. It seems that Paul wrote this letter before the Jerusalem Council mentioned in Acts 15, because although he mentions several trips to Jerusalem, he makes no mention of the council. Because the Jerusalem Council of Acts 15 dealt with the exact issues Paul writes about, it would seem strange if the Council had already happened, yet he made no mention of it. If it is true that Galatians was written around A.D. 50, then Paul would have been a Christian for about 15 years, being converted on the road to Damascus around A.D. 35.

b. **Paul, an apostle**: This emphasis on Paul's apostolic credentials is important. Paul had strong words for these Galatians, and they had to understand that he wrote with authority; indeed, *apostolic* authority. Paul expected that Christians would respect his authority as **an apostle** of Jesus Christ.

> i. "The word *apostle* as Paul uses it here does not merely refer to one who has a message to announce, but to an appointed representative with an official status who is provided with the credentials of his office." (Wuest)

> ii. It is our duty to also respect Paul's authority as an apostle. We do this by regarding this ancient letter as the Word of God, and by taking it seriously to heart.

c. **Not from men or through man, but through Jesus Christ and God the Father**: Paul's calling as an apostle was not **from** man, nor was it **through** man. It didn't *originate* with man, and it didn't *come through* man. It originated with God and came directly from God. His standing as an apostle was not based on opinion polls and it did not come from any human council. It was based on a Divine call, made through both the Father and the Son.

> i. "The bluntness of Paul's denial is due to the charge... that Paul was not a genuine apostle because not one of the twelve." (Robertson)

> ii. "When I was a young man I thought Paul was making too much of his call. I did not understand his purpose. I did not then realize the importance of the ministry... We exalt our calling, not to gain glory among men, or money, or satisfaction, or favor, but because people need to be assured that the words we speak are the words of God. This is no sinful pride. It is holy pride." (Martin Luther)

d. **And all the brethren who are with me**: Paul gave a greeting from **all the brethren who are with him**; but the use of *I* in this letter (such as in Galatians 1:6) shows that it was not really a "team effort" written by Paul and his coworkers. Paul wrote this letter and he sent greetings from his friends as a matter of courtesy.

e. **To the churches of Galatia**: This wasn't written to a *single* church in a *single* city. For example, 1 Thessalonians is addressed to *the church of the Thessalonians* (1 Thessalonians 1:1). But this was addressed to **the churches of Galatia**, because **Galatia** was a *region*, not a *city* and there were several **churches** among the cities of **Galatia**.

> i. "During the third century BC some Celtic peoples (or Gauls) migrated to this area and, after fighting with the people they encountered, they settled into the northern part of Asia Minor. In due course they came into conflict with the Romans, who defeated them, and from this time they remained under the authority of the Romans as a dependent

kingdom. The name 'Galatia' covered the territory settled by the Gauls." (Morris)

ii. There were essentially two regions of **Galatia**, one to the north (including the cities of Pessinus, Ancyra and Tavium) and one to the south (including the cities of Pisidian Antioch, Iconium, Lystra, and Derbe). There has been considerable – though mostly unimportant – debate as to if Galatians was written to the cities of the northern region or the southern region.

iii. "It is clear that Paul intended his words to have a wide circulation in the region of Galatia. The letter would be taken to each centre and read there, or several copies would be made and one taken to each church." (Morris)

f. **Of Galatia**: Paul was in southern Galatia on his first missionary journey (Acts 13:13-14:23) and he went through northern Galatia on his second (Acts 16:6) and third (Acts 18:23) missionary journeys.

i. In the end it doesn't really matter if the letter was written to the northern or southern regions of Galatia. We may not be able to know and it doesn't really matter, because this is a letter that has something to say to *every Christian*. The debate between northern Galatia and southern Galatia is interesting for scholars and adds *some* understanding to the letter, but not much.

2. (3-5) Paul sends his apostolic greeting.

Grace to you and peace from God the Father and our Lord Jesus Christ, who gave Himself for our sins, that He might deliver us from this present evil age, according to the will of our God and Father, to whom *be* glory forever and ever. Amen.

a. **Grace to you and peace**: This was Paul's familiar greeting, drawing from the traditional greetings in both Greek culture (**grace**) and Jewish culture (**peace**). Paul used this exact phrase five other times in the New Testament.

i. Paul used the word **grace** more than 100 times in his writings. Among all the other writers of the New Testament, it is only used 55 times. Paul was truly the apostle of **grace**.

ii. "These two terms, grace and peace, constitute Christianity." (Martin Luther)

b. **Who gave Himself for our sins**: Paul wished **grace** and **peace** unto his readers from both God the Father and God the Son. Now, Paul will briefly expand on the work of God the Son, **our Lord Jesus Christ**. The first thing he wrote about Jesus is that He **gave Himself for our sins**.

i. "Throughout the epistle Paul points the Galatians to the centrality of the cross. He cannot wait to make this plain, and we find a reference to it in his very first sentence." (Morris)

ii. Jesus **gave**. We know from John 3:16 that God the Father so loved the world that *He gave His only begotten Son.* Yet God the Father was not the only giver; Jesus also **gave**. Jesus is a loving, giving God and a loving, giving Savior.

iii. Jesus gave the greatest thing anyone can give – **Himself**. One might debate if it was more a gift for the Father to give the Son (as in John 3:16) or if it was more of a gift for the Son to give **Himself**. But that is like discussing how many angels can dance on the head of a pin. Jesus gave the greatest gift *He* could; He gave **himself**. There is a sense in which we do not even begin to give until we give *ourselves*.

iv. Jesus gave Himself **for our sins**. This is why Jesus *had* to give Himself. **Our sins** put us on a road to ruin and destruction. If God did not do something to save us, **our sins** would destroy us. So out of love, Jesus **gave Himself for our sins**! The love was always there; but there would never have been the need for Jesus to give Himself if our sins had not placed us in a terrible place.

v. "These words, 'who gave himself for our sins', are very important. He wanted to tell the Galatians straight out that atonement for sins and perfect righteousness are not to be sought anywhere but in Christ... So glorious is this redemption that it should ravish us with wonder." (Calvin)

c. **That He might deliver us from this present evil age**: This explains *why* Jesus gave Himself for our sins. In many ways, the Galatians battled with and sometimes lost against **this present evil age**. They needed to know that Jesus had come to save them **from this present evil age**.

i. The idea behind the word **deliver** is not deliverance from the *presence* of something, but deliverance from the *power* of something. We will not be delivered from the *presence* of **this present evil age** until we go to be with Jesus. But we can experience deliverance from the *power* of **this present evil age** right now.

d. **According to the will of our God and Father, to whom be glory forever and ever**: The purpose of this saving work is not primarily to benefit man (though that is part of the purpose). Instead, the primary purpose is to glorify God the Father.

i. False doctrine was a real problem among the Galatian churches, and their false doctrines robbed God of some of the glory due to Him. By emphasizing the rightly recognized glory of God and His plan, Paul hoped to put them on the right path.

B. The danger of a different gospel.

1. (6) Paul's amazement.

I marvel that you are turning away so soon from Him who called you in the grace of Christ, to a different gospel.

a. **I marvel that you are turning away so soon**: Paul seemed amazed not so much that they were **turning away** (this might *alarm* him, but not *amaze* him), but that they were **turning away so soon**.

i. Missing here are the expressions of thanks or praise that Paul often wrote in the beginning of his letters. Romans 1:8-15, 1 Corinthians 1:4-9, Philippians 1:3-11, Colossians 1:3-8, and 1 Thessalonians 1:2-10 are each examples of Paul giving thanks and praising the churches in his opening words. But he did not do this with the Galatians and the directness of his approach indicates the severity of their problem.

ii. "This is the sole instance where St. Paul omits to express his thanksgiving in addressing any church." (Lightfoot)

b. **From Him who called you in the grace of Christ, to a different gospel**: They were turning *away* from a Person (**from Him who called you**) as they turned *to* a false idea (**to a different gospel**). To turn away from the true gospel is always to turn away from the Person of Jesus Christ.

i. **From Him who called you in the grace of Christ** also connected their turning away to a turning away from the principle of **grace**. However the Galatians were **turning**, it was *away* from the grace of God, not *towards* it.

2. (7) Three facts about this different gospel brought to the Galatians.

Which is not another; but there are some who trouble you and want to pervert the gospel of Christ.

a. **Which is**: Galatians 1:7 tells three things about this different gospel. First, it was an *illegitimate* gospel (**which is not another**). Second, it was not good at all but *trouble* (**who trouble you**). Third, it was a *distortion* of the true gospel (**pervert the gospel of Christ**).

b. **Which is not another**: Paul recognized that this *different gospel* was not really **another** gospel at all. Those who promoted this *different gospel* perhaps said, "We know our message is different than Paul's message. He has his truth, and we have ours. He has his gospel, and we have ours." Paul rejected the idea that their message was a legitimate alternative gospel in any way.

i. The word **gospel** literally means "good news." Paul meant, "There is no 'good news' in this message. It is only bad news, so it really isn't a 'different good news.' It is bad news. This is not **another** gospel at all."

ii. The King James Version translates this passage like this: *unto another gospel: Which is not another*. Actually, the New King James Version translation is much better at this place, because it makes a distinction between *different* and **another**, accurately reflecting the difference between two distinct ancient Greek words used. *Different* has the idea of "another of different kind" and *another* has the idea of "another of the same kind." It is as if Paul wrote, "They brought you a completely different gospel. They claim it is just an alternative gospel of the same kind, but it isn't at all. It is all together different."

c. **There are some who trouble you**: Those who brought this other gospel to the Galatians brought them **trouble**. They didn't advertise their message as **trouble**, but that is what it was.

i. **Some who trouble you** means that *someone brought this false gospel to the Galatians*. False gospels don't just happen. People bring them, and the people who bring them may be sincere and have a lot of charisma.

ii. "Note the resourcefulness of the devil. Heretics do not advertise their errors. Murderers, adulterers, thieves disguise themselves. So the devil masquerades all these devices and activities. He puts on white to make himself look like an angel of light." (Martin Luther)

d. **To pervert the gospel of Christ**: The other gospel was really a *perversion* or a *distortion* of the true gospel of Jesus Christ. It didn't start from nothing and make up a new name for God and pretending to have a new Savior. It used the names and ideas familiar to the Galatian Christians, but it slightly twisted the ideas to make their message all the more deceptive.

i. **The gospel of Christ**: Notice that Paul was really not contending for the gospel of *Paul*, though it was his gospel also. Paul's gospel was only worth defending and fighting for because it was in fact **the gospel of Christ** Jesus.

e. **Want to pervert the gospel of Christ**: Paul plainly wrote that these people **want to** distort the good news of Jesus. It is sometimes hard for us to understand why someone would **want to pervert the gospel of Christ**.

i. There is something about the message of the true gospel that is deeply offensive to human nature. To understand this, we should first understand what the true gospel is. Paul stated his gospel most succinctly in 1 Corinthians 15:1-4. The message of the gospel is what

Jesus did on the cross for us as revelaed by the Scriptures and proven by the resurrection.

ii. When we understand how offensive the true gospel is to human nature, we better understand why someone would want to **pervert** it.

- The gospel offends our *pride*. It tells us we need a savior, and that we cannot save ourselves. It gives no credit to us at all for our salvation; it is all the work of Jesus for us.

- The gospel offends our *wisdom*. It saves us by something many consider foolish – God becoming man and dying a humiliating, disgraceful death on our behalf.

- Third, the gospel offends our *knowledge*. It tells us to believe something which goes against scientific knowledge and personal experience – that a dead man, Jesus Christ, rose from the dead in a glorious new body that would never die again.

3. (8-9) A solemn curse upon those who bring a false gospel.

But even if we, or an angel from heaven, preach any other gospel to you than what we have preached to you, let him be accursed. As we have said before, so now I say again, if anyone preaches any other gospel to you than what you have received, let him be accursed.

a. **But even if we, or an angel from heaven**: Paul didn't care who brought the false gospel. Even if it were himself, or **an angel from heaven**, it was to be rejected. Any person who spreads a false gospel was worthy only of a particular curse from God (**let him be accursed**).

b. **Let him be accursed**: Paul seemed to have in his mind the solemn curses pronounced by God upon those who break His covenant (Deuteronomy 27). For Paul, it wasn't enough to say, "Don't listen to these people." Paul soberly thought that they should be *cursed*.

c. **So now I say again**: The curse was repeated for extra emphasis; it is really impossible for Paul to express this idea with any more strength than he did here.

i. It might be fair to ask, "Where was Paul's love?" He asked for a "double curse" on people – people who spread a false gospel. He didn't just ask God to curse the message, but to curse the people who spread the message. So, where was Paul's love? Paul's love was for souls that were in danger of hell. If a gospel is false, and not "another good news" at all, then it can not save the lost. Paul looked at this false, perverted gospel and said, "That is a rescue ship about to sink! It can't save anyone! I want to do everything right before God to warn people away from the wrong rescue ship."

C. The Divine source of the gospel Paul preached.

1. (10) Paul's gospel did not come from a desire to please man.

For do I now persuade men, or God? Or do I seek to please men? For if I still pleased men, I would not be a bondservant of Christ.

a. **For do I now persuade men, or God?** Paul's idea was *not* "I want to persuade God to my point of view." The idea is that God was his *audience*. When Paul spoke, he spoke first to *God* and not to man.

b. **Or do I seek to please men?** Paul's first obligation was to *please God* and not to **please men**. He refused to shape his message just to please his audience. He was more concerned about pleasing God.

i. Though it is not specifically said, we sense that Paul made a contrast between himself and those who brought the *different gospel*. Apparently in some way that *different gospel* was built around the idea of pleasing man.

ii. "There have always been preachers who have sought popular acclaim above all else, and there are some still. It is part of fallen human nature that even those charged with the responsibility of proclaiming the gospel can fall into the trap of trying to be popular rather than faithful." (Morris)

c. **For if I still pleased men, I would not be a bondservant of Christ**: For Paul it was one or the other. He could not direct his ministry towards pleasing men *and at the same time* direct it towards pleasing Jesus Christ. And if his concern was not first to please Jesus Christ, then he was not **a bondservant of Christ**.

i. **Servant** is perhaps not the best translation here; it may be better translated *slave*. "It is unfortunate that... our English translations should so consistently fail to give this word its true meaning, thereby encouraging the false conception of Christian 'service' (as something essentially voluntary and part-time) so characteristic of modern religious idealism. The 'bond-servant of Christ' is not free to offer or withhold his 'service'; his life is not his own, but belongs entirely to his Lord." (Duncan, cited in Morris)

2. (11-12) The Divine source of Paul's gospel.

But I make known to you, brethren, that the gospel which was preached by me is not according to man. For I neither received it from man, nor was I taught *it*, but *it came* through the revelation of Jesus Christ.

a. **The gospel which was preached by me**: "Paul makes a play on words when he refers to 'the gospel that I gospelled to you.'" (Morris)

b. **Is not according to man**: In contrast to the different gospel brought by others, Paul's message was a revelation from God. Paul's message was not a man's attempt to reach up and understand God; it was God's effort to bow down and communicate with man.

> i. Men may have many marvelous things to teach us, but God's revelation has *all things which pertain to life and godliness* (2 Peter 1:3). Now more than ever, the world does not need the good advice and wisdom of man, it needs a revelation from God.

c. **I neither received it from man, nor was I taught it, but it came through the revelation of Jesus Christ**: Paul's own relationship to this gospel was unique. Most everyone hears the gospel from someone else; this is God's most common way of communicating the gospel (Romans 10:14-15). But Paul was not normal in this respect. He received the gospel in a dramatic, direct **revelation** when He encountered Jesus on the road to Damascus.

> i. Acts 9:1-9 describes this remarkable incident: The Lord Jesus spoke to Paul directly on the Road to Damascus, and then Paul spent three days without sight, before a Christian named Ananias came to him. It was probably during this time – either on the road or during the three days – when Jesus brought His gospel to Paul. Paul certainly had the gospel right away, because he was both saved and began to immediately preach the message Jesus gave him (Acts 9:20-22).

> ii. "Paul did not receive instruction from Ananias. Paul had already been called, enlightened, and taught by Christ in the road. His contact with Ananias was merely a testimonial to the fact that Paul had been called by Christ to preach the gospel." (Luther)

3. (13-24) Paul proves that his message did not come from man.

For you have heard of my former conduct in Judaism, how I persecuted the church of God beyond measure and *tried to* destroy it. And I advanced in Judaism beyond many of my contemporaries in my own nation, being more exceedingly zealous for the traditions of my fathers. But when it pleased God, who separated me from my mother's womb and called *me* through His grace, to reveal His Son in me, that I might preach Him among the Gentiles, I did not immediately confer with flesh and blood, nor did I go up to Jerusalem to those *who were* apostles before me; but I went to Arabia, and returned again to Damascus. Then after three years I went up to Jerusalem to see Peter, and remained with

him fifteen days. But I saw none of the other apostles except James, the Lord's brother. (Now *concerning* the things which I write to you, indeed, before God, I do not lie.) Afterward I went into the regions of Syria and Cilicia. And I was unknown by face to the churches of Judea which *were* in Christ. But they were hearing only, "He who formerly persecuted us now preaches the faith which he once *tried to* destroy." And they glorified God in me.

a. **For you have heard**: It seemed that *everyone* had heard how Paul came to the Lord. Paul's story was familiar to Christians in general and especially to those he had personally ministered to. We can trust that if Paul was among a group a people for a while and preached the gospel to them, it wouldn't be long until he shared his personal testimony.

i. The value of a personal testimony is not restricted to those who have a dramatic conversion story like Paul did. We can see the glory of God's work just as much in those who think they have a boring testimony.

b. **My former conduct in Judaism, how I persecuted the church of God beyond measure and tried to destroy it**: Paul's credentials as a zealous Jew who persecuted Christians are beyond doubt. Acts 8:1-3 and 9:1-2 describe Paul's energetic persecution of Christians.

i. This shows that Paul was not looking for some other truth when he was first confronted with the gospel of Jesus. Unfortunately, many of those who seek a new revelation will find it - and find deception that draws them away from Jesus Christ (like a young Joseph Smith, the founder of the Mormon Church).

c. **But when it pleased God**: Paul did not come to Jesus because any *man* decided that he should. It wasn't at the pleasure of any *man*, but **when it pleased God**. Additionally, God did not choose Paul because there was something in Paul that pleased him; God **called** Paul **through His grace**, God's unmerited favor.

i. We know this call wasn't because of anything Paul did because he said that he was called **from my mother's womb**. Therefore, God called Paul *before* Paul did anything to deserve it.

ii. Before Paul was a Christian, the emphasis was on what *he* had done: **I persecuted... I advanced...** (I was) **more exceedingly zealous**. Once Paul followed Jesus Christ the emphasis was on what *God* had done: **God, who separated me... called me... reveal His Son in me**.

iii. "He wanted to show that his calling depended on the secret election of God, and that he was ordained an apostle, not because he had fitted himself for undertaking such an office by his own industry or because God had discerned that he was worthy of having it bestowed on him, but because, before he was born, he had been set apart by the secret purpose of God." (Calvin)

d. **Separated**: This was an important word. The ancient Greek word *aphorizo* is related to the word used as a title for the religious elite in Paul's day, the "separated ones" known as the *Pharisees*. Before Paul came to Jesus he was an important Pharisee (Philippians 3:5), but he wasn't *really* separated to God. Now through the work of Jesus he was really **separated** to God.

> i. "The word is akin to that for 'Pharisee', and the Pharisees were in no doubt about it: they held firmly that they were 'separated' to God." (Morris)

e. **To reveal His Son in me**: In Galatians 1:12, Paul wrote of how Jesus was revealed *to* him (*the revelation of Jesus Christ*). But here is something different and perhaps more glorious: Jesus revealed **in** Paul. God wants to do more than reveal Jesus **to** us; He wants to reveal Jesus **in** us.

> i. "What begins by being a revelation of Christ to Paul becomes a revelation of Christ in Paul as the Spirit produces his fruits in unaccustomed soil." (Cole, cited in Morris)

f. **That I might preach Him among the Gentiles**: This shows that God has a sense of humor. He selected a man before he was born for the job of preaching the gospel to the Gentiles. That man grew up *hating* Gentiles, probably believing as some (not all) other Jewish people did in his day: that the only reason God made Gentiles was so they would fuel the fires of hell.

g. **I did not immediately confer with flesh and blood**: Additionally, upon his conversion, Paul did not immediately **confer with flesh and blood** (even the eminent apostles in **Jerusalem**) to discover the content of the gospel. He didn't need to, because the gospel was revealed directly to him by Jesus.

> i. We shouldn't think that Paul meant here that it was wrong to hear of the gospel through others, or that those who do hear it from someone who isn't an apostle somehow have an inferior salvation. The point is simply that the gospel Paul preached was not a gospel of *man*, and this was settled forever because he did not *receive* it from any man.

h. **But I went to Arabia**: Paul did not travel to what we would call Saudi Arabia. The area known in that day as **Arabia** in his day extended all the way to the city of Damascus. Paul probably lived in some quiet desert place outside of Damascus.

i. **Then after three years**: Paul proved here that he did not learn the gospel from the apostles, because he had been a Christian for three years before he even met the apostles Peter and James.

> i. It was unusual for him to wait so long. "A new convert, especially one who had been foremost in persecuting the believers, would surely touch base with the leaders of the movement he was now espousing, if only to make sure that he now had a correct understanding of what the Christian movement was teaching. But Paul did not do this." (Morris)

> ii. Nor was Paul commanded to appear before the apostles in some kind of examination. This is indicated when Paul wrote, "**to see Peter**." The word translated **to see** speaks of someone coming as a tourist. "'A word used,' says Chrysostom, 'by those who go to see great and famous cities.'" (Lightfoot) The idea is that Paul was *not* commanded to come to Jerusalem to give an account to Peter or the other disciples, but he came of his own accord and visited as a tourist.

j. **They were hearing only, "He who formerly persecuted us now preaches the faith he once tried to destroy."** If Paul did not learn the essential content of the gospel from any man, then it was also true that the early Christians were slow in learning just who Paul was in Jesus. All they really knew was that he had been dramatically converted – for which **they glorified God**. After his conversion, Paul was an anonymous Christian for many years.

> i. Paul's status as *unknown* is certainly different from our own habit of puffing up any prominent convert as soon as they come to Jesus. Paul was happy and well served to spend many years in obscurity before God raised him up.

> ii. In this whole section, Paul showed that there was *enough* contact between him and the other apostles to show that they were in perfect agreement, but *not so much* that it showed that Paul got his gospel from them instead of God.

> iii. Paul's whole point in the second part of this chapter is important. His gospel was true, and his experience was valid, because it *really came from God*. It is fair for every Christian to ask if their gospel has come from God, or if they have made it up themselves. Each should examine if their Christian experience has come from God, or if they have made it up themselves. The questions are important because only what comes from God can really save us and make a lasting difference in our lives.

Galatians 2 - Paul Defends the Gospel of Grace

A. Paul presents to the leaders of the church in Jerusalem the gospel of grace revealed to him by Jesus.

1. (1-2) Paul's later trip to Jerusalem.

Then after fourteen years I went up again to Jerusalem with Barnabas, and also took Titus with *me*. **And I went up by revelation, and communicated to them that gospel which I preach among the Gentiles, but privately to those who were of reputation, lest by any means I might run, or had run, in vain.**

> a. **Then after fourteen years I went up again to Jerusalem**: In Galatians 1:18-19, Paul described a trip he made to Jerusalem three years after Jesus met him on the road to Damascus. Here he describes a second trip to Jerusalem, **fourteen years** later.
>
> > i. Remember Paul's point from Galatians 1. He demonstrated that his gospel came by a revelation from Jesus and not from man, not even from the apostles in Jerusalem. Two visits to Jerusalem over 14 years demonstrated that Paul did not sit at the feet of the disciples of Jesus to learn the gospel.
>
> b. **With Barnabas, and also took Titus with me**: Traveling with Paul to Jerusalem were both **Barnabas** (who was well respected among the leadership in Jerusalem according to Acts 4:36-37 and 11:22) and **Titus** (who was a Gentile convert).
>
> > i. **Titus** was a remarkable man and associate of the Apostle Paul. A surprising number of passages show us that Paul loved and trusted Titus and regarded him as a valuable associate.
> >
> > > • In 2 Corinthians 2:13, Paul refered to *Titus my brother*, and says how he had no peace when Titus was absent.

- 2 Corinthians 7:6 says how Paul was *comforted... by the coming of Titus.*

- 2 Corinthians 8:6 shows how Paul trusted Titus to receive a collection from the Corinthians.

- 2 Corinthians 8:16 says that Titus had the same *earnest care* that filled the heart of Paul.

- In 2 Corinthians 8:23, Paul said *If anyone inquires about Titus, he is my partner and fellow worker concerning you.*

- In 2 Corinthians 12:18, Paul spoke again of Titus, and how he shared Paul's heart: *Did Titus take advantage of you? Did we not walk in the same spirit? Did we not walk in the same steps?*

- In Titus 1:4, Paul called Titus *a true son in our common faith.*

c. **And I went up by revelation**: The idea is that Paul went to Jerusalem by the express direction of God. He did not go because any man called him to come; it was because God told him to go.

d. **And communicated to them that gospel which I preach among the Gentiles**: This trip to Jerusalem is most likely the one mentioned in Acts 11:27-30, when Paul brought a gift from Christians in other cities to the Christians in Jerusalem who suffered under famine. When Paul was in Jerusalem at this time he assured the leaders there that he was obedient to God in his presentation of the gospel to the Gentiles.

> i. At this time, there was a contention rising over the place of Gentiles in the church. God used Peter to welcome Gentiles into the church in Acts 10. But some Christians from a Jewish background said that Gentiles could indeed be saved, *if* they made themselves Jews first and brought themselves under the Law of Moses. Their idea was that salvation in Jesus was only for the Jewish people, and Gentiles had to become Jews before they could become Christians.

> ii. "The believing Jews, however, could not get it through their heads that circumcision was not necessary for salvation. They were encouraged in their wrong attitude by the false apostles. The result was that the people were up in arms against Paul and his doctrine." (Luther)

> iii. Knowing this contention was present, the leaders of the church in Jerusalem wanted to know what Paul taught. When he visited Jerusalem it was the perfect time to tell them, so Paul **communicated to them that gospel which I preach among the Gentiles**.

e. **But privately to those who were of reputation**: Paul knew he had the true gospel; but he didn't know how everyone **of reputation** in Jerusalem would receive it. Perhaps some of the apostles themselves were wrong on this point, and needed to be corrected! But if there was any confrontation to be done, Paul did it **privately to those who were of reputation**. He did the best he could to not publicly embarrass **those who were of reputation** in Jerusalem.

i. This was remarkable love and sensitivity on Paul's part. It would have been easy for him to say, "I'm right and anyone who disagrees with me is wrong, and I can't wait to confront them publicly." But he didn't. He knew that being right didn't give you the privilege of being rude.

f. **Lest by any means I might run, or had run, in vain**: This probably did not come from the fear that he himself would fall away. Probably it was the fear that an unnecessary conflict with the leaders of the church in Jerusalem leaders might damage his reputation and ministry in some way. Also, the danger was that false teachers – if encouraged in some way by the leaders in Jerusalem – might undo Paul's work in planting churches and raising disciples for Jesus, and therefore would make Paul's work **in vain**.

2. (3-5) The issue over the circumcision of Titus.

Yet not even Titus who *was* with me, being a Greek, was compelled to be circumcised. And *this occurred* because of false brethren secretly brought in (who came in by stealth to spy out our liberty which we have in Christ Jesus, that they might bring us into bondage), to whom we did not yield submission even for an hour, that the truth of the gospel might continue with you.

a. **Yet not even Titus who was with me, being a Greek, was compelled to be circumcised**: Paul's point is that the leadership in Jerusalem accepted Titus (a Gentile convert) even though he was not circumcised in accord with the Mosaic Law. This shows that the Jerusalem leadership accepted the gospel of grace as Paul understood it.

i. The circumcision of Titus was a potential issue because circumcision – the cutting away of the male foreskin – was the sign of initiation into the Jewish faith and the Mosaic covenant. If a Gentile man wanted to become a Jew, he would have to be circumcised as an adult. Jewish men were circumcised as babies. Since all Jewish men were circumcised and most all Gentile men were not, it was an easy way to refer to "those who are part of the covenant" and to "those who are outside of the covenant of Moses."

ii. "Of course, if any man was going to live a life in obedience to the law he must start by being circumcised." (Morris)

iii. "Paul did not condemn circumcision as if it were a sin to receive it. But he insisted, and the conference upheld him, that circumcision had no bearing upon salvation and was therefore not to be forced upon the Gentiles." (Luther)

b. **And this occurred because of false brethren**: Yet, the lack of circumcision in Titus became an issue because of **false brethren** who attempted to bring Paul and other Christians **into bondage**.

i. It is significant that Paul calls these men **false brethren** – a severe title. Of course, they did not *think of themselves* as **false brethren**. They thought of themselves as *true brethren*. But because they opposed and contradicted the gospel revealed to Paul by Jesus Christ, they really were **false brethren**, according to the standard of Galatians 1:6-9.

ii. It is significant that Paul says these men **secretly brought in** and **came in by stealth**. They did not come in with name badges that said, "False Brother." They did not come in with a purpose statement that said, "We have come to **spy out** your **liberty** in Jesus, and to **bring you into bondage**." These men probably had the best of intentions, but they were still dangerous men who had to be confronted.

iii. Stott on **secretly brought in**: "This may mean either that they had no business to be in the church fellowship at all, or that they had gate-crashed the private conference with the apostles."

iv. It is significant that Paul says these men **might bring us into bondage**. For Paul, this wasn't just an issue between the false brethren and Gentiles. It might be easy for Paul to say, "This doesn't affect me. After all, I am a Jew and have been circumcised under the Law of Moses. I'll let Titus or other Gentiles deal with this problem, because these false brethren have a problem with them, not me." Paul realized that if the message of the gospel was compromised, it wasn't just bondage for the Gentiles, but it was bondage for *everyone* who named the name of Jesus.

c. **We did not yield submission even for an hour**: In response, Paul remained steadfast. Some might react this way out of pride or just plain stubbornness. But Paul did it so that **the truth of the gospel might continue with you** (the Gentile Christians like those in Galatia).

i. "If they had asked for it on the plea of brotherly love, Paul would not have denied them. But because they demanded it on the ground that it was necessary for salvation, Paul defied them, and prevailed. Titus was not circumcised." (Luther)

ii. "The passage is grammatically difficult… Clearly Paul was deeply moved when he wrote this and was not greatly concerned with the niceties of grammar." (Morris)

3. (6) Paul summarizes his point: his gospel or apostolic credentials did not depend on any sort of approval or influence from men, even influential men.

But from those who seemed to be something; whatever they were, it makes no difference to me; God shows personal favoritism to no man; for those who seemed *to be something* added nothing to me.

a. **But from those who seemed to be something**: Paul knew that in his day, there were leaders of high reputation – "famous" Christians, if you will. But they did not overly impress or intimidate Paul; **whatever they were, it makes no difference to me; God shows personal favoritism to no man**.

b. **Those who seemed to be something added nothing to me**: Even though Paul met with influential and famous Christians a few times, *they did not give him the gospel he preached.* The leaders in Jerusalem **added nothing** to the gospel Paul preached or to the apostolic authority he possessed.

i. Paul didn't wait for *someone else* to make him a great Christian. He knew that it came down to a personal relationship between himself and Jesus. This isn't to say that Paul received nothing from others or that no one else could ever bless him; but his Christian life was not *built* upon what other people did for him.

ii. "Paul's words are neither a denial of, nor a mark of disrespect for, their apostolic authority. He is simply indicating that, although he accepts their *office* as apostles, he is not overawed by their *person* as it was being inflated (by the false teachers)." (Stott)

4. (7-10) The leaders of the church in Jerusalem approved Paul's gospel.

But on the contrary, when they saw that the gospel for the uncircumcised had been committed to me, as *the gospel* for the circumcised *was* to Peter (for He who worked effectively in Peter for the apostleship to the circumcised also worked effectively in me toward the Gentiles), and when James, Cephas, and John, who seemed to be pillars, perceived the grace that had been given to me, they gave me and Barnabas the right hand of fellowship, that we *should go* to the Gentiles and they to the circumcised. *They desired* only that we should remember the poor, the very thing which I also was eager to do.

a. **When they saw that the gospel for the uncircumcised had been committed to me**: The leaders of the Jerusalem church (**James**, the brother of Jesus; **Cephas**, also known as Peter, and **John**) accepted Paul and his ministry to the Gentiles. They approved Paul's ministry, knowing that Paul did not require the Gentiles to come under the Mosaic Law to find favor with God.

b. **The gospel for the uncircumcised had been committed to me, as the gospel for the circumcised was to Peter**: Paul's main ministry was to Gentiles, and Peter's main ministry was to Jews. These distinctions were not absolute; each did minister to the other groups.

> i. "For the partition was not one that fixed hard and fast boundaries that they must not pass, like those of kingdoms, principalities, and provinces." (Calvin)

> ii. Yet, the distinction is interesting, especially because Roman Catholics claim that the Pope is the successor of Peter – but where through history is the Pope's ministry to the Jews? "But if Peter's apostleship pertained peculiarly to the Jews, let the Romanists ask by what right they derive from him their succession to the primacy. If the Pope of Rome claims the primacy because he is Peter's successor, he ought to exercise it over the Jews. Paul is here declared to be the chief apostle of the Gentiles; yet they deny that he was the bishop of Rome. Therefore, if the Pope would enter into the possession of his primacy, let him assemble Churches from the Jews." (Calvin)

c. **They desired only that we should remember the poor**: The only caution from the leaders in Jerusalem was that Paul should **remember the poor**. In this case, these were probably the poor saints in Jerusalem, whom Gentile believers should not forget.

> i. Paul certainly did **remember the poor** in Jerusalem. He put a lot of effort towards gathering a contribution among the Gentile churches for the sake of the saints in Jerusalem.

B. The setting of Paul's confrontation with Peter regarding the acceptance of the Gentiles.

1. (11-13) The reason for Paul's public rebuke of the apostle Peter.

Now when Peter had come to Antioch, I withstood him to his face, because he was to be blamed; for before certain men came from James, he would eat with the Gentiles; but when they came, he withdrew and separated himself, fearing those who were of the circumcision. And the rest of the Jews also played the hypocrite with him, so that even Barnabas was carried away with their hypocrisy.

a. **Now when Peter had come to Antioch**: **Peter** approved of Paul's gospel and ministry when Paul came to Jerusalem (Galatians 2:9), and God used Peter himself to welcome Gentiles into Christianity without the precondition of becoming Jews (Acts 11:1-18).

b. **He withdrew and separated himself, fearing those who were of the circumcision**: Though Peter was previously in agreement with welcoming Gentiles into the church without bringing them under the Law of Moses, when Peter came to **Antioch** (Paul's home church), it was another story. He refused to associate with Gentile Christians once certain Jewish believers from Jerusalem came.

i. These men were Christians of Jewish background. Paul called them **certain men... from James** and **those who were of the circumcision**. Knowing their background, Peter knew they would be offended at his fellowship with Gentiles who had not come under the Law of Moses. In their eyes, these uncircumcised Gentiles were not really Christians at all. Therefore, to please them and to avoid a conflict, Peter treated these Gentile Christians as if they were not Christians at all.

ii. Peter *had* known that God did not require Gentiles to come under the Law of Moses for salvation. He learned this from the vision God gave him in Acts 10:10-16. He learned this from the outpouring of the Holy Spirit upon the Gentiles who believed (apart from being circumcised) in Acts 10:44-48. He learned this by the agreement of the other leaders of the church in Acts 11:1-18. Now, Peter turned back on all that he *had* known about the place of Gentiles in the church, and he treated uncircumcised Gentiles as if they were not saved at all.

iii. "He seems to have taken this action shamefacedly. As Bishop Lightfoot says, 'the words describe forcibly the cautious withdrawal of a timid person who shrinks from observation.'" (Stott)

iv. "It is perhaps curious that nobody seems to have recalled that Jesus ate 'with publicans and sinners', which can scarcely mean that he conformed to strict Jewish practice." (Morris)

v. Sadly, others would follow Peter's lead. "The sins of teachers are the teachers of sins." (Trapp)

c. **I withstood him to his face, because he was to be blamed**: This shows how serious the matter was to Paul. He had a public confrontation with Peter over the issue (*I said to Peter before them all*, Galatians 2:14).

i. This was also serious because it involved the issue of *eating together*. Before the **certain men came from James**, Peter **would eat with the Gentiles**. Yet once they came, Peter **withdrew and separated**

himself. This separation was probably at the church potluck dinner, which they called "the agape banquet" or the "love feast." They would also remember the Lord's death at this dinner and take communion together. Therefore, it is possible that Peter turned these Gentile Christians away from the communion table.

ii. "It may be that the observance of holy communion was involved in this, for it seems that often in the early church it was celebrated at a meal shared by all the believers. If this was the case at Antioch, there would have been a division of believers at the table of the Lord." (Morris)

iii. "Paul not hearing this from the report of others, but being an eye-witness to it, doth not defer the reproof, lest the scandal should grow: nor doth he reprove him privately, because the offence was public, and such a plaster [bandage] would not have fitted the sore." (Poole)

d. **Fearing those who were of the circumcision**: This explains *why* Peter did this, even when he knew that God welcomed Gentiles into the church without placing them under the Law of Moses. Out of fear, Peter acted against what he knew was right. "Peter perhaps felt that if the members of the embassy went back and told the Jerusalem church that he was eating with Gentiles it would compromise his position with the leading church." (Morris)

i. It is easy to criticize Peter; but every person knows what it means to do something that you know is wrong. Everyone knows what it feels like to go against what you know very well is right. Everyone knows what it feels like when *social pressure* pushes you towards compromise in some way.

ii. "Their withdrawal from table-fellowship with Gentile believers was not prompted by any theological principle, but by craven fear of a small pressure group... He still believed the gospel, but he failed to practise it." (Stott)

iii. This was the kind of behavior that dominated Peter's life before he was transformed by the power of God. This was like Peter telling Jesus not to go to the cross, or Peter taking his eyes off of Jesus and sinking when walking on the water, or like Peter cutting off the ear of the servant of the High Priest when soldiers came to arrest Jesus. We see that the flesh was still present in Peter. Salvation and the filling of the Holy Spirit did not made Peter perfect; the old Peter was still there, just seen less often.

iv. We might be surprised that Peter compromised even though he knew better; but we are only surprised if we don't believe what God says about the weakness and corruption of our flesh. Paul himself knew this struggle, as he described it in Romans 7:18: *For I know that in me (that is, in my flesh) nothing good dwells; for to will is present with me, but how to perform what is good I do not find.*

v. "No man's standing is so secure that he may not fall. If Peter fell, I may fall. If he rose again, I may rise again. We have the same gifts that they had, the same Christ, the same baptism and the same Gospel, the same forgiveness of sins." (Luther)

e. **Fearing those who were of the circumcision**: We don't know what it was about these **certain men from James** that made Peter afraid. Perhaps they were men of strong personality. Perhaps they were men of great prestige and influence. Perhaps they made threats of one kind or another. Whatever it was, the desire to cater to these legalistic Jewish Christians was so strong that **even Barnabas was carried away with their hypocrisy**. When these **men from James** came, *even Barnabas* treated the Gentile Christians as if they were not Christians at all.

i. *This* was amazing. Barnabas was Paul's trusted friend and associate. Barnabas stood beside Paul when he first met the apostles (Acts 9:27). Barnabas sought out Paul and brought him to Antioch to help with the ministry there (Acts 11:25). Acts 11:24 says of Barnabas, *he was a good man, full of the Holy Spirit and of faith*. Yet, Barnabas also failed at this critical test.

ii. "The defection of Barnabas was of a far more serious nature with regard to Gentile freedom than the vacillation of Peter... Barnabas, the foremost champion of Gentile liberty next to Paul, had become a turncoat." (Wuest)

iii. "It is not impossible that this incident, by producing a temporary feeling of distrust, may have prepared the way for the dissension between Paul and Barnabas which shortly afterwards led to their separation: Acts 15:39." (Lightfoot)

f. **The rest of the Jews also played the hypocrite with him**: This shows that the matter was bigger than just Peter and Barnabas. Peter first made the compromise of acting as if the Gentile Christians were not Christians at all. Then Barnabas followed him. Then **the rest of the Jews** at the church in Antioch followed Peter and Barnabas.

i. This shows what a heavy responsibility it is to be a leader. When we go astray, others will often follow. Satan knew that if he could make Peter take the wrong path, then many others would follow him.

g. **Played the hypocrite... carried away with their hypocrisy**: The word **hypocrite**, in the original language of the New Testament, means "one who puts on a mask," referring to an *actor*. In this case Peter, Barnabas, and the rest of the Jewish Christians in Antioch *knew* that these Gentile believers were really Christians. Yet, because of the pressure from the **certain men from James**, they *acted* like they were not Christians at all.

i. But there was more to it than this. Peter **withdrew and separated himself** from Gentile believers, when before **he would eat with the Gentiles**. In fact, he used to eat with them *often*.

ii. Stott writes about the phrase **he would eat with Gentiles**: "The imperfect tense of the verb shows that this had been his regular practice. 'He... was in the habit of eating his meals with the gentiles' (JBP)."

iii. Yet now Peter refused to eat with Gentile *believers*. When a Jew refused to eat with a Gentile, he did this in obedience to Jewish rituals. Peter had already learned that obedience to these rituals (such as keeping kosher) was not essential for salvation, for either Jews or Gentiles (Acts 10 and 11). Peter had stopped keeping these Jewish rituals for himself, but now *he acted as if he did keep them*, so as to accommodate the legalism of the **certain men from James**. Peter no longer kept a strict observance of the Law of Moses for himself, but by his actions, he implied that Gentiles believers must keep the law – when he himself did not.

2. (14a) Paul confronts Peter publicly.

But when I saw that they were not straightforward about the truth of the gospel, I said to Peter before *them* all.

a. **But when I saw that they were not straightforward about the truth of the gospel**: At the foundation, this wasn't an issue of seating arrangements at the church potluck. It wasn't about table manners and being a good host. It wasn't even about being sensitive to another brother's conscience. Paul saw the issue for what it was; it was **about the truth of the gospel**.

i. When the *certain men from James*, and Peter, and Barnabas, and *the rest of the Jews* of the church in Antioch would not eat with Gentile Christians, they declared those Gentiles *unsaved unbelievers*. They said loud and clear, "You can only be right with God if you put yourself under the demands of the Law of Moses. You must be circumcised. You must eat a kosher diet. You must observe the feasts and rituals.

You must do nothing that would imply partnership with someone who is not under the Law of Moses. This is the only way to receive the salvation of Jesus." *That* message made Paul say, **I saw that they were not straightforward about the truth of the gospel**.

ii. "Peter did not say so, but his example said quite plainly that the observance of the Law must be added to faith in Christ, if men are to be saved. From Peter's example the Gentiles could not help but draw the conclusion that the Law was necessary unto salvation." (Luther)

b. **I said to Peter before them all**: What a scene this must have been! There they were, at the Antioch Christian potluck. The Gentile Christians had just been asked to leave, or were told to sit in their own section away from the real Christians. They also weren't allowed to share the same food that the real Christians ate. Peter – the honored guest – went along with all this. Barnabas – the man who led many of the Gentiles to Jesus – went along with all this. The *rest of the Jews* in the church at Antioch went along with all this. But Paul would not stand for it. Because this was a *public affront* to the Gentile Christians and because it was a *public denial of* **the truth of the gospel**, Paul confronted Peter in a *public* way.

i. It must have been hard, *knowing who Peter was*. Peter was the most prominent of all the disciples of Jesus. Peter was the spokesman for the apostles, and probably the most prominent Christian in the whole world at the time.

ii. It must have been hard, *knowing who Paul was*. This was before any of Paul's missionary journeys; before he was an apostle of great prominence. At that point, Paul was far more famous for *who he was before he was a Christian* – a terrible persecutor of the church – than he was for who he was *as* a Christian.

iii. It must have been hard, *knowing who was in agreement with Peter*. First, Paul had the strong, domineering personalities of the *certain men from James*. Then, Paul had *Barnabas*, who was probably his best friend. Finally, Paul had *the rest of the Jews*. Paul was in the minority on this issue – it was him and all the Gentile Christians against all the Jewish Christians.

iv. As hard as this was, Paul did it because *he knew what was at stake*. This wasn't a matter of personal conduct or just personal sin on Peter's part. If that were the case it is unlikely that Paul would have first used such a public approach. This was a matter **about the truth of the gospel**; proclaiming, "This is how a man is right before God."

C. What Paul said when he publicly rebuked Peter over the issue of the acceptance of Gentile Christians.

1. (14b) Paul exposes Peter's hypocrisy in appearing to live under the law.

"If you, being a Jew, live in the manner of Gentiles and not as the Jews, why do you compel Gentiles to live as Jews?"

> a. **If you, being a Jew, live in the manner of Gentiles and not as the Jews**: Paul first reminded Peter that *he himself did not live under strict obedience to the Law of Moses.* "Peter, you eat bacon and ham and lobster. You don't keep a kosher diet. Yet now, before these visitors, these *certain men... from James*, now you act as if you keep these laws all the time."

> > i. It isn't hard to imagine the scene. They all had a good time until Paul spoiled the party. He probably wasn't shouting, but he did speak with firmness in his voice. And as he told everyone that Peter didn't live under the Law of Moses, the *certain men... from James* looked amazed. Their faces showed surprise. "What? Peter – the most prominent of all the apostles – *Peter* doesn't live under the Law of Moses? *Peter* eats bacon and lobster? *Peter* eats with Gentiles?" As for Peter, his face became red, his heart beat faster, and he just felt sick to his stomach. Everyone else just felt awkward and wished the whole problem would go away.

> > ii. We also wonder if Paul was nervous or bold; perhaps he was shaking from the adrenaline of the highly charged confrontation. We know that Paul did not necessarily have a commanding physical presence. Others said of Paul – and it was probably at least partially true – *his bodily presence is weak, and his speech contemptible* (2 Corinthians 10:10). However Paul acted, *his words were memorable*, because he recalled them exactly here.

> > iii. Lightfoot on **being a Jew**: "Here it is very emphatic; 'If you, *born and bred* a Jew, discard Jewish customs, how unreasonable to impose them on Gentiles.'"

> b. **Why do you compel Gentiles to live as Jews?** Perhaps Peter and the others might say, "We're not *making* them live as Jews." But of course they were; because their message was, "Unless you **live as Jews**, you aren't saved." This did in fact **compel Gentiles to live as Jews**.

2. (15-16) Paul reminds Peter that they are justified before God by the work of Jesus, not by their keeping of the law.

"We *who are* Jews by nature, and not sinners of the Gentiles, knowing that a man is not justified by the works of the law but by faith in Jesus Christ, even we have believed in Christ Jesus, that we might be justified

by faith in Christ and not by the works of the law; for by the works of the law no flesh shall be justified."

a. **We who are Jews by nature... knowing that a man is not justified by the works of the law but by faith in Jesus Christ**: "Peter, we all grew up as observant Jews. Yet we know very well that we were not considered right before God – **justified** – by **the works of the law** that we did. We know that we, even though we grew up as observant Jews, are considered right before God **by faith in Jesus Christ**."

    i. **Not justified by the works of the law**: This is Paul's first use of the great ancient Greek word *dikaioo* (justified, declared righteous) in his letter to the Galatians. "It is a legal concept; the person who is 'justified' is the one who gets the verdict in a court of law. Used in a religious sense it means the getting of a favorable verdict before God on judgment day." (Morris)

b. **Even we have believed in Christ Jesus**: Paul knew that even a strictly observant Jew such as he was could never be considered right before God by what he did under the Law of Moses. Instead, he, Peter, and every single Christian must **have believed in Christ Jesus**.

    i. "'Faith in Jesus Christ', then, is not intellectual conviction only, but personal commitment. The expression in the middle of verse 16 is (literally) 'we have believed *into* (*eis*) Christ Jesus.' It is an act of committal, not just assenting to the fact that Jesus lived and died, but running to Him for refuge and calling on Him for mercy." (Stott)

    ii. "It would be hard to find a more forceful statement of the doctrine of justification than this. It is insisted upon by the two leading apostles ('we know'), confirmed from their own experience ('we have believed'), and endorsed by the sacred Scriptures of the Old Testament ('by works of the law shall no one be justified'). With this threefold guarantee we should accept the biblical doctrine of justification and not let our natural self-righteousness keep us from faith in Christ." (Stott)

c. **That we might be justified by faith in Christ and not by the works of the law**: This was a clear emphasis. "Peter, *we were not justified by being under the Law of Moses, but by faith in Jesus.*" By refusing fellowship with Gentile Christians, Peter said in his actions that we are – *in part* – considered right before God **by the works of the law**. Paul couldn't stand for this, because it wasn't the truth.

d. **For by the works of the law no flesh shall be justified**: Here, Paul emphasized the point in the strongest way possible. **No flesh** – not Gentile, not Jewish, not anyone – will be considered right before God **by the works of the law**.

> i. Lightfoot on **for by the works of the law no flesh shall be justified**: "The words are therefore to be regarded as a free citation of Psalm 143:2." (*For in Your sight no one living in righteous*).

> ii. "The scholastics explain the way of salvation in this manner. When a person happens to perform a good deed, God accepts it and as a reward for the good deed God pours charity into that person. They call it 'charity infused.' This charity is supposed to remain in the heart. They get wild when they are told that this quality of the heart cannot justify a person." (Luther)

> iii. Since this is true, it is plain to see how foolish and wrong it was for Peter to separate from these Gentile Christians because they had not put themselves under the Law of Moses. Because **by the works of the law no flesh shall be justified**, then what difference does it make if a Gentile is circumcised according to the Law of Moses? What difference does it make if a Gentile keeps a kosher table? All that matters is their **faith in Christ**, because that is how we are made right before God.

3. (17-18) Paul answers the main objection against the truth that we are made right before God by faith in Jesus and not by works of the law.

"But if, while we seek to be justified by Christ, we ourselves also are found sinners, *is* Christ therefore a minister of sin? Certainly not! For if I build again those things which I destroyed, I make myself a transgressor."

> a. **But if, while we seek to be justified by Christ, we ourselves also are found sinners, is Christ therefore a minister of sin?** Now Paul dealt with an objection that the *certain men from James* would raise. It's important to remember that Paul made this statement publicly, with the concerned parties right in front of him. On one side of the room were the *certain men from James*, who believed that God would not accept the Gentiles unless they put themselves under the Law of Moses. Peter sat with these men and so did Barnabas, who was Paul's best friend. In fact, *all* the Christians of Jewish background sat with these Christians from Jerusalem who didn't believe that the Gentiles in the church at Antioch were really saved at all. In a real-life setting like this, Paul couldn't just speak his mind without answering the objections – spoken or unspoken – of those who disagreed with him.

> > i. As the men from Jerusalem saw it, the idea that we are made right before God by faith in Jesus *alone* wasn't "real" enough. After all,

Christians still struggled with sin. How could they have the "accepted by God" issue settled if they still battled sin? In their thinking, this made **Christ... a minister of sin**, because Jesus' work of making them right with God apparently didn't make them right enough.

ii. "If God justifies bad people, what is the point of being good? Can't we do as we like and live as we please?" (Stott)

b. **Certainly not!** Paul's answer was brilliant. First, *yes*, **we seek to be justified by Christ** and not by Jesus *plus* our own works. Second, *yes*, **we ourselves also are found sinners**, that is, we acknowledge that we still sin even though we stand **justified by Christ**. But *no*, this **certainly** does **not** make Jesus the author or approver of sin in our life. He is not **a minister of sin**.

i. "To give a short definition of a Christian: A Christian is not somebody who has no sin, but somebody against whom God no longer chalks sin, because of his faith in Christ. This doctrine brings comfort to consciences in serious trouble." (Luther)

c. **For if I build again those things which I destroyed, I make myself a transgressor**: Paul's answer was subtle but brilliant. If he were to **build again** a way to God through keeping the Law of Moses, then he would **make** himself **a transgressor**. Essentially Paul said, "There is *more sin* in trying to find acceptance before God by our law-keeping than there is sin in everyday life as a Christian."

i. These *certain men from James* thought they had to hang on to the Law – for themselves and for Gentiles – so there wouldn't be so much sin. What Paul shows is that by putting themselves under the law again they were sinning worse than ever.

ii. How is it a sin to **build again** a way to God through the Law of Moses? In many ways, but perhaps the greatest is that it looks at Jesus, hanging on the cross, taking the punishment we deserved, bearing the wrath of God for us, and says to Him, "That's all very nice, but it isn't enough. Your work on the cross won't be good enough before God until I'm circumcised and eat kosher." This is a great insult to the Son of God.

iii. Of course, this is the great tragedy of legalism. In trying to be *more* right with God, legalists end up being *less* right with God. This was exactly the situation of the Pharisees that opposed Jesus so much during His years of earthly ministry. Paul knew this thinking well, having been a Pharisee himself (Acts 23:6).

4. (19-20) Paul describes his permanently changed relationship to the law.

"For I through the law died to the law that I might live to God. I have been crucified with Christ; it is no longer I who live, but Christ lives in me; and the *life* which I now live in the flesh I live by faith in the Son of God, who loved me and gave Himself for me."

a. **For I through the law died to the law**: Paul made a bold statement, saying that he had **died to the law**. If he was dead to the law, then it was impossible for the law to be the way that he stood accepted by God.

i. Notice that it wasn't the **law** that was dead. The law reflects, in its context, the holy heart and character of God. There was nothing wrong with the law. It wasn't the **law** that **died**, but Paul **died to the law**.

ii. How did Paul die to the law? **I through the law died to the law**. The law itself "killed" Paul. It showed him that he never could live up to the law and fulfill its holy standard. For a long time before Paul knew Jesus, he thought God would accept him because of his law-keeping. But he came to the point where he really understood the law – understanding it in the way Jesus explained it in the Sermon on the Mount (Matthew 5-7) – and then Paul realized that the law made him *guilty* before God, not *justified* before God. This sense of guilt before God "killed" Paul, and made him see that keeping the law wasn't the answer.

iii. "*To die to the law* is to renounce it and to be freed from its dominion, so that we have no confidence in it and it does not hold us captive under the yoke of slavery." (Calvin)

iv. The problem with the *certain men with James* was that they were not thinking and living as if they were dead to the law. For them, they were still alive under the law and they believed keeping the law would make them accepted by God. Not only were they living under the law, but they also wanted the Gentiles to live under the law.

b. **I through the law died to the law that I might live to God**: When Paul **died to the law**, then he could **live to God**. As long as he still tried to justify himself before God by all his law-keeping, he was dead. But when he **died to the law** then he could **live to God**.

i. "Blessed is the person who knows how to use this truth in times of distress. He can talk. He can say: 'Mr. Law, go ahead and accuse me as much as you like. I know I have committed many sins, and I continue to sin daily. But that does not bother me. You have got to shout louder, Mr. Law. I am deaf, you know. Talk as much as you like, I am dead to you. If you want to talk to me about my sins, go and talk to my flesh.

Belabor that, but don't talk to my conscience. My conscience is a lady and a queen, and has nothing to do with the likes of you, because my conscience lives to Christ under another law, a new and better law, the law of grace.'" (Luther)

c. **I have been crucified with Christ**: Again, Paul anticipated a question from those who disagree with him. "Paul, when did you die to the law? You look alive to me!" Paul was happy to answer, "**I have been crucified with Christ**. I died to the law when Jesus died on the cross. He died in my place on the cross, so it is like it was me up on the cross. He died, and I died to the law when He died."

d. **It is no longer I who live, but Christ lives in me**: Since we died with Christ on the cross we have a different life. Our old life lived under the law is dead. Now we are alive to Jesus Christ and *Jesus is alive in us* (**but Christ lives in me**).

i. Paul realized that on the cross, a great exchange occurred. He gave Jesus his old, try-to-be-right-before-God-by-the-law life, and it was crucified on the cross. Then Jesus gave Paul His life – Christ came to live in him. So Paul's life wasn't his own anymore, it belonged to Jesus Christ! Paul didn't own his own life (that life died); he simply managed the new life Jesus gave him.

e. **And the life which I now live in the flesh I live by faith**: Paul can only manage the new life Jesus gave him **by faith**. You can't live the new life Jesus gives on the foundation of law-keeping. You can only live it **by faith**.

i. When Paul said **I now live in the flesh**, he didn't mean that he lived a chronically sinful life. "By the term 'flesh' Paul does not understand manifest vices. Such sins he usually calls by their proper names, as adultery, fornication, etc. By 'flesh' Paul understands what Jesus meant in the third chapter of John, 'That which is born of the flesh is flesh'. (John 3:6) 'Flesh' here means the whole nature of man, inclusive of reason and instincts. 'This flesh,' says Paul, 'is not justified by the works of the law.'" (Luther)

ii. The focus of this verse isn't the **flesh**, it is **faith**. "Faith is not simply a topic about which Paul preached from time to time. Nor is it a virtue which he practised occasionally. It is central in all that he does." (Morris)

iii. "Faith connects you so intimately with Christ, that He and you become as it were one person. As such you may boldly say: 'I am now one with Christ. Therefore Christ's righteousness, victory, and life are mine.' On the other hand, Christ may say: 'I am that big sinner. His

sins and death are mine, because he is joined to me, and I to him.'"
(Luther)

f. **In the Son of God who loved me and gave Himself for me**: The **faith** Paul lived by was not faith in himself, faith in the law, or faith in what he could earn or deserve before God. It was **faith in the Son of God**, Jesus Christ – **who loved me and gave Himself for me**.

> i. Before, Paul's relationship with God was founded on what he could do for God – his faith was in himself. Now the foundation was what Jesus Christ had done for him – his faith was in Jesus. And Paul found a marvelous person to put his faith in! It was a person who **loved** him. It was a person who demonstrated that love when He **gave Himself for** Paul.

g. **Who loved me**: Paul can confidently give himself to Jesus because of the love Jesus has demonstrated in the *past*. "It is true that he loves us now, but Paul also wrote truly, 'Who *loved* me.' The verb is in the past tense. Jesus loved me upon the cross; loved me in the manger of Bethlehem; loved me before ever the earth was. There never was a time when Jesus did not love his people." (Spurgeon)

> i. **Loved... gave Himself**: The *past tense* is important. William Newell, in his commentary on Romans, speaks to the importance of the past tense in the word **loved**. "It is this past tense gospel the devil hates... Let a preacher be continually saying, 'God loves you, Christ loves you,' and he and his congregation will by and by be losing sight of both their sinnerhood and of the substitutionary atonement of the cross, where the love of God and of Christ was *once for all* and *supremely* set forth."

> ii. "Did the Law ever love me? Did the Law ever sacrifice itself for me? Did the Law ever die for me? On the contrary, it accuses me, it frightens me, it drives me crazy. Somebody else saved me from the Law, from sin and death unto eternal life. That Somebody is the Son of God, to whom be praise and glory forever." (Luther)

h. **Gave Himself for me**: "*For me* is very emphatic. It is not enough to regard Christ as having died for the salvation of the world; each man must claim the effect and possession of this grace for himself personally." (Calvin)

> i. "Take these blessed words of the apostle, and put them in your mouth, and let them lie there as wafers made with honey, till they melt into your very soul: 'Who loved me, and gave himself for me.'" (Spurgeon)

5. (21) Paul shows why the issue of law-righteousness is so important.

"I do not set aside the grace of God; for if righteousness *comes* through the law, then Christ died in vain."

a. **I do not set aside the grace of God**: Paul concluded his public confrontation with Peter with strength. For these Jewish Christians from Jerusalem to require for themselves or anyone else to live under the Law of Moses to be right with God was to **set aside the grace of God** – the very thing Paul does **not** do.

> i. "To nullify grace would be to put one's trust, not in salvation as God's free gift, but in one's own efforts. To do this is to reject grace altogether, and relying on one's puny effort means that one nullifies that grace." (Morris)

b. **If righteous comes through the law**: If this proposition is true, then Jesus **died in vain** – because you can be righteous before God by law-keeping, and you don't need the work of Jesus to make you righteous.

> i. In Jesus' prayer in the garden (Matthew 26:39-42), He asked that if there could be any other way to accomplish what stood before Him at the cross, He asked to be spared the cross. But Jesus was not spared the cross, because there is no other way to accomplish what He did.

> ii. This is also the great problem with seeing the **grace of God** as something that *helps* us get to heaven, as if we put forth the best we can, and then grace supplies the rest. Grace doesn't *help*, it does it *all*. *All* of our righteousness comes from the work of Jesus for us.

> iii. "If my salvation was so difficult to accomplish that it necessitated the death of Christ, then all my works, all the righteousness of the Law, are good for nothing. How can I buy for a penny what cost a million dollars?" (Luther)

c. **I do not set aside the grace of God**: We don't know the immediate effect of this bold stand for the truth. Yet we know that over time Peter came to his senses and took Paul's words to heart. We know this from Acts 15:6-11, where Peter, *in Jerusalem*, before *James and Paul and Barnabas* and the other apostles, proclaimed that Gentiles *did not* have to come under the Law of Moses to be saved.

> i. We know that Peter was already in agreement by how Paul stated the case in Galatians 2:15-17: *We... even we have believed... we might be justified by faith... we seek to be justified by Christ*. Paul is calling Peter's attention to something that Peter *believed* but did not *act* according to. One may *believe* that Jesus saves and we don't save ourself; but one must also refuse to *act* and *think* that we save ourselves.

ii. We can trust that God used this awkward encounter in Antioch for *everyone's* good.

- It was good for Paul, because he stayed true and proclaimed the gospel.

- It was good for Peter, because he was corrected, and as a result became even more convinced in the truth than before.

- It was good for Barnabas, because he came to the correct belief on this matter.

- It was good for the men who came from James and started the whole mess, because a line was drawn at the true gospel, and they had to decide.

- It was good for the Jewish believers in Antioch, because they had the truth spelled out clearly before them.

- It was good for the Gentile believers in Antioch, because their faith and liberty in Jesus was strengthened.

- It was good for us because the truth still lives today.

iii. All this good came, but only because Paul was willing to do something that was *totally right*, but extremely *uncomfortable*. Peter was willing to do that too, when he admitted he was wrong. Peter and Paul were willing to sacrifice their comfort zone for what was right.

Galatians 3 - The Christian, Law, and Living by Faith

A. The principle of continuing in faith.

1. (1) Paul confronts their blurred vision of Jesus and His work for them.

O foolish Galatians! Who has bewitched you that you should not obey the truth, before whose eyes Jesus Christ was clearly portrayed among you as crucified?

a. **O foolish Galatians!** The strong words were well deserved. Phillips even translated this, "*O you dear idiots of Galatia.*" In calling the Galatians **foolish**, Paul did not mean they were morally or mentally deficient (the ancient Greek word *moros* had that idea and was used by Jesus in parables such as in Matthew 7:26 and 25:1-13). Instead, Paul used the ancient Greek word *anoetos*, which had the idea of someone who *can* think but *fails* to use their power of perception.

i. The principles Paul referred to are things the Galatians knew, things they had been taught. The knowledge and understanding were there, but they were not using them.

b. **Who has bewitched you: Bewitched** has the idea that the Galatians were under some type of spell. Paul didn't mean this literally, but their thinking was so clouded – and so unbiblical – that it seemed that some kind of spell had been cast over them.

i. Barclay translates **bewitched** as *put the evil eye on*. The ancient Greeks were accustomed to and afraid of the idea that a spell could be cast upon them by an *evil eye*.

ii. The evil eye was thought to work in the way a serpent could hypnotize its prey with its eyes. Once the victim looked into the evil eye, a spell could be cast. Therefore, the way to overcome the evil eye was simply not to look at it. In using this phrasing and the word

37

picture of **bewitched**, Paul encouraged the Galatians to keep their eyes always and steadfastly upon Jesus.

iii. It is wonderful to have a soft, tender heart before God. But some people have softer *heads* than hearts. Their minds are too accommodating to wrong, unbiblical ideas, and they don't think things through to see if they really are true or not according to the Bible. This is a sign of spiritual immaturity, even as a baby will stick *anything* into its mouth.

c. **Before whose eyes Jesus Christ was clearly portrayed among you as crucified**: The idea behind **clearly portrayed** is something like "billboarded," to publicly display as in setting on a billboard. Paul wondered how the Galatians could have missed the message because he certainly made it clear enough to them.

i. When they left the message of Jesus and Him crucified, they left the message Paul preached. Paul's preaching was like setting up posters of Jesus all over town - if you saw anything, you saw Jesus.

ii. When we see Jesus clearly before us, we won't be deceived. "If anything contrary to this comes before him, he does not timidly say, 'Everybody has a right to his opinion'; but he says, 'Yes, they may have a right to their opinion, and so have I to mine; and my opinion is that any opinion which takes away from the glory of Christ's substitutionary sacrifice is a detestable opinion.' Get the real atonement of Christ thoroughly into your soul, and you will not be bewitched." (Spurgeon)

d. **Before whose eyes**: Paul didn't mean that they literally saw the crucifixion of Jesus or even that they had a spiritual vision of it. He meant that the truth of Jesus and Him crucified and the greatness of His work for them was clearly laid out for them so clearly that they could *see* it. Actually watching the death of Jesus on the cross might mean nothing. Hundreds, if not thousands, saw Jesus dying on the cross and most of them only mocked Him.

2. (2-3) Paul confronts their departure from the principle of faith.

This only I want to learn from you: Did you receive the Spirit by the works of the law, or by the hearing of faith? Are you so foolish? Having begun in the Spirit, are you now being made perfect by the flesh?

a. **This only I want to learn from you**: "Just tell me this," Paul said. **Did you receive the Spirit through the works of the law, or by the hearing of faith?** Obviously, the Galatians received the Holy Spirit through simple faith. The Holy Spirit is not a prize earned through the **works of the law**.

i. It worked like this: A Gentile was told he must come under the Law of Moses or God would not bless him. This meant he must be circumcised according to the Law of Moses. So he has the operation and as soon as the cut is made, the Holy Spirit is poured out upon him. Of course, this is not how it works. We receive the Holy Spirit by *faith* and not by coming under the works of the law.

b. **Having begun in the Spirit, are you now being made perfect by the flesh?** The Galatians were deceived into thinking that spiritual growth or maturity could be achieved through the works of the flesh, instead of a continued simple faith and abiding in Jesus.

i. Another way to say Paul's message is like this: "You received the greatest gift – the Holy Spirit of God – by faith. Are you going on from there, not by faith, but by trusting in your own obedience under the Law of Moses?"

ii. This lays out one of the fundamental differences between the principle of *law* and the principle of *grace*. Under law, we are blessed and grow spiritually by *earning and deserving*. Under grace, we are blessed and grow spiritually by *believing and receiving*. God deals with you under the covenant of *grace*; we should not respond on the principle of *law*.

c. **Are you so foolish?** This was indeed foolishness. This deception was cultivated by Satan to set our Christian life off-track. If he cannot stop us from being *saved* by faith, then he will attempt to hinder our *blessing* and *growth and maturity* by faith.

3. (4) A question about the past: Was it all for nothing?

Have you suffered so many things in vain - if indeed *it was* in vain?

a. **Have you suffered so many things in vain**: Apparently, the Galatians had (perhaps when Paul was among them) suffered for the principle of faith (probably at the hands of legalistic Christians). Would their departure from the principle of faith mean that this past suffering was **in vain**?

i. We know that Paul did suffer persecution in this region. Acts 14 makes it clear that Paul and his companions were persecuted vigorously (Paul even being stoned and left for dead) by the Jews when they were among the cities of Galatia. Surely some of this persecution spilled over to the Christian congregations Paul left behind in Galatia.

b. **Have you suffered so many things in vain**: Perhaps a better translation of this phrase is "Have you had such wonderful spiritual experiences, all to no purpose?" This may fit the context better. Paul wondered if all the gifts of the Spirit they had received would amount to no lasting value because they tried to walk by law, not by faith.

4. (5) Paul asks them to examine the source of the Spirit's work.

Therefore He who supplies the Spirit to you and works miracles among you, *does He do it* **by the works of the law, or by the hearing of faith?**

a. **He who supplies the Spirit to you**: Who supplied the Holy Spirit? Obviously, the Spirit was given as a gift from God.

b. **Does He do it by the works of the law, or by the hearing of faith?** God supplied the Holy Spirit in response to **faith**. Miracles are wrought by **faith**. Yet the Galatians were deceived into thinking that real spiritual riches lay in pursuing God through a *works* relationship.

c. **By the works of the law, or by the hearing of faith?** Paul repeated the phrase from Galatians 3:2 because he wanted to emphasize there was a choice to be made. Which will it be? Do you believe you will be blessed **by the works of the law, or by the hearing of faith**? Will you *earn and deserve* your blessing from God, or will you *believe and receive* it?

> i. This speaks to those who see *lack of blessing*. Why? Not from a lack of devotion, not because they haven't earned enough; but because they are not putting their faith, their joyful and confident expectation in Jesus Christ, the Son of God.

> ii. This speaks to those who are *wonderfully blessed*. How? For them to be proud is to be *blind*. They have not earned their blessing, so they should not take pride in them. All the more they should look to Jesus and put their expectation in Him.

B. Abraham: an example of those justified and walking by faith.

1. (6) How Abraham was made righteous before God.

Just as Abraham "believed God, and it was accounted to him for righteousness."

a. **Just as Abraham**: Among the Galatian Christians, the push towards a works-based relationship with God came from certain other Christians who were born as Jews and who claimed Abraham as their spiritual ancestor. Therefore, Paul used **Abraham** as an example of being right before God by **faith** and not by faith plus works.

> i. "It mattered a great deal to the apostle that God saves people by grace, not on the grounds of their human achievement, and he found Abraham an excellent example of that truth." (Morris)

b. **Abraham believed God, and it was accounted to him for righteousness**: Paul here quoted from Genesis 15:6. It simply shows that **righteousness** was **accounted** to Abraham because he **believed God**. It was *not* because he performed some work and certainly not because he was circumcised, because the covenant of circumcision had not yet been given.

i. Genesis 15:1-6 shows that when Abraham put his trust in God, specifically in God's promise to give him children that would eventually bring forth the Messiah, God credited this belief to Abraham's account as righteousness. "Abraham was not justified merely because he believed that God would multiply his seed, but because he embraced the grace of God, trusting to the promised Mediator." (Calvin)

ii. There are essentially two types of righteousness: righteousness we *accomplish* by our own efforts and righteousness *accounted* to us by the work of God when we believe. Since none of us can be good enough to accomplish perfect righteousness, we must have God's righteousness accounted to us by doing just what Abram did: **Abraham believed God**.

c. **Abraham believed God, and it was accounted to him for righteousness**: This quotation from Genesis 15:6 is one of the clearest expressions in the Bible of the truth of salvation by grace, through faith alone. It is the gospel in the Old Testament, quoted four times in the New Testament (Romans 4:3, Romans 4:9-10, Romans 4:22 and here in Galatians 3:6).

i. Romans 4:9-10 makes much of the fact this righteousness was accounted to Abraham before he was *circumcised* (Genesis 17). No one could say Abraham was made righteous because of his obedience or fulfillment of religious law or ritual. It was faith and faith alone that caused God to account Abraham as righteous.

ii. We should be careful to say that Abraham's faith did not make him righteous. Abraham's *God* made him righteous, by accounting his faith to him for righteousness. "His faith was not his righteousness, but God so rewarded his exercise of faith, as that upon it he reckoned (or imputed)... the righteousness of him in whom he believed." (Poole)

d. **Accounted to him for righteousness**: Abraham's experience shows that God *accounts* us as righteous, because of what Jesus did for us, as we receive what He did for us by faith.

i. Morris on **accounted**: "It has a meaning like 'reckon, calculate', and may be used of placing something to someone's account, here of placing righteousness to Abraham's account."

ii. If God **accounted** Abraham as righteous, then that is how Abraham should account himself. That was his standing before God, and God's accounting is not pretending. God does not account to us a pretended righteousness, but a real one in Jesus Christ.

e. **Believed God**: It wasn't that Abraham believed *in* God (as we usually speak of believing in God). Instead, it was that Abraham **believed God**. Those who only believe *in* God, in the sense that they believe He exists, are only as spiritual as demons are (James 2:19).

i. "*Believed*, of course, means more than that he accepted what God said as true (though, of course, he did that); it means that he trusted God." (Morris)

ii. Generally speaking, ancient Rabbis did not really admire Abraham's *faith*. They believed he was so loved by God because he was thought to have kept the law hundreds of years before it was given. For these and other reasons, when Paul brought up Abraham, it would have been a complete surprise to his opponents, who believed that Abraham proved *their* point. "Paul's emphasis on Abraham's faith must have come as a complete surprise to the Galatians." (Morris)

iii. However, some Rabbis had seen the importance of Abraham's faith. "It is remarkable that the Jews themselves maintained that Abraham was saved by faith. *Mehilta, in Yalcut Simeoni*, page 1, fol. 69, makes this assertion: 'It is evident that Abraham could not obtain an inheritance either in this world or in the world to come, but by faith.'" (Clarke)

iv. "Faith in God constitutes the highest worship, the prime duty, the first obedience, and the foremost sacrifice. Without faith God forfeits His glory, wisdom, truth, and mercy in us. The first duty of man is to believe in God and to honor Him with his faith. Faith is truly the height of wisdom, the right kind of righteousness, the only real religion... Faith says to God: 'I believe what you say.'" (Luther)

2. (7) The true sons of Abraham.

Therefore know that *only* those who are of faith are sons of Abraham.

a. **Therefore know**: The emphasis is clear. Paul made an important point, and he wanted each one of his readers to understand it.

i. "*Know* is imperative; Paul commands the Galatians to acquire this piece of knowledge." (Morris)

b. **Only those who are of faith are sons of Abraham**: Since Abraham was made righteous by **faith** and not by works, Abraham was therefore the father of everyone who believes God and is accounted righteous.

i. "It is always possible that we should translate *huioi Abraam*, not so much *children* (or 'sons') *of Abraham* as 'real Abrahams.'" (Cole)

c. **Are sons of Abraham**: This was a strong rebuke to the Jewish Christians who tried to bring Gentile Christians under the law. They believed they were superior because they descended from Abraham and observed the law. Paul said that the most important link to Abraham was not the link of *genetics* and not the link of *works*, but it is the link of **faith**.

i. This would have been a shocking change of thinking for these particular opponents of Paul. They deeply believed that they had a standing before God because they were *genetically* descended from Abraham. At that time, some Jewish Rabbis taught that Abraham stood at the gates of Hell just to make sure that none of his descendants accidentally slipped by. John the Baptist dealt with this same thinking when he said, *Do not think to say to yourselves, "We have Abraham as our father." For I say to you that God is able to raise up children to Abraham from these stones* (Matthew 3:9). Paul knocked down their blind reliance on *genetic* relation to Abraham and showed that what really mattered was *faith in Jesus*.

ii. It's the same today when people believe God accepts them because they come from a Christian family. God is a Father, not a grandfather; everyone must have their *own* faith in God.

d. **Are sons of Abraham**: This was a great comfort to the Gentile Christians who were regarded as "second class Christians" by others. Now they could know that they had a real, important link to Abraham and could consider themselves **sons of Abraham**.

i. Sadly, Christians have taken this glorious truth and misapplied it through the centuries. This has been a verse that many claim in support of *replacement theology* – the idea that God is *finished* with the people of Israel as a nation or a distinct ethnic group, and that the Church spiritually inherits all the promises made to Israel.

ii. Replacement theology has done tremendous damage in the Church, providing the theological fuel for the fires of horrible persecution of the Jews. If Galatians 3:7 were the only verse in the Bible speaking to the issue, there might be a place for saying that the Church has completely replaced Israel. But we understand the Bible according to its entire message, and allow one passage to give light to others.

iii. For example, Romans 11:25 (*hardening in part has happened to Israel until the fullness of the Gentiles has come in*) states clearly that God is *not* finished with Israel as a nation or a distinct ethnic group.

Even though God has turned the focus of His saving mercies away from Israel on to the Gentiles, He will turn it back again. This simple passage refutes those who insist that God is forever done with Israel as Israel, and that the Church is the New Israel and inherits every promise ever made to national and ethnic Israel of the Old Testament.

iv. We are reminded of the enduring character of the promises made to national and ethnic Israel (such as Genesis 13:15 and Genesis 17:7-8). God is not "finished" with Israel, and Israel is not "spiritualized" as the church. While we do see and rejoice in a continuity of God's work throughout all His people through all generations, we still see a distinction between Israel and the Church – a distinction that Paul understands well.

v. All who put their faith in Jesus Christ **are sons of Abraham**; but Abraham has his *spiritual* sons and his *genetic* sons, and God has a plan and a place for both. Yet no one can deny that it is far more important to be a *spiritual* son of Abraham than a *genetic* son.

3. (8-9) This blessing of righteousness by faith is for all nations.

And the Scripture, foreseeing that God would justify the nations by faith, preached the gospel to Abraham beforehand, *saying*, "In you all the nations shall be blessed." So then those who *are* of faith are blessed with believing Abraham.

a. **And the Scripture**: Paul spoke from the Scriptures. He had already spoken from his personal experience and from the experience of the Galatian Christians themselves. But this passage is even more important, because it shows how Paul's teaching is correct according to the Bible itself.

i. It would have been just fine for Paul's opponents to say, "Experiences are just fine Paul, but show us from the Scriptures." Paul was more than ready to take up the challenge.

ii. **The Scripture, foreseeing... preached... saying**: Remarkably, Paul referred to the **Scriptures** virtually as a person who *foresees*, *preaches*, and *says*. This shows just how strongly Paul regarded the Bible as God's word. Paul believed that when the Scriptures spoke, God spoke.

iii. "Paul personifies Scripture." (Morris) "Excellently spake he, who called the Scripture, *Cor et animam Dei*, The heart and soul of God." (Trapp)

b. **Foreseeing that God would justify the nations by faith**: Paul observed that even back in Abraham's day it was clear that this blessing of righteousness by faith was intended for every nation, for Gentiles as well as Jews, because God pronounced that **in you all the nations shall be blessed** (Genesis 12:3).

> i. The intention was to destroy the idea that a Gentile must first become a Jew before they could become a Christian. If that were necessary God would never have said this blessing would extend to every nation, because Gentiles would have had to become part of the *Israelite nation* to be saved.

> ii. The idea is that the gospel goes *out to* **the nations**, not that the nations come and assimilate into Israel.

> c. **Those who are of faith are blessed with believing Abraham**: The *blessing* we receive with **believing Abraham** is not the blessing of fantastic wealth and power, though Abraham was extremely wealthy and powerful. The blessing is something far more precious: the blessing of a right standing with God through faith.

> > i. "The faith of the fathers was directed at the Christ who was to come, while ours rests in the Christ who has come." (Luther)

> > ii. "*They who are of faith* are those whose characteristic is faith; it is not that they sometimes have an impulse to believe, but rather that believing is their constant attitude; faith is characteristic of them." (Morris)

C. The Law in light of the Old Testament and the New Testament.

1. (10) The Old Testament tells us that the Law of Moses brings a curse.

For as many as are of the works of the law are under the curse; for it is written, "Cursed *is* everyone who does not continue in all things which are written in the book of the law, to do them."

> a. **For as many as are of the works of the law**: Paul here addressed those who thought that their law-performance could give them a right standing before God.

> > i. The transition from believing Abraham (Galatians 3:9) to those who are **of the works of the law** had a purpose. "If even the great patriarch was accepted by God only because of his faith, then it follows that lesser mortals will not succeed in producing the good deeds that would allow them to be accepted before God." (Morris)

> > ii. "The hypocritical doers of the Law are those who seek to obtain a righteousness by a mechanical performance of good works while their hearts are far removed from God. They act like the foolish carpenter who starts with the roof when he builds a house." (Luther)

b. **For as many as are of the works of the law are under the curse**: The Christians from a Jewish background who believed Gentiles should still live under the Law of Moses thought that it was a path to *blessing*. Paul boldly declared that instead of blessing, living under **the works of the law** put them **under the curse**.

i. It isn't hard to see how these Christians believed that living under law brought blessing. They could read in the Old Testament many passages that supported this thinking. Psalm 119:1 says, *Blessed are the undefiled in the way, who walk in the law of the LORD!* Psalm 1:1-2 says, *Blessed is the man who walks not in the counsel of the ungodly, nor stands in the path of sinners, nor sits in the seat of the scornful; but his delight is in the law of the LORD, and in His law he meditates day and night.*

ii. We must understand *how* the Law can bring blessing. First, we see that the word *law* is used in two senses in the Bible. Sometimes it means "The Law of Moses, with all its commands, which a man must obey to be approved by God." Sometimes it means "God's Word" in a very general sense. Many times when the Old Testament speaks of the law, it speaks of it in the general sense of God's Word to us. When Psalm 119:97 says *Oh, how I love Your law! It is my meditation all the day*, the Psalmist meant more than just the Law of Moses; he meant all of God's Word. Seeing this, we understand how the Bible is filled with praise for the law. Secondly, we are blessed when we keep the law because we are living according to the "instruction manual" for life. There is an inherent, built-in blessing in living the way God says we should live, in fulfilling the "manufacturer's recommendation."

iii. When Paul said that **as many as are of the works of the law are under the curse**, he didn't mean that the law was bad or the Word of God is wrong. He simply meant that God never intended the law to be the way we find our approval before Him. He knew we could never keep the law, and so God instituted the system of *atoning sacrifice* along with the law. And the entire sacrificial system looked forward to what Jesus would accomplish on the cross for us.

c. **Cursed is everyone who does not continue in all things which are written in the book of the law, to do them**: To prove his point Scripturally Paul quoted from Deuteronomy 27:26. The Old Testament itself shows us that if we do not keep **all things** in the law and actually **do them**, then we are under a curse.

i. The important words are **all** and **do**. For God to approve you on the basis of the law, you first have to **do** it. Not simply *know* it, not simply *love* it, not simply *teach* it, not simply *want* it, you must **do** it.

Secondly, you have to do it **all**. Not some. Not just when you are over 18 or over 40. Not just more good than bad. Deuteronomy 27:26 specifically says that to be justified by the law, you must **do** it, and do it in **all things**.

ii. **All** means a lot. It means that while some sins are worse than others are, there are no small sins before such a great God. "Jewish keepers of the law would overlook small transgressions. Paul would not." (Morris)

iii. "It is worthy of remark that no *printed* copy of the Hebrew Bible preserves the word *col*, ALL, in Deuteronomy 27:26, which answers to the apostle's word *all*, here. St. Jerome says that the Jews suppressed it, lest it should appear that they were bound to perform *all* things that are written in the book of the law. Of the genuineness of the reading there is no cause to doubt: it exists in *six* MSS. of *Kennicott* and *De Rossi*, in the *Samaritan* text, in several copies of the *Targum*, in the *Septuagint*, and in the quotation made here by the apostle, in which there is no variation either in the MSS. or in the *versions*." (Clarke)

d. **Cursed is everyone**: Paul's point is heavy; it weighs us down with a curse. If you are under the works of the law, the only way you can stand approved and blessed before God by the law is to **do** it, and to do it **all**. If you don't, you are **cursed**.

i. **Cursed** is a word that sounds strange in our ears. Yet in the Bible, the idea of being **cursed** is important, and frightening – because it means being **cursed** by God. Not only **cursed** by our own bad choices, not only **cursed** by this wicked world, not only **cursed** by the Devil – but especially **cursed** by God. He is the one Person you don't want to be **cursed** by.

2. (11) The Old Testament tells us that a right standing before God comes by faith, not by the law.

But that no one is justified by the law in the sight of God *is* evident, for "the just shall live by faith."

a. **But that no one is justified by the law in the sight of God is evident**: Paul had already proven this point in the Scriptures by examining the life of Abraham (Galatians 3:5-9). Now he brought in another passage from the Old Testament, Habakkuk 2:4, which reminds us that the just live by **faith** and not by law.

i. The Jews themselves sensed that because none could keep the law perfectly, salvation could not come through keeping the law. This is why they placed such emphasis on their descent from Abraham, essentially trusting in Abraham's merits to save them because they sensed that their own merits could not.

b. **The just shall live by faith**: This brief statement from the prophet Habakkuk is one of the most important and most quoted Old Testament statements in the New Testament. Paul used it here to show that the **just** live **by faith**, not by law. Being under the law isn't the way to be found **just** before God; only living by faith is.

i. If you are found to be **just** – approved – before God, you have done it by a life of **faith**. If your life is all about living under the law, then God does not find you approved.

c. **The just shall live by faith**: Every word in Habakkuk 2:4 is important and God quotes it three times in the New Testament just to bring out the fullness of the meaning.

i. In Romans 1:17, when Paul quoted this same passage from Habakkuk 2:4, the emphasis was on *faith*: "The just shall live by **faith**."

ii. In Hebrews 10:38, when the writer to the Hebrews quoted this same passage from Habakkuk 2:4, the emphasis was on *live*: "The just shall **live** by faith."

iii. Here in Galatians 3:11, when Paul quoted this passage from Habakkuk 2:4, the emphasis is on *just*: "The **just** shall live by faith."

3. (12) The Old Testament tells us that approval by God through the law must be earned by actually living in obedience to the law, not just trying.

Yet the law is not of faith, but "the man who does them shall live by them."

a. **Yet the law is not of faith**: Some might come back to Paul and say, "Look, I'll do the best I can under the law and let faith cover the rest. God will look at my performance, my effort, and my good intentions and credit to me as righteousness. The important thing is that I am really trying." Paul proved from the Old Testament itself that this simply isn't good enough. No; the paths of approval by **the law** and **faith** don't run together, because **the law is not of faith**.

b. **The man who does them shall live by them**: The quote from Leviticus 18:5 is clear. If you want to **live** by the law, you must *do* it. Not *try to do it*, not *intend to do it*, and not even *want to do it*. No, it is only **the man who does them** who **shall live by them**.

i. It is very easy to comfort ourselves with our good intentions. We all mean very well; but if we want to find our place before God by our works under the law, good intentions are never enough. A good effort isn't enough. Only actual *performance* will do.

ii. This passage from Leviticus 18:5 is another often-quoted principle from the Old Testament. Nehemiah (Nehemiah 9:29) quoted it in his great prayer for Israel. The LORD Himself quoted it through the prophet Ezekiel (Ezekiel 20:11, 13, and 21). Paul also quotes it again in Romans 10:5).

iii. The effect of Paul's use of Scripture in Galatians 3:10-12 is overwhelming. We understand that we don't actually *do* the law. We understand that we don't actually do *all* the law. And we understand that this put us under a *curse*. Galatians 3:10-12 is the bad news; now Paul begins to explain the good news.

4. (13-14) Jesus redeems us from the curse of the law.

Christ has redeemed us from the curse of the law, having become a curse for us (for it is written, "Cursed *is* everyone who hangs on a tree"), that the blessing of Abraham might come upon the Gentiles in Christ Jesus, that we might receive the promise of the Spirit through faith.

a. **Christ has redeemed us from the curse of the law**: Because we didn't actually do it and do it all, the law put us under a curse. But now Jesus **has redeemed us from the curse of the law**. **Redeemed** has the idea of "buying back" or "purchasing out of." It isn't just rescuing; it is paying a price to rescue. Jesus bought us out from under the **curse of the law**.

i. Simply put, in Jesus, we aren't cursed anymore. Galatians 3:10-12 left us all under a curse, but we are not cursed any more because Jesus bought us out from under the curse.

ii. **Redemption** is an important idea. "Redemption points to the payment of a price that sets sinners free." (Morris) **Redemption** came from the practices of ancient warfare. After a battle the victors would often capture some of the defeated. Among the defeated, the poorer ones would usually be sold as slaves, but the wealthy and important men, the men who mattered in their own country, were held to ransom. When the people in their homeland had raised the required price, they would pay it to the victors and the captives would be set free. The process was called redemption, and the price was called the ransom.

iii. The image took root in other areas. When a slave had his freedom purchased – perhaps by a relative, perhaps by his own diligent work and saving – this was called "**redemption**." Sometimes the transaction took place at a temple, and a record was carved in the wall so everyone would forever know that this former slave was now a redeemed, free man. Or, a man condemned to death might be set free by the paying of a price, and this was considered "redemption." Most importantly, Jesus bought us out of defeat, out of slavery, and out of a death sentence to reign as kings and priests with Him forever.

b. **Having become a curse for us**: This explains *how* Jesus paid the price to rescue us. Jesus became cursed on our behalf; He stood in our place and took the curse we deserved.

i. It stops us in our tracks to understand that the price He paid to buy us out from under the **curse of the law** was the price of Himself. It didn't just cost Jesus something, even something great – it cost Jesus Himself. We know that men cursed Jesus as He hung on the cross; but that compares nothing to how He was cursed by God the Father. He made Himself the target of the curse, and set those who believe outside the target.

ii. "Paul does not say that Christ was made a curse for Himself. The accent is on the two words, 'for us.' Christ is personally innocent. Personally, He did not deserve to be hanged for any crime of His own doing. But because Christ took the place of others who were sinners, He was hanged like any other transgressor." (Luther)

iii. "Whatever sins I, you, all of us have committed or shall commit, they are Christ's sins as if He had committed them Himself. Our sins have to be Christ's sins or we shall perish forever." (Luther)

c. **For it is written, "Cursed is everyone who hangs on a tree."** *When* did Jesus pay this price? The principle of Deuteronomy 21:23 shows that Jesus received this curse upon Himself as He hung on the cross, fulfilling the Deuteronomy 21:23 promise of a curse to all who are not only executed but have their bodies publicly exposed to shame.

i. "This passage did not refer to crucifixion (which the Jews did not practise), but to the hanging on a tree or wooden post of the corpse of a criminal who had been executed. But in the New Testament times a cross was often called a tree and there is no doubting that that is what Paul has in mind here." (Morris)

ii. **Hangs on a tree**: In the thinking of ancient Israel, there was something worse than being put to death. Worse than that was to be put to death, and to have your corpse left in the open, exposed to shame, humiliation, and scavenging animals and birds. When it says **hangs on a tree**, it does not have the idea of being executed by strangulation; but of having the corpse "mounted" on a tree or other prominent place, to expose the executed one to the elements and supreme disgrace.

iii. However, if anyone was executed and deemed worthy of such disgrace, the humiliation to his memory and his family must not be excessive. Deuteronomy 21:23 also says "*his body shall not remain overnight on the tree*." This was a way of tempering even the most severe judgment with mercy. Significantly, Jesus fulfilled this also, being taken down from the cross before night had fully come (John 19:31-33).

d. **That the blessing of Abraham might come**: Jesus received this curse, which we deserved and He did not, so that we could receive the *blessing of Abraham*, which He deserved and we did not. It would be enough if Jesus simply took away the curse we deserved. But He did far more than that; He also gave a **blessing** that we didn't deserve.

i. **The blessing of Abraham** is what Paul already described in Galatians 3:8-9: the blessing of being justified before God by faith instead of works.

e. **The Gentiles in Christ Jesus**: This tells us to whom the **blessing of Abraham** comes. Paul didn't mean that it *only* comes upon Gentiles, as if Jews were excluded, but that it comes also upon those **Gentiles in Christ Jesus**.

i. The phrase **in Christ Jesus** is important. The blessing doesn't come *because* they are Gentiles, any more than the blessing of being right with God comes to Jewish people because they are Jews. It comes to all, Jew and Gentile alike, who are identified **in Christ Jesus** and not by their own attempts to justify themselves.

f. **Receive the promise of the Spirit through faith**: This means that this blessing is ours in Jesus on faith and not the principle of law. The promise is *received*, not *earned*.

5. (15-18) The unchanging nature of God's covenant with Abraham.

Brethren, I speak in the manner of men: Though *it is* only a man's covenant, yet *if it is* confirmed, no one annuls or adds to it. Now to Abraham and his Seed were the promises made. He does not say, "And to seeds," as of many, but as of one, "And to your Seed," who is Christ. And this I say, *that* the law, which was four hundred and thirty years later, cannot annul the covenant that was confirmed before by God in Christ, that it should make the promise of no effect. For if the inheritance *is* of the law, *it is* no longer of promise; but God gave *it* to Abraham by promise.

a. **Brethren, I speak in the manner of men**: Paul first establishes the principle that even with a covenant among men, the covenant stands firm once it is made – **no one annuls or adds to it**. Paul's point isn't really about covenants among men, but to say "How much more certain is a covenant *God* makes."

> i. But we shouldn't miss the first word of Galatians 3:15: **Brethren**. As difficult and dangerous as Paul's opponents in Galatia were, they were also his *brothers*. He confronts them and persuades them as *brothers*.

b. **Now to Abraham and his Seed were the promises made**: In Genesis 22:18, God promised Abraham that *in your seed all the nations of the earth shall be blessed*. Paul observes that the singular for **seed** is used, not the plural. The point is clear: **"And to your Seed," who is Christ**. God is referring to one specific descendant of Abraham, not all his descendants in general

c. **For if the inheritance is of the law, it is no longer of promise; but God gave it to Abraham by promise**: If the inheritance offered to Abraham was on the basis of law, it might not be permanent – because it would depend, at least in part, on Abraham's keeping of the law. But since the inheritance was offered on the basis **of promise**, *God's* promise, it stands sure.

d. **God gave it to Abraham by promise**: The word **gave** here is the ancient Greek word *kecharistai*, which is based on the Greek word *charis* - grace. God's giving to Abraham was the free giving of grace. The word is also in the perfect tense, showing that the gift is *permanent*.

> i. "Judaizers might quote Moses; Paul will quote Abraham. Let them quote law; he will quote promise. If they appeal to the centuries of tradition and the proud history of the law of Moses, he will appeal to the grander 'covenant with Abraham', older by centuries still." (Cole)

D. The purpose of the law helps us understand our freedom from the law.

1. (19-21) The law was given because of man's transgression.

What purpose then *does* the law *serve*? It was added because of transgressions, till the Seed should come to whom the promise was made; *and it was* appointed through angels by the hand of a mediator. Now a mediator does not *mediate* for one *only*, but God is one. *Is* the law then against the promises of God? Certainly not! For if there had been a law given which could have given life, truly righteousness would have been by the law.

a. **What purpose then does the law serve? It was added because of transgressions**: Part of the reason the law was given was to restrain the transgression of men through clearly revealing God's holy standard. God had to give us His standard so we would not destroy ourselves before the Messiah came. But the law is also **added because of transgressions** in another way; the law also excites man's innate rebellion through revealing a standard, showing us more clearly our need for salvation in Jesus (Romans 7:5-8).

b. **Till the Seed should come to whom the promise was made**: So as the Law was meant to prepare us for the work of the Messiah, it was given **till the Seed** (Jesus) **should come**. It isn't that the Law of Moses is *revoked* when Jesus came (Jesus said that He came to fulfill the Law, not destroy it in Matthew 5:17). Instead, the Law of Moses is not longer our ground of approaching God.

c. **It was appointed through angels by the hand of a mediator**: According to ancient traditions – true traditions, according to Paul – the Law was delivered to Moses on Mount Sinai by the hands of angels. Angels were the "go-between" or mediator for Moses when he received the Law from God.

d. **Now a mediator does not mediate for one only, but God is one**: Moses needed a mediator between himself and God, but we don't need a mediator between us and Jesus – He *is* our mediator. The law was a two-party agreement brought by mediators. Salvation in Jesus by faith is received by a promise.

> i. James Montgomery Boice called Galatians 3:20 "probably the most obscure verse in Galatians, if not the entire New Testament." Another commentator said he has read more than 250 different interpretations of it; another commentator raises the figure to 300.

> ii. "The general thought seems to be that the promise must be considered superior to the law because the law is two-sided. The law was mediated, and this means that man was a party to it. The promise, on the other hand, is unilateral; man is not a party to it." (Boice)

e. **Is the law then against the promises of God? Certainly not!** The law is not something evil, opposing God's promise. The problem with the law is found in its inability to give strength to those who desire to keep it. If the law **could have given life**, then it could have brought righteousness. But the Law of Moses brings no life; it simply states the command, tells us to keep it, and tells us the consequences if we break the command.

> i. "People foolish but wise in their own conceits jump to the conclusion: If the Law does not justify, it is good for nothing. How about that? Because money does not justify, would you say that money is good for nothing? Because the eyes do not justify, would you have them taken

out? Because the Law does not justify it does not follow that the Law is without value." (Luther)

2. (22) The picture of our imprisonment under sin.

But the Scripture has confined all under sin, that the promise by faith in Jesus Christ might be given to those who believe.

a. **The Scripture has confined all under sin**: Paul paints a picture of imprisonment. The bars of the cell are sin, keeping us confined. The **Scripture** put us in the prison, because it pointed out our sinful condition. So we sit imprisoned by sin, and the law can not help us, because the law put us in the prison.

i. "Sin is personified as a jailor, keeping sinners under its control so that they cannot break free." (Morris)

ii. Some protest and say, "I'm not a prisoner to sin." There is a simple way to prove it: stop sinning. But if you can't stop sinning, or ever have a record of sin, then you are imprisoned by the law of God.

iii. "When the Law drives you to the point of despair, let it drive you a little farther, let it drive you straight into the arms of Jesus who says: 'Come unto me, all ye that labour and are heavy laden, and I will give you rest.'" (Luther)

b. **Given to those who believe**: Only faith can break us out of our confinement to sin. The Law of Moses can show us clearly our problem and God's standard, but it cannot give us the freedom that only Jesus can give. The freedom is **given to those who believe**.

i. The bars of our sin are strong; we can't saw through them ourselves. There is no chance of a jailbreak. Instead, an offer is made by the warden Himself to simply open the door and walk out – but you have to acknowledge you are confined, that you deserve to be in the cell, and ask Him to free you. When the prosecutor accuses the warden of not being just, the warden simply points out that the freed prisoner's sentence was completely fulfilled – by Himself!

ii. "Far from being the gateway into a glorious liberty, it turns out to be a jailor, shutting people up. The result is that the only way of escape was through faith." (Morris)

3. (23-25) The Law of Moses is our tutor, a guardian to bring us to Jesus.

But before faith came, we were kept under guard by the law, kept for the faith which would afterward be revealed. Therefore the law was our tutor *to bring us* to Christ, that we might be justified by faith. But after faith has come, we are no longer under a tutor.

a. **Before faith came**: Before we were saved by faith; before we lived our lives by faith, **we were kept under guard by the law**. Here, Paul uses a different word and a different idea than when he wrote *the Scripture has confined all under sin* in the previous verse. The idea behind *confined* is imprisonment; the idea behind **under guard** is protective custody. There is a sense in which we were imprisoned by our own sin under the law; but there is also another sense in which it guarded us in *protective custody*.

　　i. How does the law protect us? It protects us by *showing us God's heart*. It protects us by *showing us the best way to live*. It protects us by *showing what should be approved and disapproved among men*. It protects us by providing a *foundation for civil law*. In these ways and more, **we were kept under guard by the law**.

b. **Kept for the faith which would afterward be revealed**: The Law of Moses prepared us to come to Jesus by the way it reveals God's character and the way it exposed our sin. **Therefore the law was our tutor to bring us to Christ, that we might be justified by faith**. The *purpose* of the Law of Moses is fulfilled when we stop trying to justify ourselves and come to faith in Jesus.

　　i. The whole purpose of **the law** is to bring us to Jesus. Therefore, if someone doesn't present the Law in a manner that brings people to faith in Jesus, they aren't presenting the Law properly. The way Jesus presented the Law was to show people that they could not fulfill it, and needed to look outside of their law-keeping to find a righteousness greater than the Scribe and the Pharisees (Matthew 5:17-48).

　　ii. "Satan would have us prove ourselves holy by the law, which God gave to prove us sinners." (Andrew Jukes, cited in Stott)

c. **But after faith has come, we are no longer under a tutor**: Once we have come to a relationship of faith, we no longer have to live under our tutor, though we remember the behavior he has taught us. So we respect our tutor, the Law; but we don't live under him. We live under Jesus by faith.

　　i. **Tutor** is not a completely accurate translation of the idea of the ancient Greek word *paidagogos*. The *paidagogos* did not simply teach a child. More than that, the tutor was the child's guardian, watching over the child and his behavior. The idea is more of a nanny than of a teacher, but since the **tutor** could discipline the child, the **tutor** was also the "dean of discipline."

　　ii. Morris translates **tutor** as *custodian*. "The *custodian* was not a teacher, but a slave whose special task was to look after a child. He exercised a general supervision over the boy's activities, and it was his responsibility to bring him to the teacher who would give him the instruction that befitted his station." (Morris)

iii. When the child has grown, he doesn't do away with the discipline and lessons he gained from the tutor; but he also doesn't live *under* the tutor any longer. This is our relation to the law of God. We learn from it; we remember our lessons from it, but we don't live *under* the law. "The simile of the schoolmaster is striking. Schoolmasters are indispensable. But show me a pupil who loves his schoolmaster." (Luther)

4. (26-27) By faith, we find our identity with Jesus Christ.

For you are all sons of God through faith in Christ Jesus. For as many of you as were baptized into Christ have put on Christ.

a. **For you are all sons of God through faith in Christ Jesus**: Compared to what was being taught among the Galatians, this was a revolutionary statement. In traditional Jewish thinking (carried into Christianity by Jewish Christians), your standing before God was measured by your obedience to the law. To truly be close to God – considered **sons of God** – you had to be *extremely observant* of the law, just as the Scribes and Pharisees were (Matthew 23). Here, Paul says we can be considered **sons of God** in a completely different way: **through faith in Christ Jesus**.

i. The *standing* is impressive. To be among the **sons of God** means that we have a special relationship with God as a loving and caring Father. It is a place of *closeness*, a place of *affection*, a place of *special care and attention*.

ii. The *method* is impressive. To become a son of God **through faith in Christ Jesus** means much more than believing that He exists or did certain things. It is to put our *trust* in Him, both for now and eternity.

b. **For as many of you as were baptized into Christ**: Here, using the picture of baptism, Paul illustrates what it means to have **faith in Christ Jesus**. He doesn't say we were **baptized** into water, but **baptized into Christ**. Just as in water baptism a person is *immersed* in water, so when we place our **faith in Christ Jesus**, we are *immersed* in Jesus.

i. Many Christians seem content with just "dipping a bit" into Jesus. God wants us to be *fully immersed* in Jesus; not sprinkled, not just a part of us dipped. When a person is immersed in water, you don't even see the person much anymore – you mostly see the water. When we live as **baptized into Christ**, you don't see so much of "me" anymore; you mostly see Jesus.

ii. It should be stressed that *this* is the baptism that really saves us: our immersion into Jesus. If a person isn't **baptized into Christ**, he could be dunked a thousand times into water and it would make no eternal difference. If a person has been **baptized into Christ**, then he should follow through and do what Jesus told him to do: receive baptism as a demonstration of his commitment to Jesus (Matthew 28:19-20).

c. **Have put on Christ**: Another way of expressing our *immersion* in Jesus is to say that we have **put on Christ**. In the original language, the phrase has the idea of *putting on a suit of clothes*. So we "clothe ourselves" with Jesus as our identity.

i. How we dress has a real impact on how we think and act. How we dress has a real impact on how we appear to others. We also need to know how to dress appropriately for each occasion. Paul says to us, "Your appropriate clothing for each day is to **put on Christ**. People should see that you belong to Him by looking at your life. You should live with the awareness that you are adorned with Jesus."

ii. Some people might wonder if this is only play-acting, if it is really an illusion, like a child playing "dress-up." The answer is simple. It is only an illusion if there is no *spiritual reality* behind it. In this verse, Paul really speaks of the *spiritual reality* – those who **were baptized into Christ** really have **put on Christ**. Now they are called to live each day consistent with the spiritual reality.

5. (28-29) Our equal standing with others who come to God through faith.

There is neither Jew nor Greek, there is neither slave nor free, there is neither male nor female; for you are all one in Christ Jesus. And if you *are* Christ's, then you are Abraham's seed, and heirs according to the promise.

a. **There is neither Jew nor Greek**: This was an amazing revolution. The whole problem among the Galatian Christians is that some wanted to still observe the dividing line between **Jew** and **Greek**. Paul writes, "In Jesus Christ that line is done away with. When we are in Jesus, **there is neither Jew nor Greek**."

b. **There is neither slave nor free, there is neither male nor female; for you are all one in Christ Jesus**: The dividing line between **Jew** and **Greek** is not the only dividing line erased. Regarding our standing before God in Jesus, every dividing line is erased. Now that Jesus is our identity, that is more important than any prior identity we possessed. We are **all one in Christ Jesus**.

i. At that time, some Rabbis quoted a morning prayer that was popular among many Jews of that day. According to William Barclay, in that prayer the Jewish man would thank God that he was not born a Gentile, a slave, or a woman. Paul takes each of these categories and shows them to be equal in Jesus.

ii. Sadly, some Christians still draw lines today. Some draw lines between denominations, some draw lines between races, some draw lines between nations, some draw lines between political parties, and some draw lines between economic classes. For example, if you feel you have more common ground with an unbeliever who shares your race or your political party than with a genuine Christian from another race or political party, you have drawn a line that Jesus died on the cross to erase.

iii. This doesn't mean that there are no *differences*. Paul knew that there was still a difference between **Jew and Greek**, and his evangelistic approach might differ to each group (1 Corinthians 9:19-21). The **slave** still had a daily obligation to obey his **master**, though he might be equal in Jesus (Ephesians 6:5-8). There are still different roles for **male** and **female** in the home and in the church (1 Timothy 2:1-15, Ephesians 5:22-33), though they are equal in standing before God. There are differences in role and in function, but none in standing before God through faith in Jesus. "When we say that Christ has abolished these distinctions, we mean not that they do not exist, but that they no longer create any barriers to fellowship." (Stott)

iv. "He is not writing about a unity that comes about as a result of human achievement. He is saying that when people are saved by Jesus Christ they are brought into a marvelous unity, a unity between the saved and the Saviour and a unity that binds together all the saved." (Morris)

c. **You are all one in Christ Jesus**: This is amazing. Some would have Paul exclude some of the Christians from a Gentile background because they hadn't come under the Law of Moses. Paul includes them saying "**You are all one in Christ Jesus**." Others might have Paul exclude some of the Christians from a Jewish background, because their theology was wrong on this point and Paul needed to correct them. Paul includes them saying "**You are all one in Christ Jesus**."

i. "Many of God's children lack a deep understanding of the Christian way, but that does not mean that they are not genuine Christians. Being a Christian is being a believer, not having an intellectual answer to all the problems we meet as we live out our Christian lives." (Morris)

d. **And if you are Christ's, then you are Abraham's seed**: Since all Christians belong to Jesus the Messiah, all Christians are spiritual descendants of Abraham and **heirs** of God. This place of high privilege comes **according to the promise**, not according to law or works. We are connected with the long line of God's people assembled throughout all the ages.

> i. Some Jewish Christians said to the Galatians that if they submitted to the law and became circumcised, they could enjoy the status of being **Abraham's seed**. Paul points out that this status was *already* theirs through faith in Jesus.

> ii. Paul has reinforced this principle throughout this section by his repeating of the title **Christ** for Jesus (used 11 times in the last 17 verses). When Paul referred to Jesus as **Christ**, he emphasized Jesus' role as the promised *Messiah* of the Jewish people – and of all the world, as Paul emphasized.

e. **If you are Christ's**: This is the issue. The issue is not "Are you under the law?" The issue is not "Are you a Jew or a Gentile?" The issue is not "Are you slave or free?" The issue is not "Are you a man or a woman?" The only issue is **if you are Christ's**.

> i. If we **are Christ's**, then...

> - We find our place in *eternity*, because we are sons and daughters of God.

> - We find our place in *society*, because we are brothers and sisters in the family of God.

> - We find our place in *history*, because we are part of God's plan of the ages, related spiritually to Abraham by our faith in Jesus.

> ii. "It enables me to answer the most basic of all human questions, 'Who am I?' and to say, 'In Christ I am a son of God. In Christ I am united to all the redeemed people of God, past, present, and future. In Christ I discover my identity. In Christ I find my feet. In Christ I come home." (Stott)

Galatians 4 - Heirs and Slaves, Grace and Law

A. No longer under bondage to the basic elements, we are God's children.

1. (1-3) An illustration and application comparing a child and slave.

Now I say *that* the heir, as long as he is a child, does not differ at all from a slave, though he is master of all, but is under guardians and stewards until the time appointed by the father. Even so we, when we were children, were in bondage under the elements of the world.

a. **The heir, as long as he is a child**: The word **child** has the idea of a *minor*. It doesn't suggest a specific age, rather someone who is not yet legally recognized as an adult.

> i. In both Jewish and Greek cultures, there were definite "coming of age" ceremonies where a boy stopped being a **child** and started being a man, with legal rights as an **heir**.

> ii. In the Roman custom, there was no specific age when the son became a man. It happened when the father thought the boy was ready. When Paul used the phrase **until the time appointed by the father**, he shows that he had the Roman "coming of age" custom more in mind than the Jewish custom.

> iii. "A Roman child became an adult at the sacred family festival known as the *Liberalia*, held annually on the seventeenth of March. At this time the child was formally adopted by the father as his acknowledged son and heir and received the *toga virilis* in place of the *toga praetexta* which he had previously worn." (Boice)

> iv. "There was a Roman custom that on the day a boy or a girl grew up, the boy offered his ball, and the girl her doll, to Apollo to show that they had put away childish things." (Barclay)

b. **As long as he is a child, does not differ at all from a slave, though he is master of all**: Think of a wealthy ancient household, with a young boy who is destined to inherit all that his father has. When the boy is just a child, he actually has less day-to-day freedom and authority than a high ranking **slave** in the household. Yet, he is *destined* to inherit everything and the slave isn't.

> i. In fact, the **heir** is under the strict care of **guardians and stewards until the time appointed by the father**.

c. **Even so**: Now comes the comparison to our own spiritual condition. We are *sons of God through faith in Christ Jesus* (Galatians 3:26), and we are *heirs according to the promise* (Galatians 3:29). The law was our guardian (Galatians 3:24-25), to watch over us when we were still "children." The law's effect on our corrupt nature was to bring us into **bondage under the elements of the world**.

d. **Elements of the world**: Paul uses an interesting phrase here. "To describe it Paul uses the word *stoicheia*. A *stocheion* was originally a line of things; for instance, it can mean a file of soldiers. But it came to mean the ABC, and then any elementary knowledge." (Barclay)

> i. Cole translates the idea: "So too, we, when we were 'young children,' were kept in slavery to the ABC of the universe."
>
> ii. The idea of the "ABC of the universe" is important. If there is any "ABC of the universe" (elementary principle) that we must break free from, and that is stressed in pagan religion just as much as Jewish law, it is the principle of *cause and effect*. One may call it karma or "you get what you deserve" or something else; yet it rules nature and the minds of men. We live under the idea that we get what we deserve; when we are good we deserve to receive good and when we are bad we deserve to receive bad.
>
> iii. Paul told the Galatians to go beyond this "ABC of the universe" into an understanding of God's grace. Grace contradicts this "ABC of the universe," because under grace God does not deal with us on the basis of what we deserve. Our good cannot justify us under grace; our bad need not condemn us. God's blessing and favor is given on a principle completely apart from the "ABC of the universe." His blessing and favor is given for reasons that are completely *in Him*, and have nothing to do with us.
>
> iv. The "ABC of the universe" is not bad in itself. We do and must use it in life, and God has a proper place for it. But we must not base our relationship to God on this principle. Since we are now under grace, He does deal not with us on the principle of earning and deserving. Because this is such an elementary principle, it is so hard for us to

shake this kind of thinking. But it is essential if we will walk in grace. When we live on the principle of earning and deserving before God, we live **in bondage under the elements of the world**.

v. False teaching is according to these elemental principles, and not according to Jesus (Colossians 2:8). In Jesus, we die to the elemental principles of the world (Colossians 2:20).

2. (4-5) The liberation of heirs from their bondage.

But when the fullness of the time had come, God sent forth His Son, born of a woman, born under the law, to redeem those who were under the law, that we might receive the adoption as sons.

a. **But when the fullness of time had come**: The idea behind the phrase **the fullness of time** is "when the time was right." Jesus came at just the right time in God's redemptive plan, when the world was perfectly prepared for God's work.

i. "*But* introduces a contrast. The control of the *elemental principles* was only for a limited time." (Morris) For those who were under bondage to the law, it may seem that Jesus' coming was late. Paul assures us that it was at *just the right time*.

ii. "It was a time when the *pax Romana* extended over most of the civilized earth and when travel and commerce were therefore possible in a way that had formerly been impossible. Great roads linked the empire of the Caesars, and its diverse regions were linked far more significantly by the all-pervasive language of the Greeks. Add the fact that the world was sunk in a moral abyss so low that even the pagan cried out against it and that spiritual hunger was everywhere evident, and one has a perfect time for the coming of Christ and for the early expansion of the Christian gospel." (Boice)

iii. The time was also right because the 483 years prophesied by Daniel were drawing to a close (Daniel 9:24-26).

b. **God sent forth His Son, born of a woman**: Jesus came not only as God's **Son**, but also as one **born of a woman, born under law**. The eternal Son of God in heaven added humanity to His deity and became a man, **born of a woman, born under law**.

i. **Born of a woman** may be a veiled reference to the Virgin Birth, because Paul never says that Jesus was *born of a man*. "The more general term 'woman' indicates that Christ was born a true man. Paul does not say that Christ was born of man and woman, but only of woman. That he has the virgin in mind is obvious." (Luther)

c. **To redeem those who were under the law**: Because Jesus is God, He has the power and the resources to **redeem** us. Because Jesus is man, He has the right and the ability to **redeem** us. He came to purchase us out of the slave market, from our bondage to sin and *the elements of the world.*

i. John Newton, the man who wrote the most popular and famous hymn in America, *Amazing Grace*, knew how to remember this. He was an only child whose mother died when he was only seven years old. He became a sailor and went out to sea at eleven years old. As he grew up, he became the captain of a slave ship and had an active hand in the horrible degradation and inhumanity of the slave trade. But when he was twenty-three, on March 10, 1748, when his ship was in imminent danger of sinking off the coast of Newfoundland, he cried to God for mercy, and he found it. He never forgot how amazing it was that God had received him, as bad as he was. To keep it fresh in his memory, he fastened across the wall over the fireplace mantel of his study the words of Deuteronomy 15:15: *You shall remember that you were a slave in the land of Egypt, and the* LORD *your God redeemed you.* If we keep fresh in our mind what we once were, and what we are now in Jesus Christ, we will do well.

d. **That we might receive the adoption as sons**: It would be enough that we are purchased out of the slave market. But God's work for us doesn't end there; we are then elevated to the place of sons and daughters of God by **adoption**.

i. Every human being is a child of God in the sense of being His offspring (Acts 17:28-29). Yet not every human being is a child of God in the sense of this close, adoptive relationship Paul writes of here. In this sense, there are children of God and children of the devil (John 8:44).

ii. Paul probably has in mind the Roman custom of adoption, where adopted sons were given absolutely equal privileges in the family and equal status as heirs.

iii. There is a sense in which this is a totally *unnecessary* blessing that God has given in the course of salvation, and a demonstration of His true and deep love for us. We can picture someone helping or saving someone, but not going so far as to make them a part of the family – but this is what God did for us.

iv. We **receive** the adoption of sons; we do not *recover* it. In this sense, we gain something in Jesus that is greater than what Adam ever had. Adam was never adopted as a son of God in the way believers are. So we are mistaken when we think of redemption as merely a restoration of what was lost with Adam. We are granted more in Jesus than Adam ever had.

3. (6-7) Celebrating our sonship.

And because you are sons, God has sent forth the Spirit of His Son into your hearts, crying out, "Abba, Father!" Therefore you are no longer a slave but a son, and if a son, then an heir of God through Christ.

a. **Because you are sons... "Abba, Father!"** It is fitting that those who are in fact sons have the **Spirit of** the **Son** in their **hearts**. This gives us both the *right* and the *ability* to cry out "Daddy!" to God our Father, even as Jesus did to His Father.

> i. Some think that translating the idea of **Abba** as "Daddy" is too intimate, and even improper. Cole writes on **Abba**: "While it was the usual informal word applied by a child to its father within the home, it is over-sentimentalizing to translate it as 'Daddy.'"

> ii. But as Boice points out, "The early church fathers - Chrysostom, Theodor of Mopsuestia, and Theodoret of Cyprus, who came from Antioch (where Aramaic was spoken and who probably had Aramaic-speaking nurses in their childhood) - unanimously testify that *Abba* was the address of a small child to his father."

> iii. "*Abba* is an Aramaic affectionate diminutive for 'father' used in the intimacy of the family circle; it passed without change into the vocabulary of Greek-speaking Christians" (Fung)

> iv. We have access to the same intimacy with God the Father that God the Son, Jesus Christ had. Jesus addressed God the Father as "Daddy" when He prayed, *Abba, Father* as recorded in Mark 14:36.

b. **Crying out, "Abba, Father!"** We don't *whisper* "Daddy" as if we were hesitant to speak so affectionately. Instead, we cry it out.

> i. Calvin on **crying out**: "I consider that this participle is used to express great boldness. Uncertainty does not let us speak calmly, but keeps our mouth half-shut, so that the half-broken words can hardly escape from a stammering tongue. 'Crying', on the contrary, is a sign of certainty and unwavering confidence."

> ii. "Let the Law, sin, and the devil cry out against us until their outcry fills heaven and earth. The Spirit of God outcries them all. Our feeble groans, 'Abba, Father,' will be heard of God sooner than the combined racket of hell, sin, and the Law." (Luther)

c. **God has sent forth the Spirit of His Son into your hearts:** We know that we are the sons and daughters of God by the witness of the Holy Spirit within us. As Paul wrote in Romans 8:16: *The Spirit Himself bears witness with our spirit that we are children of God.*

i. "Thus, God's purpose was not only to secure our sonship by His Son, but to assure us of it by His Spirit. He sent His Son that we might have the *status* of sonship, and He sent His Spirit that we might have an *experience* of it." (Stott)

ii. We also can't miss the way the truth of the Trinity is woven into the text: God the Father sends God the Holy Spirit, who is the Spirit of God the Son, into our hearts to give us an assurance that we are the sons and daughters of God.

d. **The Spirit of His Son**: The Holy Spirit can be called the Spirit of God, the Spirit of Christ, or linked to God the Father. This is because the nature of God is consistent among the persons of the Trinity. Here, the Holy Spirit is called **the Spirit of His Son** because the idea of our sonship is based on Jesus' sonship.

i. Our sonship is based on who we are in Jesus, yet there are important distinctions between our sonship and Jesus' sonship. He is the *only begotten Son* (John 3:16) making Him a Son by essential nature. We are *adopted* sons and daughters of God, made children by a legal decree of God.

e. **Therefore you are no longer a slave but a son**: Sons are never slaves and slaves are never sons in their father's house. Jesus illustrated this in the parable of the prodigal son, where the son was determined to return to his father as a slave – but the father refused, and would only receive him as a son.

f. **And if a son, then an heir**: There is a beautiful progression. First we are set free from slavery. Then we are declared sons and adopted into God's family. Then, as sons, we are made heirs.

i. Heirs inherit something and Paul made it clear just what we inherit: **an heir of God through Christ**. We inherit **God** Himself.

ii. For some, this might seem like a small inheritance. Yet for those who are really in Christ and who really love God, to be **an heir of God** is the richest inheritance of all.

g. **Through Christ**: Our release from slavery, our sonship, the Spirit of Jesus in our hearts, and our status as heirs of God are all birthrights given to us in Jesus. We receive them **through Christ**. These are things we should be living in and enjoying every day of our Christian life.

4. (8-11) A decision to make: A choice between living under the elements of the world or as a son of God.

But then, indeed, when you did not know God, you served those which by nature are not gods. But now after you have known God, or rather are known by God, how *is it that* you turn again to the weak and beggarly elements, to which you desire again to be in bondage? You observe days and months and seasons and years. I am afraid for you, lest I have labored for you in vain.

a. **But now after you have known God, or rather are known by God, how is that you turn again**: The bondage is natural when we did not know God and when we served those things that are not gods (**then, indeed, when you did not know God**). Yet now the Galatians **have known God** and yet placed themselves under **bondage**. This was what amazed Paul.

i. **Or rather are known by God**: Paul made an important point when he wrote **or rather are known by God**; it is really more important that God knows us (in the sense of an intimate, accepting relationship) than it is that we know God. Remember the terrible words of judgment in Matthew 7:21-23: *I never knew you.*

b. **How is it that you turn again to the weak and beggarly elements**: In turning to legalism, the Galatians were not turning to a new error, but coming back to an old one – the idea of a works relationship with God.

i. **The weak and beggarly elements**: Paul used the same word for **elements** used in Galatians 4:3. As Christians, we can place ourselves under the bondage of a works based, "cause and effect" relationship with God – but this is moving backward, not forward. By writing **turn again**, Paul shows that the Galatians were not turning to a new error, but coming back to an old one; the idea of a works relationship with God.

ii. "One of the tragedies of legalism is that it gives the appearance of spiritual maturity when, in reality, it leads the believer back into a 'second childhood' of Christian experience." (Wiersbe)

c. **Weak and beggarly**: These **elements of the world** are **weak** because they offer no strength; they are **beggarly** because they bestow no riches. All they can do is bring us **again** into **bondage**.

i. Stott paraphrased the thought: "If you were a slave and are now a son, if you did not know God but have now come to know Him and to be known by Him, how can you turn back again to the old slavery? How can you allow yourself to be enslaved by the very elemental spirits from whom Jesus Christ has rescued you?"

d. **You observe days and months and seasons and years**: The false teachers among the Galatians demanded the observance of **days and months and seasons and years** and other such legalistic matters acted as if this would lead them into a higher plane of spirituality. Yet all these **weak and beggarly elements** of legalism did was to bring them into **bondage**.

i. Paul seems amazed that someone would turn from the liberty of Jesus to this kind of bondage. Yet legalism caters to and recognizes our flesh by putting the focus on what we achieve for God, not on what Jesus did for us. The liberty of Jesus gives us status as sons and a rich inheritance, but it won't cater to our flesh.

ii. "Notice how such a verse is at a variance with any and every theory of a *Christian sabbath*, cutting at the root, as it does, of ALL obligatory *observance of times as such*." (Alford)

iii. "When certain days are represented as holy in themselves, when one day is distinguished from another on religious grounds, when holy days are reckoned a part of divine worship, the days are improperly observed." (Calvin)

e. **I am afraid for you, lest I have labored for you in vain**: Paul's fear was that this attraction to legalism would mean that his work among the Galatians amounted to nothing and would end up being **in vain**.

i. **Labored** is literally "to labor to the point of exhaustion." Paul worked hard among the Galatians, as he always did (1 Corinthians 15:10). Paul never thought the gospel of free grace meant laziness in serving God.

f. **In vain**: At the end of this section, Paul set a choice before the Galatians and before us. We can have a living, free, relationship with God as a loving Father based on what Jesus did for us and who we are in Him. Or we can try to please God by our best efforts of keeping the rules, living in bondage as slaves, not sons. Living that way makes the whole gospel **in vain**.

i. A good example of this is John Wesley. Before his conversion:

- He was the son of a clergyman and a clergyman himself.
- He was orthodox in belief, faithful in morality, and full of good works.
- He did ministry in prisons, sweatshops, and slums.
- He gave food, clothing, and education to slum children.
- He observed *both* Saturday and Sunday as the Sabbath.
- He sailed from England to the American colonies as a missionary.

- He studied his Bible, prayed, fasted, and gave regularly.

ii. Yet all the time, he was bound in the chains of his own religious efforts, because he trusted in what he could do to make himself right before God instead of trusting in what Jesus had done. Later, he came to "trust in Christ, in Christ only for salvation," and came to an inner assurance that he was now forgiven, saved, and a son of God. Looking back on all his religious activity before he was truly saved, he said: "I had even then the faith of a *servant*, though not that of a son."

B. A personal appeal from the Apostle Paul.

1. (12) Paul appeals: "Become like me."

Brethren, I urge you to become like me, for I *became* like you. You have not injured me at all.

a. **I urge you to become like me**: For many of us today, these are strange words from Paul. How could he ever **urge** the Galatians **to become like** him? Should he only point them to Jesus? In what way should the Galatian Christians **become like** Paul?

i. Paul knew well that he wasn't sinlessly perfect. He wasn't standing before the Galatian Christians, saying, "Look at how perfect I am. Don't worry about following Jesus, just follow me." He simply wanted them to follow him as he followed Jesus.

ii. Instead, Paul knew the Galatian Christians should imitate his *consistency*. The Galatians started out with the right understanding of the gospel, because Paul led them into the right understanding. But some of them didn't *stay* there like Paul did, and in that way, they should **become like** Paul.

iii. Paul knew the Galatian Christians should imitate his *liberty*. Paul was free in Jesus, and he wanted them to know the same freedom. In that way, they should **become like** Paul. "*Be as I am* is an exhortation to the Galatians to become Christians in the same sense as Paul is a Christian, one who is not bound by the Jewish law." (Morris)

iv. In some sense every Christian should be able to say to others, "**become like me**." "All Christians should be able to say something like this, especially to unbelievers, namely that we are so satisfied with Jesus Christ, with His freedom, joy and salvation, that we want other people to become like us." (Stott)

b. **For I became like you**: Paul could say to the Galatian Christians, "When it comes to legalism, I know where you are at. I used to live my whole life trying to be accepted by God because of what I did. In that regard, **I**

became like you and saw that it was a dead end. Take it from someone who knows where you are coming from."

i. Or, Paul may have in mind the idea that he became as a Gentile when he was among them, according to the philosophy expressed in 1 Corinthians 9:19-23. In this thinking, he became "One who lives free from the restrictions imposed by the law. This means he had thrown off his Jewish shackles and come to be like a Gentile; he beseeches his converts not to become like Jews." (Morris)

c. **You have not injured me at all**: Paul has used pretty strong words with the Galatians. It would be easy for them to think he spoke just out of a sense of personal hurt. Paul assured them that this wasn't the case at all. Paul wanted them to get this right, but for their own sakes and not for his.

i. We can feel Paul's heartfelt emotion in these verses. As Stott observed, "In Galatians 1-3 we have been listening to Paul the apostle, Paul the theologian, Paul the defender of the faith; but now we are hearing Paul the man, Paul the pastor, Paul the passionate lover of souls."

2. (13-16) Paul appeals: "Remember how you used to respond to me."

You know that because of physical infirmity I preached the gospel to you at the first. And my trial which was in my flesh you did not despise or reject, but you received me as an angel of God, *even* as Christ Jesus. What then was the blessing you *enjoyed*? For I bear you witness that, if possible, you would have plucked out your own eyes and given them to me. Have I therefore become your enemy because I tell you the truth?

a. **You know that because of physical infirmity I preached the gospel to you at the first**: Apparently, Paul was compelled to travel into the region of Galatia because of some type of physical infirmity he suffered while on his first missionary journey. The book of Acts doesn't tell us as much about this as we would like to know, but we can piece together a few facts.

i. We know that when Paul was in the region of south Galatia, persecutors tried to execute him by stoning in the city of Lystra (Acts 14:19-20). His attackers gave him up for dead, yet he miraculously survived. Some think that this was the cause of the **physical infirmity** he mentions. But Paul was already in the region of Galatia when that happened; his wording in Galatians 4 suggests that he *came into* the region because of a **physical infirmity**.

ii. "The emphatic position of the phrase suggests that Paul's original plan had been to go elsewhere (perhaps westward toward Ephesus) and that his missionary visit to the Galatians was due solely to his illness and his need for recuperation." (Fung)

iii. What exactly was Paul's **physical infirmity**? Some believe his problem was depression, or epilepsy, or that his illness was connected with the *thorn in the flesh* mentioned in 2 Corinthians 12. None of these can be established with certainty.

iv. According to Acts 13, Paul came to the region of Galatia – specifically, the city of Pisidian Antioch – from the city of Perga in the region of Pamphylia. We know a few things about Perga; first, it was the place where John Mark abandoned Paul and Barnabas (Acts 13:13), and the trials related to the **physical infirmity** may have had something to do with it. Second, Perga was in lowland, marshy area. The Galatian city of Pisidian Antioch was some 3,600 feet higher than Perga. It has been suggested that Paul's **physical infirmity** was a type of malaria common to the lowlands of Perga. William Barclay described this malaria as producing a terrible pain that was like "a red-hot bar thrust through the forehead."

v. However, we should remember what Morris quoted from Stamm: "The difficulty of diagnosing the case of a living patient should warn us of the futility of attempting it for one who has been dead almost nineteen hundred years."

b. **My trial that was in my flesh you did not despise or reject**: Even though Paul was not a great example of strength and power because of his physical infirmity, the Galatians still received him, and they received him honorably. They embraced Paul so generously that they would have **plucked out** [their] **own eyes and given them to** Paul if that could somehow meet his need.

i. "Obviously, a plucked-out eye would be a gift nobody could use, but Paul's point is that his converts had been ready to do anything for him in those early days." (Morris)

ii. This leads some to believe that Paul's physical infirmity had something to do with his eyes. Noted Greek scholars such as Wuest, Rendall, and Robertson believe that the nuances of the Greek text indicate that Paul's *physical infirmity* as an eye problem. Galatians 6:11 – where Paul makes reference to large letters written with his own hand – may also support this idea.

iii. But Cole rightly notes: "Those who see here a proof that Paul suffered from ophthalmia, or some similar eye-disease, are welcome to do so. Certainly with smoky fires, no chimneys, and oil lamps, one would expect a high incidence of eye trouble in the first-century Mediterranean world. To one who had spent years poring over crabbed

Hebrew tomes the risk might well be greater. But again we have no proof."

iv. But the real point here is that despite whatever Paul's infirmity was, the Galatians did not **despise or reject** him. "As physical infirmity and illness were regarded by Jews and Gentiles alike as a symbol of divine displeasure or punishment, there would have been a natural temptation for the Galatians to despise Paul and reject his message." (Fung) This is exactly what the Galatians *did not* do. Even though Paul seemed weak and afflicted, they embraced him and responded to his message of grace and God's love.

c. **Have I therefore become your enemy because I tell you the truth?** In light of the great love and honor the Galatians had shown towards Paul and in light of the great blessing they received from God when they showed such to him, the Galatians should not think that Paul has now become their adversary when he confronted them with the truth. They needed the **truth** more than they needed to feel good about where they were at.

i. "It is not enough that pastors be respected, if they are not also loved. Both are necessary; otherwise, their teaching will not have a sweet taste. And he declares that both had been true of him among the Galatians. He had already spoken of their respect; he now speaks of their love." (Calvin)

ii. "To the degree that ministers and teachers of the Word of God do teach the Word, to that same degree should they be received as the Galatians received the apostle Paul. Ministers should not be received and evaluated on the basis of their personal appearance, intellectual attainments, or winsome manner, but as to whether or not they are indeed God's messengers bearing the word of Christ." (Boice)

3. (17-18) Paul appeals: "Beware of the affection the legalists show you."

They zealously court you, *but* for no good; yes, they want to exclude you, that you may be zealous for them. But it is good to be zealous in a good thing always, and not only when I am present with you.

a. **The zealously court you, but for no good**: Paul will admit that the legalists **zealously court** the Galatians; and legalism often comes wrapped in a cloak of "love." But the end result is **for no good**.

i. Many cults use a technique informally known as "love bombing." They overwhelm a prospective member with attention, support, and affection. Yet it isn't really a sincere love for the prospect; it is really just a technique to gain another member. Christians can use the same technique in some way or another.

b. **They want to exclude you, that you may be zealous for them**: Paul's legalistic opponents wanted to draw the Galatian Christians away into their own divisive group. They actually wanted to *exclude* the Galatians from other Christians and to bring them into the "super-spiritual" group of the legalists.

i. The zeal cultivated by legalism is often more a zeal for the group itself than for Jesus Christ. Though they name the name of Jesus, in practice *the group itself* is exalted as the main focus, and usually exalted as the last refuge of the true "super-Christians."

c. **Exclude**: This literally means to "lock you up." For now, the legalists are courting the Galatians, but once they have alienated them from Jesus and from Paul, the legalists will demand that the Galatians serve *them*. Legalism is almost always associated with some kind of religious bondage.

i. "The Judaizers had pursued the adroit course of presenting to them only part of the requirements of the Mosaic law, those parts which might be least repulsive to them as Gentiles. Having gotten them to adopt the festivals and perhaps the fast days, the Judaizers were now urging them to adopt circumcision." (Wuest)

d. **It is good to be zealous in a good thing always**: Paul certainly wasn't against *zeal*. He wanted Christians to be **zealous in a good thing always**. But it is important to make sure that our zeal is **in a good thing** because zeal in a *bad thing* is dangerous.

i. The Galatian Christians were no doubt impressed by the *zeal* of the legalists. The legalists were so sincere, so passionate about their beliefs. Paul agreed that **it is good to be zealous** – but *only* **in a good thing always**. Zeal in the service of a lie is a *dangerous* thing.

ii. Paul knew this well, because before he became a Christian, he had plenty of zeal; even persecuting the church (Acts 7:58-8:4). Later, Paul looked back at that time of great zeal in the service of a lie and deeply regretted it (1 Corinthians 15:9, 1 Timothy 1:15).

e. **And not only when I am present with you**: Paul wanted the Galatians to be zealous for what is good when he was absent, not only when he was **present** among them.

4. (19-20) Paul appeals: "I love you like a father, please listen to me."

My little children, for whom I labor in birth again until Christ is formed in you, I would like to be present with you now and to change my tone; for I have doubts about you.

a. **My little children**: Paul rightly considers himself to be a father to the Galatians. Yet this challenge has made him feel as if he must bring them to Jesus all over again (**for whom I labor in birth again until Christ is formed in you**). Paul knew that his work of forming Christ in them was not complete until they *stayed* in a place of trusting Jesus.

i. The idea of **Christ is formed in you** is similar to the idea of Romans 8:29: *For whom He foreknew, He also predestined to be conformed to the image of His Son.*

ii. It would be wrong for Paul to seek to form *himself* in the Galatians. That is never to be the job of the pastor. He was right to seek to form *Christ* in them.

b. **My little children**: Through this section, Paul masterfully mixed metaphors to give a powerful picture.

i. Paul likens himself to a "mother" who gave spiritual "birth" to the Galatians (**my little children**).

ii. Something unnatural has happened – the Galatians are drifting away from Jesus and to the law. So Paul has to **labor in birth again**, and this is unnatural to have labor pains a second time.

iii. Paul has the **labor** pains, but **Christ is formed in** them. Paul will keep laboring until it is Christmas for the Galatians, and Jesus **is formed in** them.

iv. This is a pattern found in all Biblical ministry. "The Word of God falling from the lips of the apostle or minister enters into the heart of the hearer. The Holy Ghost impregnates the Word so that it brings forth the fruit of faith. In this manner every Christian pastor is a spiritual father who forms Christ in the hearts of his hearers." (Luther)

v. "He likens his pain to the pangs of childbirth. He had been in labour over them previously at the time of their conversion, when they were brought to birth; now their backsliding has caused him another confinement. He is in labour again. The first time there had been a miscarriage; this time he longs that Christ will be truly formed in them." (Stott)

c. **I would like to be present with you now and change my tone**: Paul wished two things. First, that he could **be present** with the Galatians. But he also wished that he did not need to speak to them in such strong words, that he could **change** his **tone**. Yet their danger of leaving the true gospel has made such strong words necessary and has made Paul's **doubts** necessary to address.

i. This section, Galatians 4:12-20, shows us principles for the attitude for people in the church toward their pastor.

- Their attitude must not be determined by his personal appearance or personality.

- Their attitude must not be determined by their own theological whims.

- Their attitude should be determined by his loyalty to the apostolic message in the Bible.

ii. This section, Galatians 4:12-20, shows us principles for the attitude for the pastor towards the people in his church.

- He must be willing to serve and sacrifice for his people.

- He must tell them the truth.

- He must love his people deeply; never for a selfish motive.

- He must desire to see more than mere excitement, but zeal for good things.

- He must desire to form Jesus in them, not himself in them.

C. Using the Old Testament, Paul shows that the systems of grace and law can't exist together as principles in our lives.

1. (21) Paul will appeal to the law to those who claim the law.

Tell me, you who desire to be under the law, do you not hear the law?

a. **Tell me, you who desire to be under the law**: Now Paul writes directly, both to those who promoted legalism and to those who succumbed to legalism. He writes to those **who desire to be under the law**, living under law keeping as the basis for their relationship with God.

i. There are many advantages to being **under the law** as your principle of relating to God. First, you always have the outward certainty of a list of rules to keep. Second, you can compliment yourself because you keep the rules better than others do. Finally, you can take the credit for your own salvation, because you earned it by keeping the list of rules.

ii. **Under the law** it is what *you do for God* that makes you right before Him. Under the grace of God, it is what *God has done for us in Jesus Christ* that makes us right before Him. **Under the law** the focus is on *my performance*. Under the grace of God, the focus is on *who Jesus is and what He has done*. **Under the law** we find fig leaves to cover our nakedness. Under the grace of God we receive the covering won through sacrifice that God provides.

iii. The Christian has no business living **under the law**. "What is God's law now? It is not *above* a Christian – it is under a Christian. Some men hold God's law like a rod *in terrorem*, over Christians, and say, 'If you sin you will be punished with it.' It is not so. The law is under a Christian; it is for him to walk on, to be his guide, his rule, his pattern... Law is the road which guides us, not the rod which drives us, nor the spirit which actuates us." (Spurgeon)

b. **Do you not hear the law?** Paul sensed that he hadn't made his point yet, so he now approached the matter with another illustration from the Old Testament. Essentially, Paul said "Let's have a Bible study. Open your Bibles to Genesis chapter 16."

i. Paul took it for granted that his readers knew the Bible. He explains his point from the story of Abraham, Hagar, and Sarah in Genesis 16 without a lot of detail from the story. He assumes that they knew the story.

ii. It is important that Paul refer back to the Scriptures again and again. The legalists among the Galatians presented themselves as the "back to the Bible" bunch. Yet Paul will show that they were not handling the Old Testament Scriptures correctly, and he will show that a true understanding of the Law of Moses will support the true gospel he preaches.

2. (22-23) The Old Testament shows the contrast between the two sons of Abraham, Isaac and Ishmael.

For it is written that Abraham had two sons: the one by a bondwoman, the other by a freewoman. But he *who was* of the bondwoman was born according to the flesh, and he of the freewoman through promise.

a. **For it is written that Abraham had two sons**: The legalists who troubled the Galatians protested that they were children of Abraham, and therefore blessed. Paul will admit they are children of Abraham, but they forget **that Abraham had two sons**.

b. **The one by a bondwoman, the other by a freewoman**: Abraham's first son was named *Ishmael*. He was born not from his wife, but from his wife's servant (**the bondwoman**), from a misguided surrogate mother scheme to "help God" when Abraham's wife Sarah couldn't become pregnant.

i. The first contrast Paul draws between real Christianity and legalism is the contrast between *freedom* and *slavery*. One son of Abraham was born by a **freewoman**, and one was born by a **bondwoman**. The real Christian life is marked by *freedom*.

c. **Born according to the flesh**: Ishmael was Abraham's son, but he was the son **according to the flesh** and *unbelief* and trying to *make your own way* before God.

> i. It often doesn't look like it, but legalism is living **according to the flesh**. It denies God's promise and tries to make your own way to God through the law. This is living like a descendant of Abraham – but it is living like *Ishmael*.

> ii. "Legalism does not mean the setting of spiritual standards; it means worshipping these standards and thinking we are spiritual because we obey them. It also means judging other believers on the basis of these standards." (Wiersbe)

> iii. "The better legalist a man is, the more sure he is of being damned; the more holy a man is, if he trust to his works, the more he may rest assured of his own final rejection and eternal portion with Pharisees." (Spurgeon)

d. **He of the freewoman through promise**: Abraham's second son was named *Isaac*. He was born, miraculously, through Abraham's wife Sarah (**the freewoman**). Isaac was Abraham's son, and he was the son of God's **promise** and *faith* and *God's miracle for Abraham*.

> i. The second contrast Paul draws between Christianity and legalism is the contrast between a work done by God's *promised miracle* and a work done by the *flesh*. The real Christian life is connected to *God's promised miracle* and not the flesh.

3. (24-27) The Old Testament shows the contrast between Mount Sinai and Mount Zion.

Which things are symbolic. For these are the two covenants: the one from Mount Sinai which gives birth to bondage, which is Hagar; for this Hagar is Mount Sinai in Arabia, and corresponds to Jerusalem which now is, and is in bondage with her children; but the Jerusalem above is free, which is the mother of us all. For it is written:

"Rejoice, O barren,
***You* who do not bear!**
Break forth and shout,
You who are not in labor!
For the desolate has many more children
Than she who has a husband."

> a. **Which things are symbolic**: Paul wanted it understood that he used *pictures* from the Old Testament. His reference to Hagar and Ishmael were

pictures, meant to illustrate his point. Now he would bring in another picture.

> i. Paul was clearly guided by the Holy Spirit here. For us, we must be careful about reading allegorical or symbolic things into the Scriptures. "Scripture, they say, is fertile and thus bears multiple meanings. I acknowledge that Scripture is the most rich and inexhaustible fount of all wisdom. But I deny that its fertility consists in the various meanings which anyone may fasten to it at his pleasure. Let us know, then, that the true meaning of Scripture is the natural and simple one, and let us embrace and hold it resolutely." (Calvin)

b. **For these are the two covenants**: In the Bible, a *covenant* is a "contract" that sets the rules for our relationship with God. Paul brought it right down to the issues confronting the Galatian Christians. The legalists wanted them to relate to God under one set of rules, and Paul wanted them to relate to God under the "rules" presented by the gospel.

c. **The one from Mount Sinai**: One covenant is associated with **Mount Sinai**, the place where Moses received the Law (Exodus 19-20).

> i. This covenant **gives birth to bondage**. Since it is all about what we must do for God to be accepted by Him, it doesn't set us free. It puts us on a perpetual treadmill of having to prove ourselves and earn our way before God.

> ii. This covenant is associated with **Hagar**, the "surrogate mother" who gave birth to Ishmael. It is therefore (if used wrongly) a covenant *according to the flesh* (Galatians 4:23).

> iii. This covenant **corresponds to Jerusalem which now is**, that is, earthly Jerusalem which was the capital of religious Judaism. This was the way most Jewish people in Paul's day tried to be right with God – by trusting in their ability to please God by keeping the law.

d. **But the Jerusalem above**: The other covenant is associated with Jerusalem, with Mount Zion – but not the Mount Zion of this earth. Instead, it is associated with the **Jerusalem above** – God's own *New Jerusalem* in heaven.

> i. The third contrast Paul draws between Christianity and legalism is the contrast between *heaven* and *earth*. Real Christianity comes from *heaven* and not earth.

e. **The Jerusalem above is free**: Paul will now tell us more about the covenant represented by the heavenly Jerusalem. This covenant brings freedom – it **is free**. It is **free** because it recognizes that Jesus paid the price, and we don't have to pay it ourselves.

f. **Which is the mother of us all**: This covenant has many children; it **is the mother of us all**. Every Christian through the centuries belongs to this new covenant, the covenant of the heavenly Jerusalem. And every birth under this covenant is a miracle, like the fulfillment of the prophecy from Isaiah 54:1, **Rejoice, O barren, you who do not bear!** Every one is born because of a miracle by God.

g. **The desolate has many more children**: The quotation from Isaiah 54:1 also suggests that there will soon be more Christians than Jews - a promise that was fulfilled.

i. The fourth contrast Paul draws between Christianity and legalism is the contrast between *many more* and *many*. The abundance and glory of the New Covenant is shown by the fact that it would soon have *many more* followers than the Old Covenant.

The "Ishmaels" - Legalism	The "Isaacs" – True Christianity
Slavery and bondage	Freedom
Ishmael: born according to the flesh	Isaac: born by God's promised miracle
Coming from the earthly Jerusalem	Coming from the heavenly Jerusalem
Many children	Many more children
Persecuting	Persecuted
Inheriting nothing	Inheriting everything
Relationship based on law-keeping	Relationship based on trusting God

4. (28-31) Paul applies the contrasts between the two systems.

Now we, brethren, as Isaac *was*, are children of promise. But, as he who was born according to the flesh then persecuted him *who was born according to the Spirit*, even so *it is* now. Nevertheless what does the Scripture say? "Cast out the bondwoman and her son, for the son of the bondwoman shall not be heir with the son of the freewoman." So then, brethren, we are not children of the bondwoman but of the free.

a. **Now we, brethren, as Isaac was, are children of promise**: As Christians, we don't identify with Ishmael. We identify with **Isaac**, as **children of** a **promise** that was received by faith.

b. **But, as he who was born according to the flesh then persecuted him who was born according to the Spirit, even so it is now**: Ishmael and his descendants persecuted Isaac and his descendants. So we should not be surprised that the modern day people who follow God in the flesh persecute those who follow God in faith through the promise.

i. The fifth contrast Paul draws between Christianity and legalism is the contrast between *persecuted* and *persecuting*. The legalists – represented by Ishmael – have always persecuted true Christianity, represented by Isaac. As we walk in the glory, in the freedom, in the miraculous power of this New Covenant, we should expect to be mistreated by those who don't.

ii. There is no specific mention of Ishmael persecuting Isaac, though Genesis 21:9 says that Ishmael did mock Isaac. Paul may be referring to this mocking, he may be recalling a Jewish tradition, or he may be adding something by the inspiration of the Holy Spirit that we didn't know before.

iii. The persecution Christians face "will not always be by the world but also and indeed more often by their half-brothers - the unbelieving but religious people in the nominal church. This is the lesson of history... Today the greatest enemies of the believing church are found among the members of the unbelieving church, the greatest opposition emanating from pulpits and church hierarchies." (Boice)

c. **Nevertheless what does the Scripture say? "Cast out the bondwoman and her son"**: The answer to this problem is clear, though not easy. We must **cast out the bondwoman and her son**. Law and grace cannot live together as principles for our Christian life.

i. Hagar and Sarah could not live together in the same house (Genesis 21:8-14). We could argue all day long whose fault it was, but that isn't the point. The point is that God told Abraham to send Hagar away. So also every Christian must send away the idea of relating to God on the principle of law, the principle of what we do for Him instead of what He has done for us in Jesus Christ.

ii. Significantly, Sarah *could* live with Hagar and Ishmael *until* the son of promise was born. Once Isaac was born, then Hagar and Ishmael had to go. In the same way, a person could relate to the law one way before the promise of the gospel was made clear in Jesus Christ. But now that it has been made clear, there is nothing to do but to **cast out the bondwoman and her son**.

d. **For the son of the bondwoman shall not be heir with the son of the freewoman**: Ishmael was not necessarily a bad man or a cursed man. But neither was he blessed with the promise of inheriting the glorious covenant of God given to Abraham and his descendants. That was the inheritance of one **heir** – Isaac, **the son of the freewoman**.

i. The sixth contrast Paul draws between Christianity and legalism is the contrast between *inheriting all* and *inheriting nothing*. While the "Isaacs" of this world may be persecuted, they also have a glorious *inheritance* that the "Ishmaels" of this world will never know. We are heirs of God through the principle of grace, not works.

e. **So then, brethren, we are not children of the bondwoman but of the free**: For Paul, one of the great issues in this was *freedom*. He knew the bondage of trying to earn his own way before God, because he lived that way for decades. Now he knew the freedom of living as a son of God, free in Jesus Christ.

i. "Barclay makes the point that anyone who makes law central is 'in the position of a slave; all his life he is seeking to satisfy his master the law'. But when grace is central, the person 'has made love his dominant principle... it will be the power of love and not the constraint of law that keeps us right; and love is always more powerful than law.'" (Morris)

Galatians 5 - Standing Fast In the Liberty of Jesus

A. A final appeal to walk in the liberty of Jesus.

1. (1) A summary statement: in light of all that Paul has previously said, he now challenges the Galatians to walk in the truth he has presented.

Stand fast therefore in the liberty by which Christ has made us free, and do not be entangled again with a yoke of bondage.

    a. **Stand fast therefore in the liberty by which Christ has made us free**: The fact is that Jesus **has made us free**. If we live in bondage to a legal relationship with God, it isn't because God wills it. God pleads with us to take His strength and walk in that freedom, and to **not be entangled again with a yoke of bondage**.

        i. Significantly, it is **Christ** who **has made us free**. We don't make ourselves free. Freedom is a gift of Jesus, given to us and received by faith. When we struggle to free ourselves, we just become more **entangled again with a yoke of bondage**.

        ii. Paul also made it emphatic: *the* **liberty**. Today, people live in the headlong pursuit of "freedom," which they think of as doing whatever they want to do, and never denying any desire. This is a kind of liberty, a false liberty; but it is not *the* **liberty**. *The* **liberty** is our freedom from the tyranny of having to earn our own way to God, the freedom from sin and guilt and condemnation, freedom from the penalty and the power and eventually freedom from the presence of sin.

    b. **Stand fast** means that it takes *effort* to stay in this place of liberty. Someone who is legally made free in Jesus can still live in bondage; they can be deceived into placing themselves back into slavery.

        i. The great evangelist D. L. Moody illustrated this point by quoting an old former slave woman in the South following the Civil War. Being a former slave, she was confused about her status and asked: *Now is*

I free, or been I not? When I go to my old master he says I ain't free, and when I go to my own people they say I is, and I don't know whether I'm free or not. Some people told me that Abraham Lincoln signed a proclamation, but master says he didn't; he didn't have any right to. Many Christians are confused on the same point. Jesus Christ has given them an "Emancipation Proclamation," but their "old master" tells them they are still slaves to a legal relationship with God. They live in bondage because their "old master" has deceived them.

c. **Yoke of bondage**: This phrase reminds us of what Peter said in Acts 15:10 about those who would bring the Gentiles under the law: *Now therefore, why do you test God by putting a yoke on the neck of the disciples which neither our fathers nor we were able to bear?* The Jews themselves were not able to justify themselves before God by the law, so they shouldn't put that heavy, burdensome **yoke** on the Gentiles.

i. Certain Jewish teachers of that day spoke of the Law of Moses as a **yoke**, but they used the term in a favorable light. Paul saw a legal relationship as a **yoke**, but as a **yoke of bondage**. It is related to slavery, not liberty. This **yoke of bondage** does nothing but *entangle* us. We try hard to pull God's plow, but the **yoke of bondage** leaves us tangled, restricted, and frustrated.

ii. It certainly was **bondage**. Jewish teachers counted up 613 commandments to keep in the Law of Moses. "Even to remember them all was a burden, and to keep them bordered on the impossible. Small wonder that Paul referred to subjecting oneself to them all as entering into *slavery*." (Morris)

2. (2-4) The danger of embracing the law as a way to walk with God.

Indeed I, Paul, say to you that if you become circumcised, Christ will profit you nothing. And I testify again to every man who becomes circumcised that he is a debtor to keep the whole law. You have become estranged from Christ, you who *attempt to* be justified by law; you have fallen from grace.

a. **If you become circumcised, Christ will profit you nothing**: When we embrace the law as our rule of walking with God, we must let go of Jesus. *He* is no longer our righteousness; we attempt to earn it ourselves. For the Galatians in this context, to receive *circumcision* – the ritual that testified that a Gentile was coming under the law – meant that he no longer trusted in Jesus as His righteousness, but trusted in himself instead. So Paul could say "**Christ will profit you nothing**."

i. The legalists among the Galatians wanted them to think that they could have *both* Jesus and a law-relationship with God. Paul tells them that this is not an option open to them - the system of grace and the system of law are incompatible. "Whoever wants to have a half-Christ loses the whole." (Calvin)

ii. "Circumcision is the seal of the law. He who willingly and deliberately undergoes circumcision, enters upon a compact to fulfill the law. To fulfill it therefore he is bound, and he cannot plead the grace of Christ; for he has entered on another mode of justification." (Lightfoot)

iii. How tragic! Jesus, dying on the cross, pouring out His blood, His life, His soul, His agony, His love for us – and it **will profit you nothing**! Two men died with Jesus; for the one who put his trust in Jesus, it was eternal life. For the one who trusted in himself, it profited him **nothing**.

iv. This point was so important to Paul that he mustered all the strength he could in a personal appeal: he began with **Indeed I, Paul**. When he continues on and wrote **I testify**, Paul remembered his former training as a lawyer - and was deadly serious. "Tongue cannot express, nor heart conceive what a terrible thing it is to make Christ worthless." (Luther)

b. **Every man who becomes circumcised... is a debtor to keep the whole law**: When we embrace the law as our rule of walking with God, we must embrace the **whole law**. We become debtors to keep the **whole law**, and that is a heavy debt.

i. Again, the legalists among the Galatians wanted them to think they could observe some aspects of the law without coming under the entire law. But when we choose to walk by law, we must walk by the **whole law**.

ii. If we come to God on the basis of our own law keeping we must keep the **whole law** and our law-keeping must be perfect. No amount of obedience makes up for one act of disobedience; if you are pulled over for speeding, it will do no good to protest that you are a faithful husband, a good taxpayer, and have obeyed the speed limit many times. All of that is irrelevant. You have still broken the speeding law and are guilty under it.

iii. This does not mean that the mere act of being **circumcised** means that someone is under a legal relationship with God, and must keep the **whole law** for salvation. Paul spoke to the Gentile Christians among the Galatians, who were being drawn to circumcision as adults, as evidence that they had come under the Law of Moses as the "first step" to salvation. We will later see that Paul didn't care one way or another about circumcision (Galatians 5:6). What he detested was the *theology* of circumcision as presented by the legalists.

c. **You have fallen from grace**: When we embrace the law as our rule of walking with God, we depart from Jesus and His grace. We are then **estranged from Christ**, separated from Him and His saving grace.

> i. The danger of falling from grace is real, but it is often misunderstood. Most people think of "falling away" in terms of immoral conduct, but we are not saved by our conduct. However, we *are* saved by our continuing reliance by faith on the grace of God. Someone may fall from grace and be damned without ever falling into grossly immoral conduct.

> ii. Boice on **you have fallen from grace**: "The phrase does not mean that if a Christian sins, he falls from grace and thereby loses his salvation. There is a sense in which to sin is to fall into grace, if one is repentant. But to fall from grace, as seen by this context, is to fall into legalism... Or to put it another way, to choose legalism is to relinquish grace as the principle by which one desires to be related to God."

> iii. Literally, Paul wrote, "you have fallen out of grace," which is not the same as the colloquial English phrase "you have fallen from grace."

3. (5-6) The answer of faith to the legalist.

For we through the Spirit eagerly wait for the hope of righteousness by faith. For in Christ Jesus neither circumcision nor uncircumcision avails anything, but faith working through love.

a. **For we through the Spirit eagerly wait for the hope of righteousness by faith**: Those walking in the Spirit **wait** for **righteousness by faith**; they are not trying to *earn* it by performing good works. No one is a legalist **through the Spirit**.

> i. Wuest on **eagerly wait**: "The word speaks of an attitude of intense yearning and an eager waiting for something. Here it refers to the believer's intense desire for and eager expectation of a practical righteousness which will be constantly produced in his life by the Holy Spirit as he yields himself to Him."

b. **For in Christ Jesus neither circumcision nor uncircumcision avails anything, but faith working through love**: Those walking in the Spirit know that being circumcised or uncircumcised means nothing. What matters is **faith working through love**, both of which were conspicuously absent in the legalists.

i. Each aspect of this verse is precious. It sets us in a *place*: **in Christ Jesus**. Morris on **in Christ**: "Paul never defines what the expression means, but it clearly points to the closest of unities."

ii. In that place, **neither circumcision nor uncircumcision avails anything** – neither one *matters at all*. You aren't better if you are circumcised or uncircumcised. You aren't worse if you circumcised or uncircumcised. The only harm is trusting in something that is completely *irrelevant*.

iii. This verse also tells us what *does matter* in this place: **faith working through love**. You have **faith**? Wonderful; but it must be **faith working through love**. If your faith doesn't *work*, it isn't real **faith**. If it doesn't work **through love**, it isn't real **faith**. But your **love** alone isn't enough; your **love** must also have **faith**: an abiding trust in Jesus and what He did for us.

iv. Faith must work **through love**. Herod had faith that John the Baptist was a true prophet, but there was no **faith working through love**, and he had John the Baptist murdered. Real faith, saving faith, will work **through love**.

4. (7-12) A final confrontation.

You ran well. Who hindered you from obeying the truth? This persuasion does not *come* from Him who calls you. A little leaven leavens the whole lump. I have confidence in you, in the Lord, that you will have no other mind; but he who troubles you shall bear his judgment, whoever he is. And I, brethren, if I still preach circumcision, why do I still suffer persecution? Then the offense of the cross has ceased. I could wish that those who trouble you would even cut themselves off!

a. **You ran well**: Paul remembered their good start in the faith, but he also knows that it isn't enough to start well. They were still in danger of falling from grace.

b. **Who hindered you from obeying the truth?** Paul knew that the false teaching came from a person (*who* **hindered you**); but it didn't come from Jesus (**This persuasion does not come from Him who calls you**).

i. At the root of it all, the Galatians were leaving Jesus to pursue the false and empty teachings of man, in this case legalism.

ii. Lightfoot on **hindered**: "A metaphor derived from military operations. The word signifies 'to break up a road'... so as to render it impassable, and is therefore the opposite of... 'to clear a way.'" The Galatians were doing well until someone broke up the road they ran on.

c. **A little leaven leavens the whole lump**: The warning is driven home – the corrupting influence of legalism and other doctrines that diminish Jesus are like **leaven** in a **lump** of dough. A little bit will soon corrupt the **whole lump**.

> i. In the Jewish way of thinking, **leaven** almost always stood for evil influence. Paul is saying that the legalistic commitment they have right now may be small, but it is so dangerous that it can corrupt everything.

d. **I have confidence in you**: Wanting to leave the confrontation on a positive note, Paul expressed his **confidence** in the Galatians (which was really a confidence in the Lord who is able to keep them). Yet, Paul was equally confident that judgment awaits those who lead them astray and away from Jesus (**he who troubles you shall bear his judgment, whoever he is**).

> i. Remember Jesus' solemn warning against those who would lead one of these *little ones* astray (Matthew 18:6-7). The judgment is sure, **whoever he is**. "It does not matter who he is; he may be highly acclaimed in the community where he teaches, but if he is perverting the gospel he is a guilty person and his rank and reputation will not shield him." (Morris)

e. **If I still preach circumcision**: Paul makes it clear that he no longer preaches the necessity of **circumcision**. The fact that he is persecuted by the legalists is evidence enough of this. Instead, Paul proudly bears **the offense of the cross**.

> i. Someone might accuse Paul of preaching **circumcision** because he asked Timothy to be circumcised (Acts 16:1-3). But Paul didn't have Timothy circumcised so Timothy could be saved or "more saved." He did it so Timothy could more freely evangelize among unsaved Jewish people.

> ii. Legalism can't handle the **offense of the cross**. The whole point of Jesus dying on the cross was to say, "You can't save yourself. I must die in your place or you have absolutely no hope at all." When we trust in legalism, we believe that we can, at least in part, save ourselves. This takes away the **offense of the cross**, which should *always* offend the nature of fallen man. In this sense, **the offense of the cross** is really the *glory of the cross*, and legalism takes this glory away.

f. **I could wish that those who trouble you would even cut themselves off!** Finally, Paul wished that those who demanded circumcision among the Gentiles would go all the way themselves, and amputate their genitalia altogether and not merely their foreskins.

i. Sacred castration was known to citizens of the ancient world; it was frequently practiced by pagan priests of the cults in the region of Galatia. Paul's idea here is something like this: "If cutting will make you righteous, why don't you do like the pagan priests, go all the way and castrate yourself?" Morris rightly observes, "This was a dreadful thing to wish, but then the teaching was a dreadful thing to inflict on young Christians."

ii. "This word was habitually used to describe the practice of mutilation which was so prevalent in the Phrygian worship of Cybele. The Galatians were necessarily familiar with it, and it can hardly bear any other sense." (Rendall)

iii. In writing this, Paul also wished that these legalists would be cut off from the congregation of the Lord as required by Deuteronomy 23:1: *He who is emasculated by crushing or mutilation shall not enter the assembly of the LORD.*

iv. With such a dramatic conclusion to this point, Paul has made one thing clear: legalism is no *little* thing. It takes away our liberty and puts us into bondage. It makes Jesus and His work of no profit to us. It puts us under obligation to the whole law. It violates the work of the Spirit of God. It makes us focus on things that are irrelevant. It keeps us from running the race Jesus set before us. It isn't from Jesus. A little bit will infect an entire church. Those who promote it will face certain judgment, no matter who they are. Legalism tries to take away some of the glory of the cross. In light of how serious all this is, it is no wonder that Paul says he wishes they would **even cut themselves off!**

B. How to live in the liberty of Jesus.

1. (13-15) Using liberty to love each other

For you, brethren, have been called to liberty; only do not *use* liberty as an opportunity for the flesh, but through love serve one another. For all the law is fulfilled in one word, *even* in this: "You shall love your neighbor as yourself." But if you bite and devour one another, beware lest you be consumed by one another!

a. **For you, brethren, have been called to liberty**: Paul has made the point over and over again – the Christian life is a life of **liberty**. Jesus came to set the captives free, not to keep them in bondage or put them in bondage all over again. It is worth asking if people *see* us as people of freedom and liberty. Often, Christians are seen as people more bound up and hung up than anyone else is.

i. "He is not saying that a certain measure of liberty was grudgingly accorded believers. He is saying that freedom is of the essence of being Christian; it is the fundamental basis of all Christian living." (Morris)

b. **Only do not use liberty as an opportunity for the flesh**: The great fear of the legalist is that liberty will be used as an opportunity for the flesh. The idea is that people will just go out and sin as they please, then say to a spineless God, "I'm sorry, please forgive me," and then go on doing whatever they want again. Paul recognized the danger of this attitude, so he warned against it here.

i. First, Paul writes to **brethren**. These are those who *are all sons of God through faith in Christ Jesus* (Galatians 3:26). These are those who *were baptized into Christ* and *have put on Christ* (Galatians 3:27).

ii. These ones **have been called to liberty**. As Paul put it earlier in the chapter, they have been made free by Jesus Christ, now they are called to *stand fast therefore in the liberty by which Christ has made us free* (Galatians 5:1). They have been set free; now the question is, "How will they use their liberty?"

iii. **Do not use liberty as an opportunity for the flesh**: Clearly, we can *choose* to **use liberty as an opportunity for the flesh**. That option – that danger – is open to us. We can take the glorious freedom Jesus has given us, spin it, and use it as a way to please ourselves at the expense of others. Because the context focuses on the way we treat one another, Paul has in mind using our freedom in a way that tramples on the toes of others.

iv. Rendall on **opportunity**: "This term was applied in military language to a base of operations, and generally to any starting-point for action." We are tempted to use our liberty in Jesus as a "base of operations" for selfish sin.

v. It is easy to think **liberty** is "the right to sin," or "the privilege to do whatever evil my heart wants to do." Instead, this **liberty** is the Spirit-given *desire* and *ability* to do what we should do before God.

c. **But through love serve one another**: This is the antidote for using liberty as an occasion for the flesh. The **flesh** expects others to conform to us, and doesn't care much about others. But when we **through love serve one another**, we conquer the flesh. It isn't through an obsessive, contemplative attitude of navel-gazing that we overcome the flesh, but by getting out and serving others.

i. This is *exactly* the pattern set by Jesus. He had more **liberty** than anyone who ever walked this earth did. Yet He used His liberty to **through love serve one another**.

d. **For all the law is fulfilled**: This attitude of service towards one another fulfills the great commandment (**You shall love your neighbor as yourself**), and it keeps us from destroying ourselves through strife (**beware lest you be consumed by one another!**). It's as if Paul addressed the legalists again, and said: "You want to keep the law? Here you have it: **Love your neighbor as yourself** and you have **fulfilled** the law **in one word**."

i. "If you want to know how you ought to love your neighbor, ask yourself how much you love yourself. If you were to get into trouble or danger, you would be glad to have the love and help of all men. You do not need any book of instructions to teach you how to love your neighbor. All you have to do is to look into your own heart, and it will tell you how you ought to love your neighbor as yourself." (Luther)

e. **Bite and devour one another**: This reminds us of a pack of wild animals. That's how the church can act when it uses its "liberty" as a platform to promote selfishness. If you want to see some action, put two selfish people together. Selfish people will eventually **be consumed by one another**.

i. "The loveless life is a life lived on the level of animals, with a concern only for oneself, no matter what the cost to other people." (Morris)

2. (16-18) Using liberty to walk in holy living.

I say then: Walk in the Spirit, and you shall not fulfill the lust of the flesh. For the flesh lusts against the Spirit, and the Spirit against the flesh; and these are contrary to one another, so that you do not do the things that you wish. But if you are led by the Spirit, you are not under the law.

a. **Walk in the Spirit, and you shall not fulfill the lust of the flesh**: Simply put, if we **walk in the Spirit** (instead of trying to live by the law), we naturally **shall not fulfill the lust of the flesh**. Again, the fear of the legalist - that walking in the Spirit gives license to sin, and that only legalism can keep us holy - is just plain wrong.

i. To **walk in the Spirit** first means that the Holy Spirit *lives in you*. Second, it means to be *open* and *sensitive* to the influence of the Holy Spirit. Third, it means to *pattern your life* after the influence of the Holy Spirit.

ii. We can tell if someone walks **in the Spirit** because they will look a lot like Jesus. Jesus told us that the mission of the Holy Spirit would be to promote and speak of *Him* (John 14:16-17, 14:26, 15:26, 16:13-

15). When someone walks **in the Spirit**, they listen to what the Holy Spirit says as He guides us in the path and nature of Jesus.

iii. "Life by the Spirit is neither legalism nor license - nor a middle way between them. It is a life of faith and love that is above all of these false ways." (Boice)

b. **And you shall not fulfill the lust of the flesh**: There is no way anyone can **fulfill the lust of the flesh** as they **walk in the Spirit**. The two simply don't go together. The Holy Spirit doesn't move in us to gratify our fallen desires and passions, but to teach us about Jesus and to guide us in the path of Jesus. *This* is the key to righteous living – walking in the Spirit, not living under the domination of the law.

i. Luther on **the lust of the flesh**: "I do not deny that the lust of the flesh includes carnal lust. But it takes in more. It takes in all the corrupt desires with which believers are more or less infected, as pride, hatred, covetousness, impatience."

c. **For the flesh lusts against the Spirit, and the Spirit against the flesh**: Walking in the Spirit is the key, but it doesn't always come easily. Often, it is a battle. There is a battle going on inside the Christian, and the battle is between the **flesh** and the **Spirit**. As Paul writes, **these are contrary to one another** – they don't get along at all. When the **flesh** is winning the inside battle, **you do not do the things that you wish**. You don't live the way you want to; you live under the **flesh** instead of under the **Spirit**.

i. When Paul uses the term **flesh**, he didn't mean our flesh and blood bodies. Precisely speaking, our flesh isn't even that fallen nature, the "old man" that we inherited from Adam, because the old man was crucified with Jesus, and is now dead and gone (Romans 6:6). Instead, as Paul uses it here, **the flesh** is the inner man that exists apart from the "old man" or the "new man," and which is trained in rebellion by the old nature, the world, and the devil.

ii. Even though the old man was crucified with Christ, and is dead and gone (Romans 6:6), his influence lives on through the flesh, and he will battle against us until we experience God's final antidote to the flesh: a resurrection body.

iii. Boice on **flesh**, and *sarx*, the Greek word translated **flesh**: "When Paul speaks of *sarx* he means all that man is and is capable of as a sinful human being apart from the unmerited intervention of God's Spirit in his life... It came to mean man as a fallen being whose desires even at best originate from sin and are stained by it. Thus *sarx* came to mean all the evil that man is and is capable of apart from the intervention of God's grace in his life."

iv. "When the flesh begins to cut up the only remedy is to take the sword of the Spirit, the word of salvation, and fight against the flesh. If you set the Word out of sight, you are helpless against the flesh. I know this to be a fact. I have been assailed by many violent passions, but as soon as I took hold of some Scripture passage, my temptations left me. Without the Word I could not have helped myself against the flesh." (Luther)

d. **But if you are led by the Spirit, you are not under the law**: The antidote to the flesh is not found in the law, but in the Spirit – and if **you are led by the Spirit, you are not under the law**. You don't need to be, because you fulfill the will of God through the *inner influence* of the Holy Spirit instead of the *outer influence* of the law of God.

i. This effectively "writes" the law of God on our hearts, inside of us. This is the great work of the New Covenant, promised in the Old Testament: *I will put My law in their minds, and write it on their hearts; and I will be their God, and they shall be My people* (Jeremiah 31:33).

ii. The *inner influence* is far more effective than the *outer influence*. "The mistake that is made so often is that the Mosaic law is substituted for the restraint of the Holy Spirit, and with disastrous results... A policeman on the street corner is a far more efficient deterrent of law-breaking than any number of city ordinances placarded for public notice." (Wuest)

3. (19-21a) Examples of the works of the flesh that walking in the Spirit helps us to overcome.

Now the works of the flesh are evident, which are: adultery, fornication, uncleanness, lewdness, idolatry, sorcery, hatred, contentions, jealousies, outbursts of wrath, selfish ambitions, dissensions, heresies, envy, murders, drunkenness, revelries, and the like.

a. **Now the works of the flesh are evident**: Paul has just written about the battle between the flesh and the Spirit in every believer. Though it is an interior, invisible battle, the results are outwardly **evident**. It's almost as if Paul apologizes for having to make this list, because **the works of the flesh are evident**. Yet, under the inspiration of the Holy Spirit, he knows it is important to be specific, because we must know *specifically* how we walk in the flesh. We can't see the **flesh**, but we can see what it *does*.

i. Lists of good and bad behavior would be a familiar form to many of Paul's readers. "In many writings in antiquity there are lists of virtues or vices or both, and such lists are found in the Old Testament, and elsewhere in the New." (Morris)

ii. Some have sought to organize this list in four categories: *sensual* sins, *religious* sins, *interpersonal* sins, and *social* sins. We shouldn't regard this as an exhaustive list, but it adequately gives the idea of what the person who walks in the flesh *does*.

iii. "It you will read the chapter, you will notice that the apostle has used no less than seventeen words, I might almost say eighteen, to describe the works of the flesh. Human language is always rich in bad words, because the human heart is full of the manifold evils which these words denote." (Spurgeon)

b. **Adultery, fornication, uncleanness... lewdness**: These are all *sensual* sins, relating to sex. We are often appalled at the sexual immorality of our day, but we should remember that the times Paul wrote in were as bad if not worse. "There is ample evidence to show that the sexual life of the Greco-Roman world at the time of the New Testament was sheer chaos. Such evidence has come not from Christian writers but from pagans who were disgusted with the unspeakable sexual immorality." (Fung)

i. **Adultery** is violating the marriage covenant by sexual immorality. This word isn't included in the list of many ancient manuscripts, so many translations (such as the NIV) don't include it. But that doesn't mean that God gives a free pass on **adultery**, because even if Paul didn't write the word in this list, it is included under the next word, "fornication." **Adultery** is sin, and those guilty of it should confess their sin and repent of it instead of excusing it. The Holy Spirit never led anyone into **adultery**.

ii. **Fornication** is the ancient Greek word *porneia*, and it speaks of sexual immorality in a broad sense. *Pornia* started out meaning "the use of a prostitute," but by Paul's day it was "used for a wide variety of sexual sin." (Morris) Therefore, **fornication** covers "Illicit connection between *single* or *unmarried* persons; yet often signifying *adultery* also." (Clarke) Webster's dictionary defines **fornication** as "Voluntary sexual intercourse between two unmarried persons or two persons not married to each other." Sex before and outside of marriage – which Paul calls here **fornication** – "was so widespread that it was apparently accepted as a normal part of life... Paul cannot accept any such view of the practice; he sees it as totally wrong." (Morris) The Holy Spirit never led anyone into **fornication**.

iii. **Uncleanness** is another broad word, referring to sexual impropriety in general. It should be thought of as the *opposite* of *purity*. If it isn't pure before God, then it is **uncleanness**. It covers many sexual sins that are not actual intercourse or even interaction with another person (such as pornography). **Uncleanness** also covers impure speech, or suggestive speaking filled with double meanings. The Holy Spirit never led anyone into **uncleanness**.

iv. **Lewdness** (sometimes translated *licentiousness*) has the idea of "ready to sin at any time." It speaks of someone who flaunts their immorality, throwing off all restraint and having no sense of *shame, propriety*, or *embarrassment*. Morris defines it as "a disregard of accepted rules... conduct that knows no restraint." **Lewdness** can be thought of as *public* and *open* **uncleanness**. "A man may be *unclean* and hide his sin; he does not become *licentious* until he shocks public decency." (Lightfoot) We live in an incredibly *lewd* culture, yet the Holy Spirit never led anyone into **lewdness**.

c. **Idolatry... sorcery**: These are *religious* sins. They are sins of worship, and remind us that it isn't only tragic to worship the wrong God, or seek the wrong spiritual power – it is *sinful* as well.

i. **Idolatry** is the worship of any god except the LORD God revealed to us by the Bible and in the person of Jesus Christ. When people serve a god of their own opinion, of their own creation, they reject the true and living God – and that is sin. Someone might say, "Well, I can believe whatever I want!" and they certainly can; but they also bear the consequences of their wrong belief. The Holy Spirit never led anyone into **idolatry**.

ii. **Sorcery** (translated *witchcraft* in the NIV) is the service and worship of occult and spiritual powers apart from the true God. It also has another dimension, revealed by the word for **sorcery** in the original language Paul uses: *pharmakeia*, from which we get our word for "pharmacy." Morris defines **sorcery** as "the use of any kind of drugs, potions, or spells." In the ancient world, the taking of drugs (especially hallucinogens) was always associated with the occult, and the Bible's association with drug taking and sorcery points out that drugs open up doors to the occult that are better left closed. William Barclay wrote, "this literally means *the use of drugs*... it came to be very specially connected with the use of drugs for sorcery, of which the ancient world was full." The Holy Spirit never led anyone into **sorcery** or getting high on drugs.

d. **Hatred, contentions, jealousies, outbursts of wrath, selfish ambitions, dissensions, heresies, envies... murders**: These are each *"people"* sins. They are sins that primarily express themselves in how we treat others. God cares about our sexual and moral purity, and He cares about the purity of our religion and worship. But He also passionately cares about how we treat one another. The fact that Paul uses more words to describe these *interpersonal* sins shows how important our treatment of each other is to God.

i. **Hatred** (*ekthra*) is an attitude of heart, and it somehow expresses itself in actions such as **contentions**, **outbursts of wrath**, or many other works of the flesh. But **hatred** is the inner motivation for the ill treatment of others. Just as **love** is the inner motivation for the kind and good treatment of others, **hatred** is an inner motivation. Laws can be passed to punish the evil that men do against each other; but no law can answer the problem of **hatred**, which motivates those acts. But the Holy Spirit never led anyone into **hatred**.

ii. **Contentions** translates the ancient Greek word *eris*. "Originally, this word had mainly to do with *the rivalry for prizes*... it means the rivalry which has found its outcome in quarrellings and wrangling." (Barclay) Most commonly it is translated as *strife* (as in Romans 13:13 and 1 Corinthians 3:3), and simply speaks of a combative and argumentative spirit. The Holy Spirit never led anyone into **contentions**.

iii. **Jealousies** translates an ancient Greek word (*zelos*) that is sometimes used in a positive sense - as for being zealous for something good. But here, clearly, the connotation is wrong. In this context it means "the desire to have what someone else has, wrong desire for what is not for us." (Barclay) The Holy Spirit never led anyone into **jealousies**.

iv. **Outbursts of wrath** translates an ancient Greek word (*thumos*) that speaks of a sudden flash of anger, not a settled state of anger. It means to lose your temper, being unable to control your anger. The Holy Spirit never led anyone into **outbursts of wrath**.

v. **Selfish ambitions** translates the ancient Greek word *eritheia*, and the word has an interesting history. It started out as a perfectly respectable word meaning "to work for pay." Over time, it began to mean the kind of work that is done for money and for no other reason. Then it was used to describe politicians who campaign for election, not for what service they can give to the government and the people, but only for their own glory and benefit. "It ended up meaning 'selfish ambition', the ambition which has no conception of service and whose only aims are profit and power." It is the heart of a person whose first question is always, "What's in it for me?" To be sure, the Holy Spirit never led anyone into **selfish ambitions**.

vi. **Dissensions** translates the ancient Greek word *dichostasia*, and it literally means "standing apart." Romans 16:17 and 1 Corinthians 3:3

translate this word as *divisions*. "*Dissension* describes a society... where the members fly apart instead of coming together." (Barclay) The Holy Spirit never led anyone into **dissensions**.

vii. **Heresies** translates an ancient Greek word (*hairesis*) which originally simply meant "to choose." Over time, it came to mean someone who divisively expressed their "choices" or opinions. We think today of *heresies* in terms of wrong ideas and teachings; but the emphasis in the word is actually the *wrongful dividing* over opinions. **Heresies** can be thought of as *hardened* **dissensions**. "There is all the difference in the world between believing that we are right and believing that everyone is wrong. Unshakable conviction is a Christian virtue; unyielding intolerance is a sin." (Barclay, *Flesh and Spirit*, cited in Morris) The Holy Spirit never led anyone into **heresies**.

viii. **Envy** is the ancient Greek word *phthonos*. It doesn't so much want what someone else has (as in **jealousies**), but it is bitter just because someone else has something and we don't. The ancient Stoics called this "grief at someone else's good," and the ancient philosopher Euripides said it was "the greatest of all diseases among men." The Holy Spirit never led anyone into **envy**.

ix. **Murders** translates the ancient Greek word *phonos*, which is well translated by the English word **murders**. This is another word (like **adultery** earlier) that is not in every ancient Greek text, and isn't included in translations such as the NIV. But there is no dispute that murder is a work of the flesh, and that the Holy Spirit never led anyone into **murders**.

e. **Drunkenness... revelries**: These can be thought of as *social* sins – sins that are often committed in the company of other people. The fact that Paul includes these two sins in his list shows that they were **works of the flesh** that the Galatian Christians had to be on guard against. Romans 13:12-13 lists **drunkenness** and **revelries** as part of the Christians' past of darkness that now need to be cast off as we walk in the light.

i. "They let us see that the early church was not made up of people whose pre-Christian lives were of the highest standard... Paul recognizes reality and reminds his readers that whatever kind of sin they had favoured in their pre-Christian days should be decisively abandoned." (Morris)

ii. **Drunkenness** is clearly described as one of the **works of the flesh**. While Christians may differ as to if a Christian can drink alcohol, the Scriptures *precisely* forbid **drunkenness**. We must not think that only being "falling down drunk" is a sin; but being impaired in any way by drink is sin, as well as drinking with the *intention* of becoming impaired. Ephesians 5:18 also describes **drunkenness** as *dissipation*, which means "wastefulness." Getting drunk is a *waste*; Trapp writes of drinking "all the three outs" – "that is, ale out of the pot, money out of the purse, and wit out of the head." For certain, the Holy Spirit never led anyone into **drunkenness**.

iii. **Revelries**, translating the ancient Greek word *komos*, doesn't mean simply having a party or a good time. It means *unrestrained* partying. Barclay says, "It describes the kind of revelry which lowers a man's self and is a nuisance to others."

f. **And the like**: This demonstrates that Paul understands that his list is not exhaustive. These are not the only **works of the flesh**. It isn't as if one could find a work of the flesh that is not described in this list, then one would be free to do it.

4. (21b) The danger and the destiny of those who live in the *works of the flesh*.

Of which I tell you beforehand, just as I also told *you* in time past, that those who practice such things will not inherit the kingdom of God.

a. **Of which I tell you beforehand, just as I also told you in time past**: This shows that Paul often instructed Christians in how they should live, and this wasn't just an occasional emphasis. Paul knew that we are saved by God's grace and Jesus' work alone, not by what we have done, are doing, or promise to do. But he also knew that those who *are saved* by God's grace have a high moral obligation to fulfill – not to *earn* salvation, but in *gratitude* for salvation, and in *simple consistency* with who we are in Jesus.

b. **Those who practice such things will not inherit the kingdom of God**: To walk in these **works of the flesh** is to be in plain rebellion against God, and those in plain rebellion against God **will not inherit the kingdom of God**.

i. What is at stake here? **The kingdom of God**, which describes where God rules, and the benefits of His rule are realized. Because Paul speaks of *inheriting* the **kingdom of God**, we understand he means "heaven." Paul says plainly, that **those who practice such things will not** go to heaven. Neither will they know the wonder and the glory of the **kingdom of God** on earth.

ii. Who are the people in danger? **Those who practice such things**. This means more than someone who *has committed* **adultery**, or **fornication**, or **sorcery**, or **drunkenness**, or any of these. This speaks of those who continue on in these sins, ignoring the voice of the Holy Spirit telling them to "stop."

iii. "The tense of the verb (present) indicates a habitual continuation in fleshly sins rather than an isolated lapse, and the point is that those who continually practice such sins give evidence of having never received God's Spirit." (Boice)

iv. **Practice** "represents a present participle, 'people doing such things', and it carries the implication that they do them constantly." (Morris)

v. "The verb *prassontes* [**practice**] referring to habitual practice rather than an isolated lapse." (Stott)

c. **Will not inherit the kingdom of God**: The *strength* and *certainty* of Paul in this verse is striking. Paul may sound rigid or even harsh here, but he is consistent with the Biblical idea of *conversion*. When we come to Jesus to have our sins forgiven and our soul saved, He also changes our life. It doesn't happen all at once, and the work will never be perfected on this side of eternity, but there will be a real change none the less (1 John 3:5-9). As Charles Spurgeon is said to have put it, "The grace that does not change my life will not save my soul." The idea isn't that a Christian could never *commit* these sins, but that they could never *stay* in these sins.

i. "Christians also fall and perform the lusts of the flesh. David fell horribly into adultery. Peter also fell grievously when he denied Christ. However great as these sins were, they were not committed to spite God, but from weakness. When their sins were brought to their attention these men did not obstinately continue in their sin, but repented. Those who sin through weakness are not denied pardon as long as they rise again and cease to sin. There is nothing worse than to continue in sin. If they do not repent, but obstinately continue to fulfill the desires of the flesh, it is a sure sign that they are not sincere." (Luther)

5. (22-23) Examples of the fruit of the Spirit that walking in the Spirit produces in our lives.

But the fruit of the Spirit is love, joy, peace, longsuffering, kindness, goodness, faithfulness, gentleness, self-control. Against such there is no law.

a. **But the fruit of the Spirit**: The *works of the flesh* seem overwhelming – both *in* us and *around* us. God is good enough and big enough to change everything with **the fruit of the Spirit**. The fruit of the Spirit can always conquer the works of the flesh.

i. Significantly, it is the **fruit of the Spirit** set across from the *works of the flesh*. Works are works, and fruit is fruit. Fruit has several important characteristics.

- Fruit isn't achieved by working, but is birthed by abiding.
- Fruit is fragile.
- Fruit reproduces itself.
- Fruit is attractive.
- Fruit nourishes.

b. **Fruit of the Spirit**: Paul used the plural in describing life after the flesh (*works of the flesh*), but he uses the singular (**fruit**, not *fruits*, **of the Spirit**). In the big picture, the Spirit has one work to do in all of us. These aren't the *gifts of the Spirit*, which are distributed on an individual basis by the will of the Spirit; this is something for every Christian.

> i. "It may be significant that the word *fruit* is singular; Paul is not speaking of a series of fruits that would be shared around, so that one believer has one, another another. Rather he is referring to a cluster, such that all the qualities are to be manifested in each believer." (Morris)

c. **The fruit of the Spirit is love**: It is fitting that **love** be the first mentioned, because it encompasses all of the following. It may even be said that the following eight terms are just describing what **love** in action looks like. "It would have been enough to mention only the single fruit of love, for love embraces all the fruits of the Spirit." (Luther)

> i. **Love** translates the ancient Greek word *agape*. In that language there were four distinct words for "love." *Eros* was the word for romantic or passionate love. *Philia* was the word for the love we have for those near and dear to us, be they family or friends. *Storge* is the word for the love that shows itself in affection and care, especially family affection. But *agape* describes a different kind of love. It is a love more of *decision* than of the *spontaneous heart*; as much a matter of the *mind* than the *heart*, because it chooses to love the undeserving. "*Agape* has to do with the *mind*: it is not simply an emotion which rises unbidden in our hearts; it is a principle by which we deliberately live." (Barclay)

> ii. We could say that this is a *love of the Spirit*, because it is a **fruit of the Spirit**. This is above and beyond natural affection, or the loyalty to blood or family. This is loving people who aren't easy to love; loving people you don't *like*.

> iii. "When you wax indignant because you have been badly treated, and you think of returning evil for evil, remember this text, 'The fruit of the Spirit is love.' 'Ah,' you say, 'it was shameful!' Of course it was: and therefore do not imitate it: do not render railing for raiding, but contrariwise blessing, for 'the fruit of the Spirit is love.'" (Spurgeon)

iv. It is also helpful to understand the *works of the flesh* in the light of this **love** of the Spirit. Each one of the works of the flesh is a violation or a perversion of this great **love**.

- *Adultery, fornication, uncleanness,* and *lewdness* are counterfeits of love among people.

- *Idolatry* and *sorcery* are counterfeits of love to God.

- *Hatred, contentions, jealousies, outbursts of wrath, selfish ambitions, dissensions, heresies, envy,* and *murders* are all opposites of love.

- *Drunkenness* and *revelries* are sad attempts to fill the void only love can fill.

d. **The fruit of the Spirit is... joy**: One of the greatest marketing strategies ever employed was to position the kingdom of Satan as the place where the fun is and the kingdom of God as the place of gloom and misery. But the fruit of the Spirit is **joy**.

i. We could say that this is *joy of the Spirit*, because it is a higher joy than just the thrill of an exciting experience or a wonderful set of circumstances. It is a joy that can abide and remain, even when circumstances seem terrible. Paul knew this joy personally; he could sing when manacled in a dark prison dungeon (Acts 16:25).

ii. Barclay on *chara*, the ancient Greek word used here for **joy**: "It is not the joy that comes from earthly things, still less from triumphing over someone else in competition. It is a joy whose foundation is God."

iii. "Believers are not dependent upon circumstances. Their joy comes not from what they have, but from what they are; not from where they are, but from whose they are; not from what they enjoy, but from that which was suffered for them by their Lord." (Spurgeon)

e. **The fruit of the Spirit is... peace**: This **peace** is peace with God, peace with people, and it is a *positive* peace, filled with blessing and goodness – not simply the absence of fighting.

i. We could say that this **peace** is a *peace of the Spirit*, because it is a higher peace than just what comes when everything is calm and settled. This is a *peace of God, which surpasses all understanding* (Philippians 4:7).

ii. The ancient Greek word used here for **peace** is *eirene*, and it "means not just freedom from trouble but everything that makes for a man's highest good. Here it means that tranquility of heart which derives from the all-pervading consciousness that our times are in the hands of God." (Barclay)

iii. The early Christians really knew and loved the **joy** and the **peace** of the Spirit. Two very common Christian names in the early church were *Chara* (Cara) and *Eirene* (Irene).

f. **The fruit of the Spirit is... longsuffering**: **Longsuffering** means that one can have **love, joy,** and **peace** even over a period of time when people and events annoy them. God is not quickly irritated with us (Romans 2:4, 9:22), so we should not be quickly irritated with others.

> i. **Longsuffering** in itself is a work of the Spirit. "Longsuffering is that quality which enables a person to bear adversity, injury, reproach, and makes them patient to wait for the improvement of those who have done him wrong. When the devil finds that he cannot overcome certain persons by force he tries to overcome them in the long run... To withstand his continued assaults we must be longsuffering and patiently wait for the devil to get tired of his game." (Luther)

g. **The fruit of the Spirit is... kindness, goodness**: These two words are closely connected. About the only difference is that **goodness** also has with it the idea of *generosity*.

h. **The fruit of the Spirit is... faithfulness**: The idea is that the Spirit of God works faithfulness in us, both to God and to people. "It is the characteristic of the man who is reliable." (Barclay)

> i. "The ability to serve God faithfully through the years and through the temptations of life is not something we achieve by heroic virtue. It comes from the Spirit." (Morris)

i. **The fruit of the Spirit is... gentleness**: The word has the idea of being teachable, not having a superior attitude, not demanding one's rights. It isn't timidity or passiveness; "It is the quality of the man who is always angry at the right time and never at the wrong time." (Barclay)

> i. Morris on **gentleness**: "It is important for the Christian to see that the self-assertiveness that is so much part of the twentieth-century life should not be valued highly. It is much better that each of us curtails the desire to be pre-eminent and exercises a proper meekness (or gentleness)."

j. **The fruit of the Spirit is... self-control**: The world knows something of **self-control**, but almost always for a selfish reason. It knows the self-disciple and denial someone will go through for *themselves*, but the *self-control of the Spirit* will also work on behalf of others.

k. **Against such there is no law**: Paul wrote with both irony and understatement. There is certainly **no law** against **love, joy, peace, longsuffering, kindness, goodness, faithfulness, gentleness,** and **self-**

control. But more so, if a person has this **fruit of the Spirit**, he doesn't *need the Law*. He already fulfills it.

i. Morris on **against such there is no law**: "This is a masterly understatement. It draws our attention to the fact that the kind of conduct that Paul has outlined is that which lawmakers everywhere want to bring about."

6. (24-26) Keeping in step with the Spirit.

And those *who are* Christ's have crucified the flesh with its passions and desires. If we live in the Spirit, let us also walk in the Spirit. Let us not become conceited, provoking one another, envying one another.

a. **And those who are Christ's have crucified the flesh with its passions and desires**: God has a place for our flesh, with all its passions and desires. He wants us to nail it to His cross, so that it may be under control and under the sentence of death.

i. **Crucified** is an important word. Paul could have simply chosen the word "killed," but he used the word **crucified** because it speaks of many things:

- It reminds us of what Jesus did for us on the cross.
- It reminds us that we are called to take up our cross and follow Him (Matthew 16:24).
- It reminds us that the death of the flesh is often *painful*.
- It reminds us that our flesh must be dealt with *decisively*.

b. **Those who are Christ's have crucified the flesh**: This speaks of something that the *believer does*, being directed and empowered by the Spirit of God. It was not and is not the sovereign, "unilateral" work of God.

i. The *old man*, the self inherited from Adam, is crucified with Jesus as the sovereign work of God when we are born again. Romans 6:6 says, *Knowing this, that our old man was crucified with Him*. We are simply told to *reckon*, or account, the old man as dead (Romans 6:11), we are not told to put him to death. But the flesh is another matter. We are called to choose to work with God to do to the flesh exactly what God did all by Himself to the old man: crucify the flesh.

ii. "Please notice that the 'crucifixion' of the flesh described here is something that is done not *to* us but *by* us... Galatians 5:24 does not teach the same truth as Galatians 2:20 or Romans 6:6. In those verses we are told that by faith-union with Christ 'we have been crucified with him'. But here it is we who have taken action." (Stott)

iii. Boice on **have crucified**: "The verb is in the active voice and points rather to what the believer has himself done and must continue to regard as being done."

iv. The problem of our **flesh** will not be finally dealt with until we are resurrected. Until then, we are to constantly "nail it to the cross," so that it hangs there, alive yet powerless over us. "To resist the flesh... is to nail it to the Cross. Although the flesh is still alive it cannot very well act upon its desires because it is bound and nailed to the Cross." (Luther)

c. **With its passions and desires**: In Jesus Christ, you can live above the **passions and desires** of your flesh. The resources are there in Jesus. Look to Him. See your life in Him. If you are one of **those who are Christ's**, then you belong to Him – not to this world, not to yourself, and not to your **passions and desires**.

d. **If we live in the Spirit, let us also walk in the Spirit**: We can better understand what Paul wrote here if we understand that the ancient Greek words for **walk** are different in Galatians 5:16 and 5:25. The first (*peripateo*) is the normal word for walking, used there as a picture of the "walk of life." The second (*stoicheo*) means "to walk in line with" or "to be in line with." Paul here is saying, "Keep in step with the Spirit."

i. The idea is, "The Spirit has given you life. Now let Him direct your steps." Or, as the *Revised English Bible* has it, "If the Spirit is the source of our life, let the Spirit also direct its course."

ii. "The verb *stoicheo* means '*to be in line with, stand beside* a person or a thing, *hold to, agree with, follow*'. The present imperative indicates that this is to be the habitual practice." (Morris)

e. **Let us not become conceited**: Paul concluded this section of walking in the Spirit with this warning, knowing that some will become **conceited** in their own **walk in the Spirit**. This can be a masterful stroke of Satan. We can think of a child of God finally walking in the Spirit – then Satan tempts him to be **conceited** about it. Soon, he is sure that he is almost always right and everyone else is wrong. It often happens gradually, so Paul warned, "Do not **become** conceited."

i. Morris on **conceited**: "To be *conceited*, to be sure that we are always right (even if that means that other people are always wrong!) is a perennial temptation to believers... It is easy to assume that because we are Christ's we will always say and do the right thing. Paul is warning his readers that believers can be too confident that they are right in what they are contemplating."

f. **Provoking one another**: When we are **conceited** – always sure we are right, always confident in our opinions and perceptions – it definitely *provokes* other people. It will rub them the wrong way and be the source of many conflicts.

g. **Envying one another**: When we are **conceited**, we also are open to the sin of *envy*. If we know someone is more right, or more successful than we are, we resent it and *envy* them.

i. This whole chapter lends itself to a searching examination of ourselves. We often think that our problems and difficulties are all outside of ourselves. We think that we would be fine if everyone just treated us right and if circumstances just got better. But that ignores the tenor of this chapter: the problems are *in us*, and need to be dealt with by the Spirit of God. Augustine used to often pray, "Lord, deliver me from that evil man, myself." With that kind of reality check, *we can see a new world, and a new life* – and not one other person or one other circumstance has to change. All we must do is yield to the Spirit of God, and begin to truly walk in the Spirit.

Galatians 6 - Final Instructions

A. Personal responsibility and helping others.

1. (1) Restoring those overtaken in sin.

Brethren, if a man is overtaken in any trespass, you who *are* spiritual restore such a one in a spirit of gentleness, considering yourself lest you also be tempted.

> a. **If a man is overtaken in any trespass**: Paul recognized that there may be those among the Christians in Galatia who had been **overtaken in** a **trespass**. Paul didn't seem to exclude the **overtaken** one from the **brethren**, yet they should never *stay* in the place of being **overtaken**.

> > i. Paul's wording here speaks not of a determined and hardened sinner. Instead, the idea is of someone who has fallen into sin, finding themselves trapped in a place they never thought they would be. **Overtaken** "Contains the idea of falling. It is not the deliberate, the planned, aspect of sin that is stressed here, but rather the unwitting element. Mistake rather than misdeed is the force of the word, though without absolution of responsibility." (Ridderbos, cited in Morris)

> > ii. "If we carefully weigh the words of the Apostle we perceive that he does not speak of doctrinal faults and errors, but of much lesser faults by which a person is overtaken through the weakness of his flesh. This explains why the Apostle chooses the softer term 'fault.' To minimize the offense still more, as if he meant to excuse it altogether and to take the whole blame away... he speaks of him as having been 'overtaken,' seduced by the devil and of the flesh... This comforting sentence at one time saved my life." (Luther)

> b. **Restore such a one**: The **overtaken** ones need to be restored. They are not to be *ignored*. They are not to be *excused*. They are not to be *destroyed*. The goal is always *restoration*.

i. Stott on **restore**: "The verb is instructive. *Kataritzo* means to 'put in order' and so to 'restore to its former condition'… It was used in secular Greek as a medical term for setting a fractured or dislocated bone. It is applied in Mark 1:19 to the apostles who were 'mending' their nets."

ii. This job of restoration is often neglected in the church. We have a tendency to either pretend the sin never happened, or we tend to react too harshly towards the one who has sinned. The balance between these two extremes can only be negotiated by the **spiritual**. It should be normal to do what God says here, but it isn't. It is all too easy to respond to someone's sin with gossip, harsh judgment, or undiscerning approval.

c. **Restore such a one in a spirit of gentleness**: Restoration must always be done **in a spirit of gentleness**, with full understanding of *our own* weakness and corruption. Those doing the restoring must guard against the temptation of pride, as well as the same temptation the overtaken one struggled with.

i. "Let the ministers of the Gospel learn from Paul how to deal with those who have sinned. 'Brethren,' he says, 'if any man be overtaken with a fault, do not aggravate his grief, do not scold him, do not condemn him, but lift him up and gently restore his faith." (Luther)

ii. "This suggests that gentleness is born of a sense of our own weakness and proneness to sin." (Stott)

iii. The influence of the legalists among the Galatians made this warning necessary; "Nothing reveals the wickedness of legalism better than the way the legalists treat those who have sinned." (Wiersbe)

2. (2-5) Bearing each other's burdens and bearing our own load.

Bear one another's burdens, and so fulfill the law of Christ. For if anyone thinks himself to be something, when he is nothing, he deceives himself. But let each one examine his own work, and then he will have rejoicing in himself alone, and not in another. For each one shall bear his own load.

a. **Bear one another's burdens**: When Paul brought up the idea of the one *overtaken in any trespass*, it painted the picture of a person sagging under a heavy load. Here he expanded the idea to encourage every Christian to **bear one another's burdens**.

i. The focus isn't on "expect others to bear your burdens." That is *self-focused*, and always leads to pride, frustration, discouragement, and depression. Instead, God always directs us to be *others-focused*, and says, "**Bear one another's burdens.**"

ii. This is a *simple* command to obey. Look for a brother or a sister with a burden, and help them with it. It isn't complicated, and it doesn't take a huge program or infrastructure to do it. Just look for a burden to bear and bear it.

iii. "Notice the assumption which lies behind this command, namely that we all have burdens and that God does not mean us to carry them alone." (Stott)

b. **And so fulfill the law of Christ**: As we **bear one another's burdens**, we are fulfilling the simple **law of Christ**: *A new commandment I give to you, that you love one another; as I have loved you, that you also love one another. By this all will know that you are My disciples, if you have love for one another* (John 13:34-35).

i. Through this whole letter Paul battled the legalists among the Galatian Christians. Here, he hit them again. Paul essentially said, "Do you want to **fulfill the law**? Here is your **law** to fulfill. **Bear one another's burdens and so fulfill the law of Christ**."

ii. "So Paul may be saying to them, in effect, that instead of imposing the law as a burden upon others, they should rather lift their burdens and so fulfill Christ's law." (Stott)

c. **If anyone thinks himself to be something, when he is nothing, he deceives himself**: Pride prevents us from bearing **one another's burdens** and fulfilling the **law of Christ**. It is often pride that keeps us from ministering to one another as we should.

i. As much as anything, pride is *self-focus*. Pride doesn't necessarily say, "I'm *better* than you are." Pride simply says, "I'm more *important* than you are, so I deserve more of my own attention and love than you do." Instead, Biblical humility tells us, "I am no more important than you are. Let me care about your burdens and needs."

ii. When **anyone thinks himself to be something, when he is nothing**, it also stifles ministry in another way. Out of pride, people will refuse to *receive* help when someone else reaches out to help bear their burden.

iii. It is important to understand that Paul wrote to *every Christian* when he said, "**When he is nothing**." In the sense Paul uses the idea here, it isn't that some Christians are **something**, and others are **nothing**, and the problem is that the *nothings* think they are one of the *somethings*. Instead, Paul writes with the same idea behind Philippians 2:3b-4: *In lowliness of mind let each esteem others better than himself. Let each of you look out not only for his own interests, but also for the interests* *of others*. If I esteem you above me, and you esteem me above you, a marvelous thing happens: we have a community where everyone is looked up to, and no one is looked down on.

iv. "The meaning is more general and should therefore be expressed thus, 'Since all men are nothing, he who wishes to appear something and persuades himself that he is somebody, deceives himself.'" (Calvin)

d. **He deceives himself**: There are few things more self-deceptive than *pride*. To be proud is to be blind – blind to the freely given favor and gifts of God, blind to our sin and depravity, blind to the good in others, and blind to the foolishness of self-centeredness.

i. We often get angry when someone deceives us. Yet we don't take the danger of self-deception as seriously as we should. It is a serious and terrible thing to deceive yourself.

ii. This helps explain the greatest deception of the greatest of deceivers – Satan himself. If there was anyone who thought **himself to be something when he is nothing**, it was Satan both before and after his fall. And if there is anyone who **deceives himself**, surely it is Satan – who works on and on against God in the self-delusion that he may one day triumph.

e. **But let each one examine his own work**: Instead of deceiving ourselves, we must take a careful and a sober examination of our works before God. If we don't, and if we carry on under our self-deception, then we may *think* our works are approved before God, when really they aren't. We want to have our work approved before God, so that our **rejoicing** on the day of reward can be for our own work (**himself alone**), and **not in** the work of **another**.

i. There is another aspect to **rejoicing in himself**. It means having joy at your own walk with the Lord, instead of feeling spiritual because someone around you perhaps is *overtaken in any trespass*.

f. **For each one shall bear his own load**: The Bible speaks of a day when our works will be examined before the Lord. This is *the judgment seat of Christ* described in Romans 14:10 and 2 Corinthians 5:10. On that day, **each one shall bear his own load**.

i. There is no contradiction between *bear one another's burdens* (Galatians 6:2) and **each one shall bear his own load** (Galatians 6:5). In Galatians 6:5, Paul spoke of our final accountability before God. In Galatians 6:2, he spoke of our need to care for others in the body of Christ.

ii. There is also a difference in the wording Paul uses. The word for **load** in Galatians 6:5 was a common term for a man's backpack. The word for *burdens* in Galatians 6:2 was a different word meaning "heavy burdens" - those that are more than a man should carry. In the end, we will are all responsible for our own work, but we can help bear the burdens of others.

3. (6-10) Doing good to others in the household of faith.

Let him who is taught the word share in all good things with him who teaches. Do not be deceived, God is not mocked; for whatever a man sows, that he will also reap. For he who sows to his flesh will of the flesh reap corruption, but he who sows to the Spirit will of the Spirit reap everlasting life. And let us not grow weary while doing good, for in due season we shall reap if we do not lose heart. Therefore, as we have opportunity, let us do good to all, especially to those who are of the household of faith.

a. **Let him who is taught the word share in all good things with him who teaches**: In this context of caring for one another, Paul instructs those who are **taught** to support (**share in all good things**) those who teach them.

i. To **share in all good things** has the idea *focused* on financial support, but not *limited* to it. "Of the variety of interpretations of Paul's words here the most common is also the most likely: this takes *share* in the sense of active giving and *all good things* in the sense of physical goods (Luke 1:53; 12:18-19; 16:25)." (Fung)

ii. Lightfoot translates the sense of this: "I spoke of bearing one another's burdens. There is one special application I would make of this rule. Provide for the temporal needs of your teachers in Christ."

iii. Passages like this are important, yet can be awkward for the preacher. Martin Luther wrote, "These passages are all meant to benefit us ministers. I must say I do not find much pleasure in explaining these verses. I am made to appear as if I am speaking for my own benefit."

iv. "The right relationship between teacher and taught, or minister and congregation, is one of *koinonia*, 'fellowship' or 'partnership'. So Paul writes: 'Let him who is taught the word *share* (*koinoneito*) all good things with him who teaches.'" (Stott) It isn't *payment*; it is *sharing*.

v. This is a basic, though sometimes neglected spiritual principle. Those who feed and bless you spiritually should be supported by you financially. Paul repeated this principle in several other places. *If we have sown spiritual things for you, is it a great thing if we reap your material things?* (1 Corinthians 9:11). *Even so the Lord has commanded that those who preach the gospel should live from the gospel* (1 Corinthians 9:14). *Let the elders who rule well be counted worthy of double honor, especially those who labor in the word and doctrine* (1 Timothy 5:17). If you trust them with your spiritual health, you should also trust them to steward the gifts of God's people (Luke 16:11).

vi. "I have often wondered why all the apostles reiterated this request with such embarrassing frequency... We have come to understand why it is so necessary to repeat the admonition of this verse. When Satan cannot suppress the preaching of the Gospel by force, he tries to accomplish his purpose by striking the ministers of the Gospel with poverty." (Luther)

b. **Do not be deceived, God is not mocked; for whatever a man sows, that he will also reap**: For those who are hesitant to **share in all good things** with those who teach them, Paul reminded them of God's principle of sowing and reaping. Their giving (to **share in all good things with him who teaches**) isn't like throwing away money; it is like planting seeds, and **whatever a man sows, that he will also reap**.

i. To regard sharing **in all good things with him who teaches** as a waste is to mock God. It is selfishness that mocks God's generosity towards those who give to Him. Luther put it strongly: "Be careful, you scoffers. God may postpone His punishment for a time, but He will find you out in time, and punish you for despising His servants. You cannot laugh at God."

ii. Paul's point is that God's people should not **share in all good things with him who teaches** because it is good for the teacher. They should do it because it is good for the one who is taught and shares, and the principle of reaping and sowing demonstrates this.

c. **For he who sows to his flesh will of the flesh reap corruption, but he who sows to the Spirit will of the Spirit reap everlasting life**: If we want to reap to the Spirit, we should not hesitate to sow to the Spirit with whatever resources God has given us.

i. A farmer reaps the same as he has sown. If he plants wheat, wheat comes up. In the same way, if we sow to the flesh, the flesh will increase in size and strength.

ii. The farmer reaps the same as he has sown, but not *exactly*. The apple seed doesn't just grow more apple seeds, but more apples with seeds. Even so, when we sow **to the Spirit** – even with material things – what we reap is not necessarily material things, but something better:

of the Spirit we **reap everlasting life**. So we don't give as a crude "investment" or money-making scheme, though we are completely confident we will never be the loser for giving.

iii. The farmer also reaps more if he has sown more, and the relationship between what he sows and what he reaps is exponential. A farmer can plant one apple seed and receive hundreds of apples over time.

d. **Whatever a man sows, that he will also reap**: This principle has application beyond giving and supporting teachers and ministers. It has a general application in life; what we get out of life is often what we put in. Yet, Paul is not promoting some law of spiritual karma that ensures we will get good when we do good, or always get bad when we do bad. If there were such an absolute spiritual law, it would surely damn us all. Instead, Paul simply relates the principle of sowing and reaping to the way we manage our resources before the Lord. He used the same picture in 1 Corinthians 9:11 and 2 Corinthians 9:6-10.

i. We may fool ourselves by expecting much when we sow little, but we cannot fool God and the results of our poor sowing will be evident.

e. **Let us not grow weary while doing good, for in due season we shall reap if we do not lose heart**: As we wisely manage our resources before God under the principle of sowing and reaping, we need patience. This is because the harvest does not come immediately after the seeds are sown.

i. It is easy but dangerous to **lose heart**. In the ancient world, this phrase translated **lose heart** was used for the kind of fear and weariness a woman experiences during labor before delivery. It describes a time when the work is hard and painful, but also unfinished and unrewarded. It's easy to **lose heart** when we feel like that, but that is exactly when we must hang on and **not grow weary while doing good**.

f. **As we have opportunity, let us do good to all, especially to those who are of the household of faith**: Not losing heart, we seek to do good with our resources, and **to do good to all** - but especially to those who are of God's family.

i. When Paul wrote **as we have opportunity** and **let us do good**, he clearly included *himself* in what he wrote. He spoke to himself here as much as to the Galatians. Because of the danger brought in by the legalists, Paul's work among them had not yet really been rewarded, so he needed to remember not to lose heart himself.

B. Final words.

1. (11) Introduction to Paul's personal postscript.

See with what large letters I have written to you with my own hand!

a. **I have written to you with my own hand**: Paul's custom, typical in the ancient world, was to dictate his letters to a secretary. But he would often personally write a short portion at the end, both to authenticate the letter and to add a personal touch.

i. Other examples of this kind of postscript are 1 Corinthians 16:21-24 (*The salutation with my own hand – Paul*) and Colossians 4:18 (*This salutation by my own hand – Paul*). One reason Paul may have done this was to prove that he really wrote the letter, as in 2 Thessalonians 3:17: *The salutation of Paul with my own hand, which is a sign in every epistle; so I write.*

b. **See with what large letters I have written**: Paul points out that he wrote his postscript with **large letters**. Many speculate this was because he had poor eyesight and could not read or write small print. But it is more likely that he made the letters **large** simply for emphasis.

i. "At this point the Apostle takes the pen from his amanuensis, and the concluding paragraph is written with his own hand... He writes it too in large bold characters, that his handwriting may reflect the energy and determination of his soul." (Lightfoot)

ii. "Most commentators consider that he used large letters deliberately, either because he was treating his readers like children (rebuking their spiritual immaturity by using baby writing) or simply for emphasis... much as we would use capital letters or underline words today." (Stott)

2. (12-13) A final word regarding the motives of the legalists among the Galatians.

As many as desire to make a good showing in the flesh, these *would* compel you to be circumcised, only that they may not suffer persecution for the cross of Christ. For not even those who are circumcised keep the law, but they desire to have you circumcised that they may boast in your flesh.

a. **As many as desire to make a good showing in the flesh, these try to compel you to be circumcised**: Paul here referred to the legalistic Christians among the Galatians and wrote frankly about their motive – **to make a good showing in the flesh**. They worked to bring the Galatian Christians from a Gentile background under circumcision because it would be a **good showing** for them – but a **good showing in the flesh**.

i. The legalists *pretended* to be motivated out of concern for the ones they tried to bring under the law. But Paul saw through this deception and saw their motive was really selfish, simply desiring the honor and glory of a **good showing in the flesh**. They wanted the Galatians to become circumcised so they could wear the submission of these Gentiles as a badge of achievement. Even as David had boasted in the two hundred foreskins of the Philistines he had killed, so these legalists wanted the allegiance of these Gentiles primarily as a trophy.

ii. **Compel** is an important word. There was nothing wrong with a Gentile being circumcised. There was everything wrong in *compelling* a Gentile to be circumcised, saying he could not be right with God without coming under the law of Moses.

b. **Only that they may not suffer persecution for the cross of Christ**: Beyond their own glory, their other motive was to *avoid* **persecution for the cross of Christ**. If these legalists had said, "We are saved only by the work of **the cross of Christ**, not by our obedience under the law," they would have been persecuted. Probably the **persecution** would have come from other legalistic Christians or from those still in Judaism. Their unwillingness to stand in the face of this pressure made them stand for false doctrines.

i. There is also another way to consider this. By aligning Christianity with Judaism through emphasizing circumcision and the Law of Moses, men could escape **persecution** from the Romans. "To advocate circumcision was to align the new movement with Judaism, a religion that had official Roman sanction, and therefore one that avoided persecution. The preachers Paul was opposing may have included the cross in their proclamation, but by adding the necessity of circumcision they avoided persecution." (Morris)

3. (14-15) Paul writes about his motives.

But God forbid that I should glory except in the cross of our Lord Jesus Christ, by whom the world has been crucified to me, and I to the world. For in Christ Jesus neither circumcision nor uncircumcision avails anything, but a new creation.

a. **But God forbid that I should glory except in the cross of our Lord Jesus Christ**: Paul's heart cared nothing for the **glory** that came from fame. He cared nothing for the **glory** that came from riches. He cared nothing for the **glory** that came from status and power among men. He only cared about the **glory** of **the cross of our Lord Jesus Christ**.

i. It is hard for us to appreciate how *strange* Paul's words are here. For people who knew what crucifixion was all about, the words "**cross**" and "**glory**" just did not go together. They were direct opposites because there was not a more humiliating, shameful way to be executed than

the cross. It seemed much more logical to *glory* in your *good showing in the flesh*, instead of **the cross**. But Paul thinks and writes with a heavenly logic that surpasses anything of this earth.

ii. "The word *crux* was unmentionable in polite Roman society... even when one was condemned to death by crucifixion the sentence used was an archaic formula which served as sort of an unlucky euphemism: *arbori infelici suspendito*, 'hang him on the unlucky tree.'" (Bruce, cited in Morris) But Paul not only *used* this unmentionable word; he *gloried* in it.

iii. "What did he mean, however, by the cross? Of course he cared nothing for the particular piece of wood to which those blessed hands and feet were nailed, for that was mere materialism, and has perished out of mind. He means the glorious doctrine of justification-free justification-through the atoning sacrifice of Jesus Christ." (Spurgeon)

b. **By whom the world has been crucified to me, and I to the world**: In Galatians 5:24, Paul wrote about having *crucified the flesh with its passions and desires*. Now with the *flesh* on the cross he also put **the world** on the cross, and considers himself dead to the world. **The world** could not have any influence over Paul if it were dead, and Paul could not respond to any influence from it if he were dead to **the world**.

i. The **world**, in the sense Paul means it here, was not the global earth; nor was it the mass of humanity (which God Himself loves, John 3:16). Instead, it was the community of sinful humanity that is united in rebellion against God.

ii. There is nothing more *worldly* than trying to make *a good showing in the flesh*. When we live for the glory that comes from fame, from riches, from status, or from power among men we are very alive to the world and the world is very alive to us.

iii. Paul and the world could agree together on one thing: they didn't like each other. "'The world is crucified unto me,' means that I condemn the world. 'I am crucified unto the world,' means that the world in turn condemns me." (Luther) "The world and I are well agreed. The world cares not a pin for me, and I care as little for the world." (Trapp)

iv. "To live to serve men is one thing, to live to bless them is another; and this we will do, God helping us, making sacrifices for their good. But to fear men, to ask their leave to think, to ask their instructions as to what we shall speak, and how we shall say it – that is a baseness we cannot brook. By the grace of God, we have not so degraded ourselves, and never shall." (Spurgeon)

c. **For in Christ Jesus neither circumcision nor uncircumcision avails anything, but a new creation**: Without doubt, Paul knew Christians had a moral standard to live by (described in passages like Galatians 5:19-21). But what really mattered was not what we do in keeping the law, especially in its ceremonies, but what God has done in us – making us **a new creation**.

i. For the legalists among the Galatian Christians, **circumcision** was a big issue, because it was the initiation to living under the Mosaic Law. Even though it was important to the legalists, Paul knew that it didn't matter at all (**avails nothing**). If you were circumcised, but not **a new creation**, you did not belong to Jesus. If you were uncircumcised, but were **a new creation**, you did belong to Jesus.

ii. We don't make ourselves **a new creation**; God does it in us. At root, Christianity is something God does in us, not something we do for God. This can simply define the difference between the systems of grace and law.

4. (16) A blessing on those who walk in God's truth.

And as many as walk according to this rule, peace and mercy *be* upon them, and upon the Israel of God.

a. **And as many as walk according to this rule**: Lightfoot on **rule**, the ancient Greek word *kanon*: "The carpenter's or surveyor's line by which a direction is taken." There is a **rule** for the Christian life, revealed by God's Word. We just don't make it up as we go along. We are to measure ourselves according to this **rule**.

b. **Peace and mercy be upon them**: Just as Paul was willing to pronounce a curse on those who taught false doctrines (Galatians 1:8-9), he was also willing to give a blessing to those who **walk according to this rule**. These are those who are the true **Israel of God**, the descendants of Abraham according to faith.

5. (17-18) Last words.

From now on let no one trouble me, for I bear in my body the marks of the Lord Jesus. Brethren, the grace of our Lord Jesus Christ *be* with your spirit. Amen.

a. **I bear in my body the marks of the Lord Jesus**: Paul wrote as one who had suffered for Jesus, who bore those marks on his body. Having suffered so, he can say **from now on let no one trouble me**, in the sense that it is fruitless for anyone to try, because he has already endured the worst.

i. In 2 Corinthians 11:23-25, Paul described his physical suffering for Jesus' sake. What he endured was plenty enough to leave scars, **marks of the Lord Jesus**.

ii. Some think "**let no one trouble me**" was Paul's way to say to the Christians of Galatia, "Don't be a trouble to me by continuing to play around with these false doctrines - I've suffered enough already."

b. **The marks of the Lord Jesus**: Some have thought that Paul speaks here of a phenomenon known as the *stigmata*. These are said to be marks on the body similar to wounds of Jesus, such as wounds in the hands, feet, side, or head as a result of an intense mystical identification with Jesus. Such a view reads too much into the simple words of the text, and often they are used to justify an unhealthy mysticism.

i. **The marks of the Lord Jesus** were not wounds similar to Jesus' wounds; they are **marks** that identify – or even "brand" – Paul as a follower of Jesus. In the ancient world, slaves were branded with the name of their master. "Often a master branded his slaves with a mark that showed them to be his. Most likely what Paul means is that the scars of the things he had suffered for Christ are the brands which show him to be Christ's slave." (Barclay)

ii. The practice of branding was also known in military life: "Instances are recorded of soldiers branding themselves with the name of their general in token of their absolute devotion to his cause." (Rendall) Paul said that his **marks** were his "brands" of allegiance.

iii. "For even as earthly warfare has its decorations with which generals honour the bravery of a soldier, so Christ our leader has His own marks, of which He makes good use in decorating and honouring some of His followers. These marks, however, are very different from the others; for they have the nature of the cross, and in the sight of the world they are disgraceful... but before God and the angels they surpass all the honours of the world." (Calvin)

c. **The grace of the Lord Jesus Christ be with your spirit**: Paul could wish nothing greater for the Galatians than this. If this were so, they would walk in a **grace** relationship with God instead of the legal, performance-based relationship that endangered them so. This is an appropriate end for the letter and prayer for all our lives.

i. "After the storm and stress and intensity of the letter comes the peace of the benediction. Paul has argued and rebuked and cajoled but his last word is GRACE, for him the only word that really mattered." (Barclay)

Ephesians 1 - God's Ultimate Plan

A. Introduction to Paul's letter to the Ephesians.

1. The character and themes of Paul's letter to the Ephesians.

a. Paul's letter to the Ephesians is different compared to many of the other New Testament letters he wrote. Like Romans, Ephesians was not written so much to address problems in a particular church; more so, it was written to explain some of the great themes and doctrines of Christianity.

i. The elevated themes of Ephesians make it highly praised and prized by commentators. Ephesians has been called "the Queen of the Epistles," "the quintessence of Paulinism," "the divinest composition of man" and even "the Waterloo of commentators." Some say that Ephesians reads "like a commentary on the Pauline letters" and probably it has been best termed "the crown of Paulinism." (Bruce)

ii. "It sums up in large measure the leading themes of the Pauline writings... But it does more than that; it carries the thought of the earlier letters forward to a new stage." (Bruce)

iii. "Among the Epistles bearing the name of St. Paul there is none greater than this, nor any with a character more entirely its own... There is a peculiar and sustained loftiness in its teaching which has deeply impressed the greatest minds and has earned for it the title of the 'Epistle of the Ascension.'" (Salmond)

iv. "The Epistle to the Ephesians is a complete Body of Divinity. In the first chapter you have the doctrines of the gospel; in the next, you have the experience of the Christians; and before the Epistle is finished, you have the precepts of the Christian faith. Whosoever would see Christianity in one treatise, let him 'read, mark, learn, and inwardly digest' the Epistle to the Ephesians." (Spurgeon)

b. If the Letter to the Romans focuses more on God's work in the individual Christian, Ephesians includes the great themes of God's work in the church, the community of believers.

i. Karl Marx wrote about a new man and a new society, but he saw man and society both in almost purely economic terms and offered only economic answers. In his letter to the Ephesians, Paul also saw the new man and a new society, but he saw it all accomplished by the work of Jesus.

c. Ephesians has many similarities with Paul's letter to the Colossians. Since Paul wrote both of them from his Roman imprisonment, his mind may have worked on the same themes when he wrote each letter.

i. "He wrote to the Colossians to meet a particular situation and danger in the church at Colossae. Then with his mind still working over the theme of the greatness and glory of Christ, but moving on to consider the place of the Church in the purpose of God, he wrote Ephesians, this time without the limitation of any polemical aims." (Foulkes)

ii. In looking at the great, majestic themes of Ephesians, it is important to remember that Paul wrote this letter *from prison*.

d. Paul wrote in 1 Corinthians 2:9-10: *But as it is written: "Eye has not seen, nor ear heard, nor have entered into the heart of man the things which God has prepared for those who love Him." But God has revealed them to us through His Spirit. For the Spirit searches all things, yes, the deep things of God.* Ephesians is the fulfillment of this. It reveals the things God has prepared for those who love Him.

2. (1-2) Paul's greeting to the Ephesians.

Paul, an apostle of Jesus Christ by the will of God, To the saints who are in Ephesus, and faithful in Christ Jesus: Grace to you and peace from God our Father and the Lord Jesus Christ.

a. **Paul, an apostle of Jesus Christ**: The opening of the letter is brief, without the more detailed greetings from Paul often found in his other letters.

b. **To the saints who are in Ephesus**: In a few ancient manuscripts there is a blank space instead of the words **in Ephesus**. Based partly on this, some believe that this letter was actually a circular letter written not to any one congregation, but meant to be passed on to many different congregations in different cities.

i. There is little doubt this letter was intended for Ephesus, and Ephesus was an important city to Paul. "Here was his well-known

Ephesus. Here for the space of three complete years – a unique length of stationary work for him – he had lived and laboured, not as the apostolic missionary only but as the apostolic pastor. Here he had taken that critical and momentous step, the 'separation' of the disciples from the Synagogue to a distinct place of teaching and no doubt of worship, 'the school of one Tyrannus,' the lecture-hall, we may suppose, of a friendly professor in what we may call the Ephesian University. Here he had laboured, watched, and wept, for both the community and individuals." (Moule)

ii. At the same time, we can gather that the letter was also intended in a more general sense - to circulate among Christians as a great statement of God's eternal plan, worked out in the church and in individual Christian lives. If there is a blank space in a manuscript where others read **in Ephesus**, it is certainly because we are to put *our city* in that blank space.

c. **Grace to you and peace from God our Father**: This greeting is typical of Paul. The apostle knew the essential place of **grace** and **peace** from God in the life of the believer, and He knew that receiving God's grace comes *before* a walk in peace with Him.

B. The work of the Triune God on behalf of the believer.

In ancient Greek (the language Paul originally wrote in), Ephesians 1:3 through 1:14 form one long sentence. As an opera has an overture, setting the tone for all the melodies that will follow, so Ephesians 1:3-14 sets the tone for the rest of Ephesians.

1. (3-6) The work of God the *Father*.

Blessed *be* the God and Father of our Lord Jesus Christ, who has blessed us with every spiritual blessing in the heavenly *places* in Christ, just as He chose us in Him before the foundation of the world, that we should be holy and without blame before Him in love, having predestined us to adoption as sons by Jesus Christ to Himself, according to the good pleasure of His will, to the praise of the glory of His grace, by which He has made us accepted in the Beloved.

a. **Blessed be the God and Father of our Lord Jesus Christ**: Paul called for a blessing upon the Father (in the sense of recognizing His glory and honor and goodness), because the Father has *already* blessed the believer with every spiritual blessing (**who has blessed us with every spiritual blessing**).

i. Moule wrote that the idea behind **blessed** is, "Praised with worshipping love."

b. **Who has blessed us**: This blessing is ours. God's resources are there for us always. This speaks of an attitude of certainty and assurance.

i. "We are not sitting here, and groaning, and crying, and fretting, and worrying, and questioning our own salvation. He has blessed us; and therefore we will bless him. If you think little of what God has done for you, you will do very little for him; but if you have a great notion of his great mercy to you, you will be greatly grateful to your gracious God." (Spurgeon)

ii. The "**us**" includes both Jews and Gentiles in the church at Ephesus and beyond. It was important to point out that these blessings are for both Jewish and Gentile believers. First century Jews had a strong sense of being blessed, called, and predestined. Paul showed that these things are now given to Christians, be they Jew or Gentile.

c. **With every spiritual blessing in the heavenly places in Christ**: This describes both the *kind* of blessings and the *location* of those blessings. These are **spiritual** blessings, which are far better than material blessings. These blessings are ours **in the heavenly places in Christ**, they are higher, better, and more secure than earthly blessings.

i. "Our thanks are due to God for all temporal blessings; they are more than we deserve. But our thanks ought to go to God in thunders of hallelujahs for spiritual blessings. A new heart is better than a new coat. To feed on Christ is better than to have the best earthly food. To be an heir of God is better than being the heir of the greatest nobleman. To have God for our portion is blessed, infinitely more blessed than to own broad acres of land. God hath blessed us with spiritual blessings. These are the rarest, the richest, the most enduring of all blessings; they are priceless in value." (Spurgeon)

ii. If we have no appreciation for spiritual blessing, then we live at the level of *animals*. Animals live only to eat, sleep, entertain themselves, and to reproduce. We are made in the image of God and He has something much higher for us, yet many choose to live at the level of *animals*. God wants us know **every spiritual blessing in the heavenly places in Christ**.

iii. We also note that this includes **every spiritual blessing**.

- This means that *every blessing we receive,* we receive *in Christ.*

- This means that God wants to bless us with *every blessing available to us.*

d. **Just as He chose us in Him**: Our possession of **every spiritual blessing** is as certain as our being chosen by Him, and chosen **before the foundation of the world**.

i. We dare not diminish what Paul writes here. Believers are chosen by God, and they are chosen before they *have done* anything or *have been* anything for God. The great light of this truth casts some shadows; namely, in trying to reconcile human responsibility with divine sovereignty. Yet the purpose of light is not to cast shadows but to guide our steps. The light of God's selection gives us assurance to the permanence of His plan and His love towards us.

ii. The reasons for God's choosing are not capricious, nor are they random. Though they are past our finding out, we know that they are altogether wise and good, but the reasons are all in Him, not in us. His choosing is *according to the good pleasure of His will* (Ephesians 1:5).

iii. We are chosen **in Him**. "For if we are chosen in Christ, it is outside ourselves. It is not from the sight of our deserving, but because our heavenly Father has engrafted us, through the blessing of adoption, into the Body of Christ. In short, the name of Christ excludes all merit, and everything which men have of themselves." (Calvin)

e. **That we should be holy and without blame before Him in love**: We are chosen not only for salvation, but also for *holiness*. Any understanding of God's sovereign choosing that diminishes our personal responsibility for personal holiness and sanctification falls far short of the whole counsel of God.

i. "The words [**holy and without blame**] are a metaphor taken from the *perfect* and *immaculate* sacrifices which the law required the people to bring to the altar of God." (Clarke)

ii. We cannot forget the words **in love**. Holiness and blamelessness are nothing without love. "But as *love* is the *fulfilling of the law*, and *love* the *fountain* whence their salvation flowed, therefore *love* must fill their hearts towards God and each other." (Clarke)

f. **Having predestined us to adoption as sons by Jesus Christ to Himself**: This is the Father's destiny for His chosen - that they would enjoy **adoption as sons**. God's unfolding plan for us not only includes salvation and personal transformation, but also a warm, confident relationship with the Father.

i. In Roman law, "When the adoption was complete it was complete indeed. The person who had been adopted had all the rights of a legitimate son in his new family and completely lost all rights in his old family. In the eyes of the law he was a new person. So new was he that even all debts and obligations connected with his previous family were abolished as if they had never existed." (Barclay)

ii. Gaebelein takes the thought even further: "Believers in the Lord Jesus Christ are not adopted into the family of God; they are born into the family. The Greek has only one word 'Sonplace.' We are placed into the position of Sons."

iii. This high position in the family of God gives us something in Jesus that Adam never had. "When people ask us the speculative question why God went ahead with the creation when he knew that it would be followed by the fall, one answer we can tentatively give is that he destined us for a higher dignity than even creation would bestow on us." (Stott)

g. **To the praise of the glory of His grace, by which He has made us accepted in the Beloved**: The relational aspect is emphasized again as Paul describes the status of **accepted** (*charito*, "highly favored" or "full of grace" as in Luke 1:28) that is granted to every believer because of God's grace.

i. Jesus was completely accepted by the Father. All His character, all His words, all His work was acceptable to God the Father. And now we are **accepted in the Beloved**.

ii. Paul realized this plan gave glory to the **grace** of God. "By the giving of the Law, God's *justice* and *holiness* were rendered most glorious; by the giving of the Gospel, his *grace* and *mercy* are made equally glorious." (Clarke) God's plan in the gospel is often rejected because it glorifies God and His grace and not the effort or achievement of man.

iii. Bruce on the idea of being **accepted** by God on the standing of grace: "God's grace has extended to his people and enfolded them: he has 'be-graced' them, says Paul (using a verb derived from the Greek word for 'grace')."

iv. Chrysostom, speaking of the work by which God makes us **accepted in the Beloved**: "It is as if one were to take a leper and change him into a lovely youth."

2. (7-8) The work of God the *Son*.

In Him we have redemption through His blood, the forgiveness of sins, according to the riches of His grace which He made to abound toward us in all wisdom and prudence,

a. **In Him we have redemption through His blood**: The **Him** is the *Beloved* of Ephesians 1:6. **In Him** we have redemption and nowhere else. There is no possible redemption outside of Jesus and His redeeming **blood**.

i. **Redemption** always implies a price being paid for the freedom that is purchased. It uses the ancient Greek word *lootruo*, which means, "to liberate on the receipt of a ransom." (Gaebelein) Here the price is **His blood**, showing that the blessing from the Father and the Son comes not only from a divine decree, but it also comes according to His righteousness and holiness. He cannot bless in opposition to His righteousness and holiness.

ii. Jesus does not redeem us by His sinless life or His moral example, but only by His death in our place - by **His blood**. "Observe, it is not redemption through his power, it is *through his bloo*d. It is not redemption through his love, it is through his blood." (Spurgeon)

iii. We should not take a superstitious or mystical view of "the blood." It was not Jesus' physical blood that saved anyone, but His real and total payment for the sins of man in His whole person on the cross. This is what the New Testament means when it talks about "the **blood**."

b. **According to the riches of His grace**: The redemption and forgiveness given to us comes according to the measure of the **riches of His grace**. It is not a "small" redemption or forgiveness won by Jesus on the cross. It is immense.

c. **Which He made to abound toward us in all wisdom and prudence**: Many think it is unwise of God to lavish such redemption and forgiveness on guilty sinners. But it was **in all wisdom and prudence** that He gave this to us.

3. (9-12) The mystery of His will.

Having made known to us the mystery of His will, according to His good pleasure which He purposed in Himself, that in the dispensation of the fullness of the times He might gather together in one all things in Christ, both which are in heaven and which are on earth; in Him. In Him also we have obtained an inheritance, being predestined according to the purpose of Him who works all things according to the counsel of His will, that we who first trusted in Christ should be to the praise of His glory.

a. **Having made known to us the mystery of His will**: Part of what belongs to us under the *riches of His grace* is the knowledge of **the mystery of His will**, God's great plan and purpose which was once hidden but is now revealed to us in Jesus. Through the Apostle Paul, God called us to consider the greatness of God's great plan for the ages and our place in that plan.

i. "In the New Testament sense a mystery is something which is hidden to the heathen but clear to the Christian." (Barclay)

ii. The idea behind the word **dispensation** also reflects a plan or a strategy. "The plan which the master of a family, or his steward, has established for the management of the family... it signifies, also, a plan for the management of any sort of business." (Clarke)

b. **That... He might gather together in one all things in Christ, both which are in heaven and which are on earth; in Him**: God's ultimate plan is to bring together – to ultimately resolve – all things in Christ, either through Jesus as a Savior or Jesus as a Judge; this will happen in the **fullness of the times**.

i. The word for **gather together** has the idea of "to unite" or "to sum up." It was used for the process of adding up a column of figures and putting the sum up at the top. Paul's idea is that God will make all things "add up" at the end, and right now He is in the process of coming to that final sum.

ii. This shows that God wants to unify all things in our lives under Him. "It is a heresy of our times to divide life into sacred and secular." (Foulkes)

iii. This is the great resolution and deliverance that even the creation groans for (Romans 8:18-22), the day when every wrong will be righted and every matter resolved according to God's holy love and justice.

iv. Bruce on **the fullness of the times**: "When the time is ripe for the consummation of his purpose, in his providential overruling of the course of the world, that consummation will be realized."

c. **In Him also we have obtained an inheritance**: For believers, Jesus is not a judge, but the One in whom we have an inheritance. Believers are predestined for this according to the **counsel of His will** - again, the reasons for His choosing reside in Him, not in us.

d. **Being predestined according to the purpose of Him who works all things according to the counsel of His will**: We see three aspects of God's plan working together. It begins with His **purpose**, then the **counsel of His will**, and finally results in His **work**. God made His plan carefully according to an eternal purpose, taking **counsel** within the Godhead, and then He works with all wisdom.

i. "Our God is a God who not only wills; He works; and He works according to His will... The word *counsel* stands for deliberate planning and arranging, in which the ways and means of carrying out the will are considered and provided for." (Morgan)

ii. **By the counsel of His will**: "God doth all by counsel, and ever hath a reason of his will, which though we see not for present, we shall at last day. Meanwhile submit." (Trapp)

e. **That we who first trusted in Christ should be to the praise of His glory**: God's purpose in all this is so that those who have trusted Christ will exist **to the praise of His glory**. The goal of God's ultimate plan is to glorify Him.

f. **We who first trusted in Christ**: This speaks of Jewish believers. The words *you also* in Ephesians 1:13 speak of Gentile believers. God's great plan has a place for both Jew and Gentile, and it brings them both together in Jesus.

4. (13-14) The work of the Holy Spirit.

In Him you also *trusted,* after you heard the word of truth, the gospel of your salvation; in whom also, having believed, you were sealed with the Holy Spirit of promise, who is the guarantee of our inheritance until the redemption of the purchased possession, to the praise of His glory.

a. **In Him you also trusted, after you heard the word of truth**: God's sovereign choice works, but it does not exclude human cooperation. These ones who were so sovereignly chosen were also the ones who **trusted, heard the word of truth**, and **believed**.

b. **You were sealed with the Holy Spirit of promise**: Also essential in God's work is the sealing work of the Holy Spirit. His presence in our lives acts as a seal which indicates ownership, and which is a **guarantee of our inheritance**.

i. "The seal is therefore the Holy Spirit Himself, and His presence in the believer denotes ownership and security. The sealing with the Spirit is not an emotional feeling or some mysterious inward experience." (Gaebelein)

ii. The word **guarantee** ("down payment") is used only in the New Testament of the Holy Spirit. He is our *only* down payment of coming glory; nothing else is provided - or *needed*.

c. **Having believed, you were sealed**: The sealing does not come *before* we believe, and those who demand some assurance from God before they will believe treat God as if His word could not be trusted.

i. "For sealing there are needed the softened wax; the imprint of the beloved face; the steady pressure. Would that the Spirit might impress the face of our dear Lord on our softened hearts, that they may keep it for evermore!" (Meyer)

d. **Until the redemption of the purchased possession**: We have this **guarantee** until we are "completely purchased" by God through resurrection and glorification - again, all to the **praise of His glory**.

C. Paul prays in light of God's ultimate plan and the work of the Triune God.

1. (15-16) Paul's statement of prayer and declaration of thanksgiving.

Therefore I also, after I heard of your faith in the Lord Jesus and your love for all the saints, do not cease to give thanks for you, making mention of you in my prayers:

a. **After I heard of your faith in the Lord Jesus and your love for all the saints**: When Paul heard of the **faith** and **love** of the Ephesians, he could do nothing else but **give thanks** for them. This was because their **faith** and **love** were evidence of their participation in this great work of God.

i. Faith and love do not *earn* us participation in this great work of God. They are *evidence* of our participation in God's plan.

b. **Love for all the saints**: Significantly, Paul gave thanks not for their love for God, but for their **love for all the saints**. The real evidence of God's work in us is not the love we claim to have for Him, but our love for His people that others can see (1 John 4:20, John 13:14 and John 13:34-35).

c. **Making mention of you in my prayers**: Paul not only gave thanks for God's work among the Ephesians; he also prayed that it would continue with greater strength, as the prayer in Ephesians 1:17-23 makes clear.

i. Paul shows us here that preachers must do more than preach to their audience - they must also *pray* for them. "Whether a minister shall do more good to others by his prayers or preaching, I will not determine, but he shall certainly by his prayers reap more comfort to himself." (Trapp)

ii. Paul often prayed **making mention** of others in prayer. When he prayed he mentioned the Christians in Rome (Romans 1:9), the Christians in Thessalonica (1 Thessalonians 1:2), and Philemon (Philemon 1:4).

2. (17) Paul prays that they would know God.

That the God of our Lord Jesus Christ, the Father of glory, may give to you the spirit of wisdom and revelation in the knowledge of Him,

a. **May give to you the spirit of wisdom and revelation**: Paul prayed that the Father would grant the Ephesians **the spirit of wisdom** and that He would give them **revelation**. But these are not so they may see into the lives of others, have the ability to predict events, or do what we commonly think of as "prophet stuff." He wanted them to have **the spirit of wisdom** and **revelation** simply so that they would have a better **knowledge of Him** (God).

b. **In the knowledge of Him**: Our Christian life must be centered around this purpose - to know God as He is in truth, as revealed by His Word, and to correct our false, idolatrous ideas of who God is.

c. **The knowledge of Him**: It is important for us to have an accurate knowledge and understanding of who *we* are. Yet it is far more important (and beneficial) for us to know and understand who God is.

i. A famous writer named Alexander Pope wrote, "Know then thyself, presume not God to scan; the proper study of mankind is man." Charles Spurgeon responded to this famous statement: "It has been said by someone that 'the proper study of mankind is man.' I will not oppose the idea, but I believe it is equally true that the proper study of God's elect is God; the proper study of a Christian is the Godhead. The highest science, the loftiest speculation, the mightiest philosophy which can ever engage the attention of a child of God, is the name, the nature, the person, the work, the doings, and the existence of the great God whom he calls his Father."

ii. "For philosophy comes to man with the message, *Know thyself*; the Gospel meets him with the far more glorious and fruitful watchword, *Know thy God*." (Alford)

3. (18-19a) Paul prays that they would understand everything God gave them in Jesus Christ.

The eyes of your understanding being enlightened; that you may know what is the hope of His calling, what are the riches of the glory of His inheritance in the saints, and what *is* the exceeding greatness of His power toward us who believe,

a. **The eyes of your understanding being enlightened**: If the Ephesians will know all God has given them in Jesus, it will take a supernatural work. It will require that **the eyes of your understanding** be **enlightened** by God.

i. Paul used a great expression when he speaks of *the eyes of your heart* (*heart* is more literal than *understanding*). Too many Christian *hearts* have no eyes (places where they gain real knowledge and understanding), and too many Christian *eyes* have no heart – God wants both to be combined in us.

ii. "The word '*heart*' in Scripture signifies the very core and centre of life, where the intelligence has its post of observation, where the stores of experience are laid up, and the thoughts have their fountain." (Alford)

b. **What is the hope of His calling**: Paul wanted them to know this. Few things give us a more secure and enduring **hope** in life than simply knowing that God has called us and has a specific **calling** for us to fulfill.

i. The **hope of His calling** has its perspective on the *future*. The believer has a glorious future of resurrection, eternal life, freedom from sin, perfected justification, and glorious elevation above the angels themselves.

c. **What are the riches of the glory of His inheritance in the saints**: Paul wanted them to know the greatness of God's inheritance in His people. We usually think only of *our* inheritance in God, but Paul wanted the Ephesians to understand that they are so precious to God that He considered them *His* own **inheritance**.

i. Several commentators believe that Paul also spoke of God's inheritance in His people back in Ephesians 1:11. But that is certainly his idea here, with Paul probably drawing his idea from Deuteronomy 32:8-9: *When the Most High divided their inheritance to the nations, when He separated the sons of Adam, He set the boundaries of the peoples according to the number of the children of Israel. For the Lord's portion is His people; Jacob is the place of His inheritance.*

ii. Knowing our spiritual poverty, we wonder how God can find *any* inheritance in the saints. Yet God can make riches out of poor men and women because He invests so much in them. He has invested riches of love, riches of wisdom, riches of suffering, riches of glory. These things accrue to a rich inheritance in the saints.

d. **The exceeding greatness of His power toward us who believe**: Paul wanted them to know how great the **power** of God is **toward us who believe**. Christians should know they serve and love a God of living power who shows His strength on behalf of His people.

i. Many Christians do not know this power - or they only know it from a distance. God wants resurrection life to be *real* in the life of the believer. "The very same power which raised Christ is waiting to raise the drunkard from his drunkenness, to raise the thief from his dishonesty, to raise the Pharisee from his self-righteousness, to raise the Sadducee from his unbelief." (Spurgeon)

ii. This ends the "request" portion of Paul's prayer. The following section explains more of this mighty power and what it did. Paul asked these things because they were important to ask for. We could say that the prayer of Ephesians 1:17-19 is essentially a request that the promises of Ephesians 1:3-14 be found as real in the lives of the Ephesian Christians.

iii. In the same way, your prayers for the spiritual growth and enlightenment of others are important. If Paul believed it was important to pray these things for the Ephesian Christians, it is important for us to pray them for others – and for ourselves.

4. (19b-21) A description of the great power of God that Paul wants the Ephesians to know.

According to the working of His mighty power which He worked in Christ when He raised Him from the dead and seated *Him* at His right hand in the heavenly *places*, far above all principality and power and might and dominion, and every name that is named, not only in this age but also in that which is to come.

a. **According to the working of His mighty power**: The power that works in us is the **mighty power** that raised Jesus **from the dead**. With this **mighty power** available to us, there never needs to be a "power shortage" in the Christian life.

i. "If the death of Christ is the supreme demonstration of the love of God... the resurrection of Christ is the supreme demonstration of his power." (Bruce)

b. **And seated Him at His right hand**: It is the **mighty power** that raised Jesus to heaven after His resurrection, raising Him above all demonic foes and every potential enemy of all time - this *same* power is at work in Christians.

i. "The *right hand* is the place of friendship, honour, confidence, and authority." (Clarke)

c. **Far above all principality and power and might and dominion**: From other passages in Ephesians (Ephesians 3:10 and 6:12) we know that this refers to angelic beings, both loyal and lethal. We don't completely understand the ranks of the angelic realm, but we do know that Jesus is raised above them. "We know that the king is above all, though we cannot name all the officers of his court. So we know that Christ is above all, though we are not able to name all His subjects." (Alford)

i. "Think of the paradox. The Apostle is speaking of a Personage of history, of recent, almost contemporary, history... He had worked with His hands, He had walked from place to place like other men, and man could no doubt accurately describe His look and manner when He talked... He is now 'seated at the right hand of' Almighty God, on His very throne." (Moule)

5. (22-23) Where this great power has placed Jesus.

And He put all *things* under His feet, and gave Him *to be* head over all *things* to the church, which is His body, the fullness of Him who fills all in all.

a. **He put all things under His feet**: This great resurrection power placed Jesus above all things. Now all things are **under His feet**. It set Jesus as the **head over all things**, including the church.

i. "He says that Christ in his exaltation over the universe is God's gift to the church." (Wood)

b. **The church, which is His body**: If Jesus is the head, then the community of Christians make up **His body**. The idea of **the fullness of Him** here is probably connected to the manner in which Jesus fills His church with His presence and blessings.

i. "Yes, this is here given as the final glory of the infinitely exalted Christ. Angels and archangels are subject to Him. But believing men are *joined to Him*, with a union such that He and they, by this same messenger of His, are called elsewhere (1 Corinthians 12:12) one '*Christ*.'" (Moule)

Ephesians 2 - God's Way of Reconciliation

A. The need for reconciliation.

1. (1) Christians are alive from the dead.

And you *He made alive,* who were dead in trespasses and sins,

a. **And you He made alive**: The words **He made alive** are in italics, which indicates that they are added to the text but implied from the context. Paul wrote to believers who were **made alive** by God's work.

i. Paul ended the last chapter by considering that the ultimate example of God's power was the resurrection of Jesus. Now Paul considers what the implications of Jesus' resurrection power are for our life.

b. **Who were dead in trespasses and sins**: Though Christians are now **alive**, they must never forget where they came *from*. They were **dead in trespasses and sins**.

i. There are many kinds of life: vegetable life, animal life, mental life, moral life, and spiritual life. A being might be alive in one sense but dead in another. To be spiritually dead does not mean that we are physically dead, socially dead, or psychologically dead. Yet it is a real death, a "dead death" nonetheless. "The most vital part of man's personality – the spirit – is dead to the most important factor in life – God." (Wood) "Not in a moral sense, nor a mental sense, but in a spiritual sense, poor humanity is dead, and so the word of God again and again most positively describes it." (Spurgeon)

ii. This touches on one of the most controversial areas in theology - in what manner, and to what extent, is a person **dead** before conversion? Must a person be converted *before* he can believe, or can there be a prior work of God to instill faith that is still short of conversion? Those who argue that man must be regenerated *before* he can believe like to say that a dead man cannot believe. This takes this particular description further than intended, to say that unredeemed man is *exactly like* a dead man, because a dead man also *cannot sin*.

iii. We err if we think that **dead in trespasses and sins** says *everything* about man's lost condition. It is an err because the Bible uses many different pictures to describe the state of the unsaved man, saying he is:

- Blind (2 Corinthians 4:3-4).
- A slave to sin (Romans 6:17).
- A lover of darkness (John 3:19-20).
- Sick (Mark 2:17).
- Lost (Luke 15).
- An alien, a stranger, a foreigner (Ephesians 2:12, 2:19).
- A child of wrath (Ephesians 2:3).
- Under the power of darkness (Colossians 1:13).

iv. Therefore, in some ways man apart from God is dead; in other ways he is not. Therefore, it is valid to *appeal to all men to believe*. We need not look for evidence of regeneration before we tell men to believe and be saved. As the Puritan John Trapp wrote, "Howbeit, the natural man, though he be theologically dead, yet is ethically alive, being to be wrought upon by arguments; hence Hosea 11:4, 'I drew them by the cords of a man,' that is, by reason and motives of love, befitting the nature of a man. So the Spirit and Word work upon us still as men by rational motives, setting before us life and good, death and evil."

c. **In trespasses and sins**: The idea behind the word **trespasses** is that we have crossed a line, challenging God's boundaries. The idea behind the word **sins** is that we have missed a mark, the perfect standards of God.

i. **Trespasses** speaks of man as a rebel, **sins** speaks of man as a failure. "Before God we are both rebels and failures." (Stott)

2. (2-3) The life of death.

In which you once walked according to the course of this world, according to the prince of the power of the air, the spirit who now works in the sons of disobedience, among whom also we all once conducted ourselves in the lusts of our flesh, fulfilling the desires of the flesh and of the mind, and were by nature children of wrath, just as the others.

a. **In which you once walked**: At one time we lived in *trespasses and sins*, **according to the course of this world**, which is orchestrated by Satan. Satan (**the prince of the power of the air**) is still very much active among those in rebellion against God - **the sons of disobedience**.

b. **You once walked**: The self that **once walked** was the old man, now crucified with Jesus at the time of conversion. The sin nature inherited from Adam influenced the old man, but the world system and Satan do also. One might say that the influence of the old man lives on in what the New Testament calls the flesh.

i. **Once walked** means it should be different for those who are made alive by Jesus Christ. A dead man feels comfortable in his coffin; but if he were to be made alive again, he would instantly feel suffocated and uncomfortable. There would be a strong urge to escape the coffin and leave it behind. In the same way, when we were spiritually dead we felt comfortable in trespasses and sins; but having come to new life we feel we must escape that coffin and leave it behind.

c. **Who now works in the sons of disobedience**: In sin we respond to Satan's "guidance." The same ancient Greek verb is used in Ephesians 2:2 for the work of Satan in unbelievers as is used in Ephesians 3:20 for the power of God that works in believers.

d. **The prince of the power of the air**: This unique title for Satan speaks of his authority (**prince**) and his realm (**the air**, a way of referring to Satan's "environment").

i. "The *domain of the air*, in fact, is another way of indicating the *heavenly realm*, which, according to Ephesians 6:12, is the abode of those principalities and powers, *world-rulers of this darkness* and *spiritual forces of wickedness* against which the people of Christ wage war." (Bruce)

ii. Satan is not the ultimate ruler, but he is a prince in the sense that "Evil men set him up for their sovereign, and are wholly at his beck and obedience." (Trapp)

e. **We all once conducted ourselves in the lusts of our flesh**: We once were among the *sons of disobedience*, proven by our conduct. We embraced **the lusts of the flesh**, which are primarily perversions of the legitimate desires of human nature.

i. "The converts are to be reminded what they have been delivered from, as well as what they have been lifted into. They must be led to look down again into the pit, into the grave, from which grace called them out and set them free." (Moule)

f. **And were by nature children of wrath**: Because of our surrender to the old man, the world, and the devil, we **were by nature children of wrath**. We rightfully deserved God's wrath, and deserved it because of who we were by our heritage.

i. The Bible knows nothing of the idea that all men are "children of God," except in the sense that He is our common creator (Acts 17:28). Here Paul says that there is a "family" of wrath that has its children, and Jesus called the Pharisees "a family of snakes" (*brood of vipers* in Matthew 3:7, 12:34, and 23:33) and said that their father was the Devil (John 8:44).

B. The process of personal reconciliation to God.

1. (4) God's motive in reconciliation.

But God, who is rich in mercy, because of His great love with which He loved us,

a. **But God... because of His great love**: With **but** and **because**, Paul explained God's reason behind reconciling man to Himself, and these reasons are found totally in God. The reasons are His rich **mercy** and **His great love**, which He focuses on **us**.

i. "As they were *corrupt* in their *nature*, and *sinful* in their *practice*, they could possess no *merit*, nor have any *claim* upon God; and it required much *mercy* to remove so much *misery*, and to pardon such transgressions." (Clarke)

b. **With which He loved us**: We might imagine a God of rich **mercy** and **great love** who did not focus that mercy and love upon *us*. But behind the good news of God's salvation offered in Jesus is the fact that this mercy and love *is* extended to **us**.

c. **His great love with which He loved us**: Some warp the idea of God's great mercy and love into something that justifies our pride. Some imagine that God loves us *because we are so lovable*. Instead, God's love is so great that it extends even to the unlovely - to the *children of wrath*.

i. Every reason for God's mercy and love is found in Him. We give Him no *reason* to love us, yet in the greatness of His love, He loves us with that great love anyway.

ii. Therefore, we must stop trying to make ourselves lovable to God, and simply receive His great love while recognizing that we are unworthy of it. This is the *grace secret* of the Christian life.

2. (5-7) The past, present, and future of God's work of individual reconciliation.

Even when we were dead in trespasses, made us alive together with Christ (by grace you have been saved), and raised *us* up together, and made *us* sit together in the heavenly *places* in Christ Jesus, that in the ages to come He might show the exceeding riches of His grace in *His* kindness toward us in Christ Jesus.

a. **When we were dead**: This is when God started loving us. He did not wait until we were lovable. He loved us even when we were **dead in trespasses**, providing nothing lovable to Him.

i. This is the requirement for being saved. You must first be dead, dead to every attempt to justify yourself before God. *He who hears My word and believes in Him who sent Me... has passed from death into life* (John 5:24).

b. **Made us alive together with Christ**: This is what God did to those who were dead in sin. He shared in our death so that we could share in His resurrection life. The old man is crucified and we are new creations in Jesus with the old things passing away and all things becoming new.

i. **By grace you have been saved**: Paul is compelled to add here that this is the work of God's **grace**, in no way involving man's merit. Our salvation - our rescue - from spiritual death is God's work done for the undeserving.

c. **Sit together in the heavenly places in Christ Jesus**: This is the present position of the Christian. We have a new place for living, a new arena of existence - we are not *those who dwell on the earth* (as Revelation often calls them), but our *citizenship is in heaven* (Philippians 3:20).

i. We don't sit in the heavenly places *with* Christ Jesus, or at least not yet. Instead, we sit in the heavenly places **in Christ** Jesus. Since our life and identity is **in Christ**, as He sits in heavenly places, so do we.

ii. "And now we *sit in heavenly* places – we have a *right* to the kingdom of God, anticipate this glory, and are indescribably happy in the possession of this salvation, and in our fellowship with Christ Jesus." (Clarke)

d. **In the ages to come He might show the exceeding riches of His grace**: *In the future*, God will continue to **show the exceeding riches of His grace** to us. God will never stop dealing with us on the basis of grace, and will forever continue to unfold its riches to us through eternity.

i. **He might show**: "The original implies, that the exhibition is for His own purpose, for his own glory." (Alford) This work in us reflects infinitely more on the glory of *God* than on *our* glory, and God will use His work in the Church to display His glory throughout the ages.

ii. "From this verse it is clear that Paul fully expected the gospel of the grace of God to be preached in the ages to come. He had no notion of a temporary gospel to develop into a better, but he was assured that the same gospel would be preached to the end of the dispensation. Nor this alone; for as I take it, he looked to the perpetuity of the gospel, not only through the ages which have already elapsed since the first advent of our blessed Lord, but throughout the ages after he shall have come a second time. Eternity itself will not improve upon the gospel." (Spurgeon)

iii. "When all the saints shall be gathered home they shall still talk and speak of the wonders of Jehovah's love in Christ Jesus, and in the golden streets they shall stand up and tell what the Lord has done for them to listening crowds of angels, and principalities, and powers." (Spurgeon)

iv. **Exceeding riches of His grace**: "So is it with the grace of God: he has as much grace as you want, and he has a great deal more than that. The Lord has as much grace as a whole universe will require, but he has vastly more. He overflows: all the demands that can ever be made on the grace of God will never impoverish him, or even diminish his store of mercy; there will remain an incalculably precious mine of mercy as full as when he first began to bless the sons of men." (Spurgeon)

v. One way to see the greatness of the grace of God is to see how He *begs* man to receive it. When we offer a gift to someone and they refuse it, we are likely to allow them to refuse and leave them alone. God does not do this with us; even when we refuse His mercy He reaches into His storehouse of grace and persists with us, *begging* us to receive the free gift.

3. (8-10) A summing up of God's work of individual reconciliation.

For by grace you have been saved through faith, and that not of yourselves; *it is* the gift of God, not of works, lest anyone should boast. For we are His workmanship, created in Christ Jesus for good works, which God prepared beforehand that we should walk in them.

a. **For by grace you have been saved**: Paul cannot speak of this glorious work God does without reminding us that it is a gift of **grace**, given to the undeserving. We are not even saved by our faith (though faith itself is not a work), but **by** grace **through** faith.

i. We can think of water flowing through a hose. The water is the important part, but it is communicated through the hose. The hose does not quench your thirst; the water does. But the hose brings water to the place you can benefit from it.

ii. "The precise form of words here stresses two things. As consistently emphasized by Paul, it is entirely of His *grace*, His free, undeserved favour to mankind. Then also this salvation is presented as an accomplished fact." (Foulkes)

b. **And that not of yourselves, it is the gift of God**: The work of salvation is God's gift. Paul's grammar here indicates that the words apply to the gift of *salvation* mentioned in Ephesians 2:4-8, and not directly to the **faith** mentioned in this verse.

i. Clarke emphatically states that the original Greek is clear in noting that when it says **it is the gift of God**, the **it** referred to is *salvation*, not *faith*. The great Greek scholar Dean Alford also clearly pointed out that the **this not of yourselves** referred to *salvation*, not to *faith*.

ii. Yet, even our faith is a **gift of God**. We *cannot* believe in Jesus unless God does a prior work in us, for we are blinded by our own deadness and by the god of this age (2 Corinthians 4:4).

iii. "But it may be asked: Is not *faith* the *gift of God*? Yes, as to the *grace* by which it is produced; but the *grace* or *power* to believe, and the act of believing, are two different things. Without the *grace* or *power* to believe no man ever did or can believe; but with that *power* the *act of faith* is a man's own. God never believes *for* any man, no more than he *repents* for him; the penitent, through this grace enabling him, believes for himself." (Clarke)

iv. This shows us the essential place of *prayer* in evangelism. Since God initiates salvation, we should begin our evangelism with asking God to do the initiating, and granting the ability to believe to those we want to see saved.

c. **Not of works, lest anyone should boast**: God did it **not of works** simply so that no one could **boast**. If salvation was the accomplishment of man in any way, we could boast about it. But under God's plan of salvation, God alone receives the glory.

i. "I thought Napoleon did a good thing, when, on the day of his coronation, he took his crown, and put it on his own head. Why should he not take the symbol that was his due? And if you get to heaven, one half by grace and one half by works, you will say, 'Atonement profited me a little, but integrity profited me much more.' " (Spurgeon)

d. **For we are His workmanship**: God saves us not merely to save us from the wrath we rightly deserve, but also to make something beautiful of us. We are **His workmanship**, which translates the ancient Greek word *poiema*. The idea is that we are His beautiful poem. The Jerusalem Bible translates **workmanship** as "work of art."

i. God's love is a transforming love. It meets us right where we are at, but when we receive this love it always takes us where we should be going. The love of God that saves my soul will also change my life.

ii. We are **His workmanship**, His creation – something new He has made of us in Jesus Christ. "The spiritual life cannot come to us by development from our old nature. I have heard a great deal about evolution and development, but I am afraid that if any one of us were to be developed to our utmost, apart from the grace of God, we should come out worse than before the development began." (Spurgeon)

iii. "Our new life is as truly *created out of nothing* as were the first heavens, and the first earth. This ought to be particularly noticed, for there are some who think that the grace of God improves the old nature into the new. It does nothing of the sort." (Spurgeon)

e. **Created in Christ Jesus for good works**: That beautiful thing God is making of us is active in **good works**. These are just as much a part of God's predestined plan as anything else is. These good works are valid evidence that someone is walking as one of God's chosen.

i. "Works play no part at all in securing salvation. But afterwards Christians will prove their faith by their works. Here Paul shows himself at one with James." (Wood)

C. The reconciliation of Jews and Gentiles in Jesus.

1. (11-12) The need for the reconciliation of Gentile and Jew.

Therefore remember that you, once Gentiles in the flesh; who are called Uncircumcision by what is called the Circumcision made in the flesh by hands; that at that time you were without Christ, being aliens from the commonwealth of Israel and strangers from the covenants of promise, having no hope and without God in the world.

a. **You, once Gentiles in the flesh**: God's work of reconciliation is not only between God and the individual, though it must begin there. It is also between groups of people that are at odds, such as Jews and Gentiles were in the days of Paul.

b. **Who are called Uncircumcision by what is called the Circumcision**: Gentiles were in a desperate place, being **aliens, strangers, having no hope** and being **without God**. This shows that they were not only spiritually dead, but they also did not have the access to God that the Jews enjoyed.

i. Before coming to Jesus, Gentiles were "Christless, stateless, friendless, hopeless and Godless." (Stott quoting Hendriksen)

ii. **Having no hope**: "The absence of hope in the face of death is amply attested in the literature and epigraphy of the Gaeco-Roman world of that day." (Bruce)

iii. **Without God in the world**: Some people believe in God, but they believe He lives in heaven and has nothing to do with this **world**. In that way, a person can still believe in God and be **without God in the world**.

c. **Without Christ**: These are terrible words, and the implications of them are the sum of the woeful condition of the lost man or woman. To be **without Christ** means to be:

- Without spiritual blessings.
- Without light.
- Without peace.
- Without rest.
- Without safety.
- Without hope.
- Without a Prophet, Priest, or King.

    i. "Without Christ! If this be the description of some of you, we need not talk to you about the fires of hell; let this be enough to startle you, that you are in such a desperate state as to be without Christ. Oh! What terrible evils lie clustering thick within these two words!" (Spurgeon)

d. **Aliens from the commonwealth of Israel**: This likely includes separated Jews as well as Gentiles. "For there were also Israelites who were outside the commonwealth, not only as foreigners but as lax Jews, and lost their part in the covenants, not as foreigners, but as unworthy." (Alford)

2. (13) Gentiles brought near to God.

But now in Christ Jesus you who once were far off have been brought near by the blood of Christ.

a. **But now in Christ Jesus**: Those Gentiles who are **now in Christ Jesus** are no longer **far off**. They are **made near** to the things of God, and the **blood of Christ** accomplishes this, by His sacrificial death.

    i. This coming near happens only **by the blood of Christ**.

    Gentiles who are not **in Christ Jesus** are just as **far off** as they ever were. This reconciliation only happens in Jesus.

    ii. It is important the Paul connects the ideas of the great love of Jesus and His sacrificial death. Many people think that preaching Christ crucified is all about a bloody, gory Jesus. But the point of Christ crucified is not gore, but love. Preaching Christ crucified means we preach Jesus full of love - sacrificial, giving, saving love.

b. **By the blood of Christ**: Many people suggest different ways to come **near** to God. Some think you can come by keeping the law or by belonging to a group (such as Israel or even the church). But the only way to be **brought near** to God is **by the blood of Christ**. What Jesus did on the cross, suffering as a guilty sinner in the place of guilty sinners, brings us **near** to God.

3. (14-16) Jew and Gentile brought together in the Church.

For He Himself is our peace, who has made both one, and has broken down the middle wall of separation, having abolished in His flesh the enmity, *that is,* the law of commandments *contained* in ordinances, so as to create in Himself one new man *from* the two, *thus* making peace, and that He might reconcile them both to God in one body through the cross, thereby putting to death the enmity.

a. **For He Himself is our peace**: Jesus Himself is our peace; He hasn't simply *made* peace between God and man and Jew and Gentile; He *is* **our peace**.

b. **Who has made both one, and has broken down the middle wall of separation**: The work of Jesus on the cross is the common ground of salvation for both Jew and Gentile. Therefore, there is no longer any dividing wall between Jew and Gentile. Jesus broke that wall down.

i. In the temple, in between the court of the Gentiles and the court of the women, there was a physical barrier, an actual **wall of separation** between Jew and Gentile.

ii. Paul was, at the time of this writing, under house arrest in Rome, awaiting trial because he was falsely accused by the Jews of taking a Gentile into the temple past the literal **wall of separation** dividing Jew and Gentile. Paul made it clear that in Jesus, the wall is gone.

iii. The **wall of separation** is gone because the common Lordship is greater than any previous division. If the Lordship of Jesus Christ is not greater than any difference you have with others - be it political, racial, economic, language, geography or whatever, then you have not fully understood what it means to be under the Lordship of Jesus.

c. **Having abolished in His flesh the enmity, that is, the law of commandments contained in ordinances**: The source of contention between Jew and Gentile was the fact that the Gentiles did not keep the law. But since Jesus fulfilled the law on our behalf, and since He bore the penalty for our failure to keep the law, we are reconciled through His work on the cross - putting to death the *source* of contention.

i. "The *enmity* of which the apostle speaks was reciprocal among the *Jews* and *Gentiles*. The *former* detested the *Gentiles*, and could hardly allow them the denomination of *men*; the *latter* had the *Jews* in the most sovereign contempt, because of the peculiarity of their religious rites and ceremonies, which were different from those of all the other nations of the earth." (Clarke)

ii. "And the separation was intensified and emphasized by those institutions which were, in part, *designed* to isolate Israel from the world, until the fit time for the wider blessing. And He 'annulled' them by fulfilling them, in His sacrificial work; thus at once reconciling man to God and man to man." (Moule)

iii. The law as a source of righteousness is no longer an issue. That source of **enmity** between Jew and Gentile is dead.

d. **That He might reconcile them both to God in one body through the cross**: Gentiles and Jews are brought together into **one body**, the Church, where our unity in Jesus is far greater than our previous differences.

i. **So as to create in Himself one new man from the two**: Early Christians called themselves a "third race" or a "new race." Early Christians recognized that they were not Jews, not Gentiles, but **one new man** embracing all who are in Jesus.

ii. "As Chrysostom explained, it is not that Christ has brought one up to the level of the other, but that he has produced a greater: 'as if one should melt down one statue of silver and another of lead, and the two together should come out gold.' " (Wood)

e. **Through the cross**: We see the emphasis Paul places on the work of Jesus on the cross. He repeats the idea several times: **made near by the blood... having abolished in His flesh the enmity... in one body through the cross**. This unity didn't just happen, it was the hard-fought accomplishment of Jesus.

i. This means that Jesus' prayer in John 17 (*that they all may be one*) wasn't "just" a prayer. It was a prayer Jesus prayed knowing that His work of the cross would *accomplish* the answer, and a prayer He was willing to pray knowing that His *agony* would be used to answer.

ii. This bringing together of Jew and Gentile in Jesus is a partial fulfillment of God's eternal purpose as stated in Ephesians 1:10: *that... He might gather together in one all things in Christ*. God uses the bringing together Jew and Gentile into the Church as a preview of His ultimate work of summing up all things into Jesus Christ. Since He can do this, He can also do that.

4. (17-18) How Jews and Gentiles are brought together.

And He came and preached peace to you who were afar off and to those who were near. For through Him we both have access by one Spirit to the Father.

a. **He came and preached peace to you who were afar off and to those who were near**: As they respond to the same gospel, the same **peace** that is **preached** to those **afar off** (Gentiles) and those **near** (Jews).

b. **Through Him we both have access by one Spirit to the Father**: They enjoy the same **access** to God, access that comes **by one Spirit to the Father**. Not only are Jews and Gentiles saved by the same gospel, but they also have the same essential walk with God and **access** to Him. One group does not have a greater **access** than the other does.

i. "*Access* is probably the best translation of *prosagoge*, though it could be 'introduction.' In oriental courts there was a *prosagoges* who brought a person into the presence of the king." (Foulkes)

ii. When conflict arises among Christian groups of different backgrounds, you can be sure that they forget that they were saved by the same gospel and that they have the same access to God. One or both groups usually feel they have superior access to God.

iii. "This text is a plain proof of the *holy Trinity*. Jews and Gentiles are to be presented unto *God the* FATHER; the SPIRIT of God works in their hearts, and prepares them for this presentation; and JESUS CHRIST himself *introduces* them." (Clarke)

5. (19-22) A picture of God's work of reconciliation, both individual and among groups.

Now, therefore, you are no longer strangers and foreigners, but fellow citizens with the saints and members of the household of God, having been built on the foundation of the apostles and prophets, Jesus Christ Himself being the chief corner*stone*, in whom the whole building, being joined together, grows into a holy temple in the Lord, in whom you also are being built together for a dwelling place of God in the Spirit.

a. **You are no longer strangers and foreigners**: Paul refers to Christians of Gentile background. They should not regard themselves as "second-class citizens" in God's kingdom in any regard. They are not only full **citizens**, but also full and equal members of God's **household**.

b. **Built on the foundation of the apostles and prophets**: Because we are one body and have the same access to God, it also follows that we are all built upon a common **foundation**. That foundation is the original

apostles and prophets, and their enduring revelation, recorded in the New Testament. May no one ever lay any other foundation.

i. Though Chrysostom, Jerome, Calvin and others saw the **prophets** mentioned as Old Testament prophets, it is better to see them as New Testament prophets, perhaps New Testament authors who were not strictly members of the core apostolic group.

ii. "Those who ranked next to the Apostles in the government of the church... They were not in every case distinct from the Apostles: the apostleship probably always including the gift of *prophecy*: so that all the Apostles themselves might likewise have been *prophets*." (Alford)

iii. In this sense of laying a foundation of supremely authoritative revelation for all God's people, there are no more **apostles** or **prophets** today. The foundation is already set. In a *lesser* sense there may be apostles and prophets today, but not in the sense Paul means here.

c. **Jesus Christ Himself being the chief corner stone**: This **corner stone** "literally means at the tip of the angle. It refers to the capstone or binding stone that holds the whole structure together... often the royal name was inscribed on it. In the East it was considered to be even more important than the foundation." (Wood)

i. Salmond on **corner stone**: "It denotes the stone placed at the extreme corner, so as to bind the other stones in the building together - the most important stone in the structure, the one on which its stability depended."

ii. "That structure and cohesion may have for its *scaffolding* the sacred order of the Church in her visible aspect. But the *cement* is not of these things; it is wholly divine; it is the Spirit, possessing each saint for God, and binding them all together by articulating them all to their Head." (Moule)

d. **In whom the whole building, being joined together, grows into a holy temple in the Lord**: As we keep to our common foundation, the **whole building** of God's people grows together in a beautiful way, as a **holy temple** where God dwells in beauty and glory.

i. This tells us that the Church is a **building**, perfectly designed by the Great Architect. It is not a haphazard pile of stones, randomly dumped in a field. God *arranges* the Church for His own glory and purposes.

ii. This tells us that the Church is a **dwelling place**, a place where God lives. It is never to be an empty house that is virtually a museum, with no one *living* inside. The Church is to be both the living place of God and His people.

iii. This tells us that the Church is a **temple**, holy and set apart to God. We serve there as priests, offering the spiritual sacrifices of our lips and hearts, our praises to God (Hebrews 13:15).

e. **You also are being built together for a dwelling place of God in the Spirit**: When Solomon's temple was built, the stones were prepared at a place far from the temple building site. It was said that you couldn't hear the sound of a hammer or axe or other iron tools at the sight (1 Kings 6:7). In the same way, God prepares us first, then He fits us into His building.

i. "The Father makes choice of this house, the Son purchaseth it, the Holy Ghost taketh possession of it." (Trapp)

ii. "And the everlasting FATHER will perfectly reveal Himself, to all the watchers of all the regions of the eternal world, not anyhow but *thus* – in His glorified Church, in the Race, the Nature, once wrecked and ruined, but rebuilt into this splendour by His grace." (Moule)

iii. Adam Clarke explained how God's work in the Church gave glory to the wisdom, power, and love of God. See all this, we should praise God for His glorious Church.

- There is nothing as *noble* as the Church, seeing that it is the temple of God.
- There is nothing so worthy of *reverence*, seeing God who *dwells* in it.
- There is nothing so *ancient*, since the *patriarchs* and *prophets* worked to building it.
- There is nothing so *solid*, since *Jesus Christ* is the *foundation* of it.
- There is nothing so *high*, since it reaches as high as to the *heavenly places in Christ Jesus*.
- There is nothing so *perfect* and *well proportioned*, since the *Holy Spirit* is the *architect*.
- There is nothing more *beautiful*, because it is adorned with building stones of every age, every place, every people; from the highest kings to the lowest peasants; with the most brilliant scientists and the simplest believers.
- There is nothing more *spacious*, since it is spread over the whole earth, and takes in all who have washed their robes, and made them white in the blood of the Lamb.
- There is nothing so *Divine*, since it is a *living* building, *animated* and *inhabited* by the *Holy Spirit*.

Ephesians 3 - The Revealing of God's Mystery

A. God's mystery and man's place in it revealed.

1. (1-5) Preface to the revelation of the mystery.

For this reason I, Paul, the prisoner of Christ Jesus for you Gentiles; if indeed you have heard of the dispensation of the grace of God which was given to me for you, how that by revelation He made known to me the mystery (as I have briefly written already, by which, when you read, you may understand my knowledge in the mystery of Christ), which in other ages was not made known to the sons of men, as it has now been revealed by the Spirit to His holy apostles and prophets:

a. **I, Paul, the prisoner of Christ Jesus for you Gentiles**: During his Roman imprisonment Paul was under house arrest. In the day he was free to move around the house with the supervision of soldiers, but every night he was chained to a soldier to make sure he did not escape before his trial before Caesar. Yet he saw himself as **the prisoner of Jesus Christ**. He knew that Jesus was the Lord of his life, not the Roman government, so if he was a prisoner, he was Jesus' prisoner.

b. **For you Gentiles**: The entire reason he was under arrest and awaiting trial was because of his missionary efforts on behalf of the Gentiles.

i. Paul suffered for the very truth he would explain to the Ephesians, and this did not make him back down one bit.

ii. The last thing Paul wanted was people to feel sorry for him because he was imprisoned. He wanted his readers to realize that it was a benefit for them that he was a prisoner.

c. **If indeed you have heard**: This suggests Paul knew his particular calling to the Gentile world was well known among Gentile Christians.

d. **You have heard of the dispensation of the grace of God which was given to me for you**: The word **dispensation** speaks of the "implemented strategy" of God's plan in the church. "Here as in Ephesians 1:10, however, it is to be interpreted rather as the implementation of a strategy." (Wood)

> i. "By the *dispensation of the grace of God* we may understand, either the *apostolic office* and *gifts* granted to St. Paul, for the purpose of preaching the Gospel among the Gentiles... or the *knowledge* which God gave him of that gracious and Divine *plan* which he had formed for the conversion of the Gentiles." (Clarke)

e. **How that by revelation**: Paul wanted them to know, "I'm not making this up. This isn't my invention. God gave me the **revelation** and I am only His messenger of this truth." It cost Paul a lot to hold on to this mystery, so he probably would not have made it up himself.

> i. It is indeed amazing that God would take a Hebrew of the Hebrews, a Pharisee, and a persecutor of the church to be the main minister of the mystery, the mystery of the work of the gospel in bringing Jew and Gentile together into one new body.

f. **He made known to me the mystery**: The principle Paul will describe is a **mystery**, yet it is known. However, it would never be known if God did not make it **known**.

> i. "In English a 'mystery' is something dark, obscure, secret, puzzling. What is 'mysterious' is inexplicable, even incomprehensible. The Greek word *mysterion* is different, however. Although still a 'secret', it is no longer closely guarded but open... More simply, *mysterion* is a truth hitherto hidden from human knowledge or understanding but now disclosed by the revelation of God." (Stott)

g. **He made known to me the mystery**: Paul did not hesitate to claim that the mystery he will reveal was given to him **by revelation**. But it was not given to *only him* by revelation. It was also given specifically to Peter by revelation (Acts 11:1-18), and it is consistent with prophecy in the Old Testament (such as Isaiah 49:6) and the specific words of Jesus (Acts 1:8).

> i. However, it seems that God used Paul to declare specifically how Jews and Gentiles would be joined together in one body of Christ. This was something hinted at through others, but only specifically detailed through Paul's revelation. Paul trusted that his readers would understand what God revealed to him.

h. **Was not made known to the sons of men, as it now has been revealed**: The nature of the union of Jews and Gentiles into this new body is the aspect that was **not made known**. In the Old Testament, the salvation of Gentiles in the Messiah is prophesied, the coming together of Jew and Gentile into the Church is never spoken of.

2. (6-7) The mystery described.

That the Gentiles should be fellow heirs, of the same body, and partakers of His promise in Christ through the gospel, of which I became a minister according to the gift of the grace of God given to me by the effective working of His power.

a. **That the Gentiles should be fellow heirs, of the same body**: This describes the mystery itself – that believing Jews and believing Gentiles are joined together into one body of Christ, into one Church, and no longer separated before God as such.

b. **Partakers of His promise in Christ**: The truth of this mystery means that Gentiles are now full **partakers of His promise**. This was a privilege no longer reserved only for the believing Jewish person.

c. **Through the gospel**: This could only happen **through the gospel**, where all men have an equal standing in Jesus. This is the same gospel Paul is a servant of, because of **the gift of grace given** to him by the working of God's power.

i. Paul says he is a **minister**, but that is a title of service, not exaltation. In classical literature of ancient Greece, the **minister** (*diakonos*) "is a table waiter who is always at the bidding of his customers." (Wood)

3. (8-9) Paul's presentation of the mystery.

To me, who am less than the least of all the saints, this grace was given, that I should preach among the Gentiles the unsearchable riches of Christ, and to make all see what *is* the fellowship of the mystery, which from the beginning of the ages has been hidden in God who created all things through Jesus Christ;

a. **To me, who am less than the least of all the saints**: Paul marveled at the **grace** given to him, by which he was called to preach the gospel that makes the mystery a reality. When we consider Paul's personal history, we see that his calling really was all of **grace**.

i. "But while Paul was thus thankful for his office, his success in it greatly humbled him. The fuller a vessel becomes the deeper it sinks in the water. A plenitude of grace is a cure for pride." (Spurgeon)

ii. "Preachers ought to grow in grace, for their very calling places them at a great advantage, since they are bound to search the Scriptures, and to be much in prayer. It is a choice mercy to be permitted to preach the gospel. I wish some of you would be ambitious of it, for earnest preachers are wanted." (Spurgeon)

b. **That I should preach**: The ancient Greek word translated "**preach**" literally means "to announce good news." Paul's *preaching* was simply the announcement of the good news of what God has done in Jesus.

c. **The unsearchable riches of Christ**: This mystery is like great **riches** for the Gentiles. They can now come before God in a standing they could only dream of before.

> i. Paul tried to figure out the greatness of God's grace, and started tracking it out as one might track out the shore of a lake. He soon discovered that it wasn't a lake at all, but an ocean, an immeasurable sea. God's riches are unsearchable; we will never know them completely.

> ii. "I am bold to tell you that my Master's riches of grace are so unsearchable, that he delights to forgive and forget enormous sin; the bigger the sin the more glory to his grace. If you are over head and ears in debt, he is rich enough to discharge your liabilities. If you are at the very gates of hell, he is able to pluck you from the jaws of destruction." (Spurgeon)

d. **To make all see what is the fellowship of the mystery**: Having been entrusted with such riches, Paul's passion was to make this gospel known to *all people*. He wants everybody to see and share in the fellowship of this **mystery** - which is a **mystery** precisely because it was unknown and unknowable until God revealed it.

e. **Fellowship of the mystery**: We should carefully consider what this phrase means. It demonstrates that these are not only facts to know but also a life to live, united in Jesus with other believers, without any separation such as existed between Jew and Gentile.

f. **Which from the beginning of the ages has been hidden in God**: This great truth - the **fellowship of the mystery** - was **hidden** before it was revealed after the finished work of Jesus on the cross. This reinforces the idea that there is genuinely something *new* in the New Covenant, and that it is wrong to consider Israel simply the Old Testament Church and the Church the New Testament Israel.

> i. "This statement settles the question once for all concerning the existence of the church, the body of Christ, in and during the Old Testament dispensations. Yet it is one of the most widespread views that the church existed from the beginning of creation and the words of promise contained in the Old Testament prophetic Word are the promises of the church, and its glorious future on the earth, in reigning over the nations." (Gaebelein)

4. (10-12) The purpose of the mystery.

To the intent that now the manifold wisdom of God might be made known by the church to the principalities and powers in the heavenly *places*, **according to the eternal purpose which He accomplished in Christ Jesus our Lord, in whom we have boldness and access with confidence through faith in Him.**

a. **That now the manifold wisdom of God might be made known**: God is a being of infinite wisdom and glory, and He wants His creatures to know His great and **manifold wisdom**. One purpose in His great plan of the ages is to reveal this wisdom.

i. Understanding the character of God, we can say that this is not for a *selfish* or *self-glorying* motive, in the way we think of the proud man showing his brains and accomplishments to everyone. God does this for the glory of His *creatures*, because the glory of the creature is directly connected to the glory of the *Creator*.

ii. This wisdom is **manifold**. The ancient Greek word *polupoikilos* has the ideas of intricacy, complexity, and great beauty. "That hath abundance of curious variety in it, such as is seen in the best pictures or textures." (Trapp)

iii. It also *must* **be made known**. Dean Alford points out that the words **might be made known** are emphatic, strongly contrasting the idea of *hidden* in Ephesians 3:9.

b. **Might be made known by the church to the principalities and powers**: This explains *how* God will reveal His wisdom, and to *whom* He reveals it. He will reveal it *by* His work in **the church**, and He will reveal it *to* angelic beings (**principalities and powers**).

i. Of course, God also wants to reveal this wisdom to the church. Yet in the big picture, God doesn't use the angels to reveal His wisdom to the saints, but He does use the saints to reveal His wisdom to the angelic beings, both faithful and fallen angels. This reminds us that we are called for something far greater than our own individual salvation and sanctification. We are called to be the means by which God teaches the universe a lesson, and a beautiful lesson.

ii. We are surrounded by invisible spiritual beings, and they intently look upon us. Here, Paul draws back the invisible curtain that hides these beings just as Elisha prayed at Dothan, *LORD, I pray, open his eyes that he may see* (2 Kings 6:17). These angelic beings see us perfectly and know us far better than we know them.

iii. "What then have they to learn *from us*? Ah, they have to learn something which makes them watch us with wonder and with awe. They see in us indeed all our weakness, and all our sin. But they see a nature which, wrecked by itself, was yet made in the image of their God and ours. And they see this God at work upon that wreck to produce results not only wonderful in themselves but doubly wonderful because of the conditions." (Moule)

iv. "In his immortality, never touched by one drop of our cold river, it is instructive to him beyond all our thought to see his God triumphing over pain and death in some sufferer in the fire of martyrdom, or in the torture of cancer, or in the shipwreck, or just in the silent awe of any form of our departure from the body... They see these fallen and mortal beings, this Community of the lost and saved, not only bearing and doing for God here on earth, but spiritually present with Him in the Holy of Holies above." (Moule)

v. Sometimes Christians get the crazy idea that God saved them and works in their life because they are somehow such great people. The angels see right through this. We might believe that it is because of us; the angels know better. We may think our lives are small and insignificant; the angels know better. We may doubt our high standing, seating in heavenly places; the angels see this spiritual reality with eyes wide open.

vi. "It is as if a great drama is being enacted. History is the theatre, the world is the stage, and the church members in every land are the actors. God himself has written the play, and he directs and produces it. Act by act, scene by scene, the story continues to unfold. But who are the audience? They are the cosmic intelligences, *the principalities and powers in the heavenly places.*" (Stott)

vii. "The Angels are instructed in God's wisdom... by the fact of the great spiritual body, constituted in Christ, which they contemplate, and which is to them the *theatre of the glory of God.*" (Alford) "The history of the Christian church becomes a graduate school for angels." (Stott, quoting Mackay)

c. **To the principalities and powers in the heavenly places**: This means that angelic beings are *interested* and *instructed* by the lives of Christians. This is why the conduct of the church is so important: because angelic and demonic beings are looking on, and God's intent is to teach them through us. Several passages refer to this:

• *For this reason the woman ought to have a symbol of authority on her head, because of the angels* (1 Corinthians 11:10).

- *The things which now have been reported to you through those who have preached the gospel to you by the Holy Spirit sent from heaven; things which angels desire to look into* (1 Peter 1:12).

- *I charge you before God and the Lord Jesus Christ and the elect angels that you observe these things without prejudice, doing nothing with partiality* (1 Timothy 5:21).

    i. We should take this responsibility seriously, for angels are given the responsibility to carry souls to heaven at death (Luke 16:22) and are the reapers of the final harvest (Matthew 13:39-43).

    ii. "And, lastly, what think some of you, would angels say of *your* walk and conversation? Well, I suppose you don't care much about them, and yet you should. For who but angels will be the reapers at the last, and who but they shall be the convoy to our spirits across the last dark stream? Who but they shall carry our spirit like that of Lazarus into the Father's bosom? Surely we should not despise them." (Spurgeon)

    iii. "O be not, ye converts, ignorant of the word of God; be not oblivious of the operations of God in your own souls! The angels desire to look into these things. Do you look into them?" (Spurgeon)

    iv. A popular interpretation today sees the **principalities and powers** as modern political states and economic structures. The idea is that the church primarily is a witness to them, and should redeem governments and social structures through its witness. But Paul specifically wrote that these **principalities and powers** are **in the heavenly places**, not in earthly places.

d. **According to the eternal purpose which He accomplished**: The mystery reveals and furthers God's **eternal purpose** in Jesus, previously described in Ephesians 1:10 - that in the fullness of the times, God will gather together (essentially, to sum up or resolve) all things in Jesus.

    i. The mystery of the unified body of Christ is **according** to that purpose. It is a preview of what Jesus will ultimately do in the fulfillment of summing up all things in Himself.

    ii. "The church thus appears to be God's pilot scheme for the reconciled universe of the future, the mystery of God's will *to be administered in the fullness of the times* when *the things in heaven and the things on earth* are brought together in Christ." (Bruce)

e. **Which He accomplished**: There is a sense in which Paul can say that this eternal purpose is already **accomplished**. Its fulfillment is a certainty (as shown by the initial work of bringing Jew and Gentile together in Jesus), so he can speak of it as already finished.

f. **Through faith in Him**: The fact of this unity is shown by the truth that **we** (Jew and Gentile collectively) have the identical **boldness, access,** and **confidence** before God - because it has nothing to do with national or ethnic identity, only with **faith in Him** (Jesus).

i. The word for **boldness** has the idea of "freedom of speech." We have the freedom to express ourselves before God, without fear or shame. "The Greek word 'parresia' translated by 'boldness' means really 'free speech' – that is, the speaking of all. It is the blessed privilege of prayer." (Gaebelein)

ii. Divisions in the church have not always been between Jew and Gentile. The Reformers spoke out against the division between "clergy" and "laity" and the teaching of the priesthood of all believers insisted that all had the same access to God.

5. (13) Paul's current personal participation in the mystery.

Therefore I ask that you do not lose heart at my tribulations for you, which is your glory.

a. **Therefore I ask that you do not lose heart**: Though under arrest for the sake of the gospel, Paul asked his readers to not **lose heart**. Paul didn't want them to be discouraged for *his* sake, because Paul was still being used in the service of God's eternal plan.

b. **My tribulations for you**: Paul wrote the Letter to the Ephesians from prison, and it is useful to remember why Paul was in prison. He lived his whole life with the passion to bring salvation to his own people, the Jews (Romans 9:1-3). On a strategic visit to Jerusalem he had the opportunity to preach to a vast crowd on or near the temple mount (Acts 21:39-22:22), but the opportunity ended in disaster because the Jewish crowd could not stand the idea of the good news of the Messiah being extended to the Gentiles (Acts 22:21-22). The ensuing riot put Paul in a legal dilemma, from which he used his right as a Roman citizen and appealed to Caesar. Now Paul was imprisoned in Rome, waiting for his trial before Caesar - and there because he knew God wanted Gentiles to share in the good news of the Messiah, and he wasn't afraid to preach that truth.

c. **Which is your glory**: Paul was being used, and probably in a greater way than he ever imagined. This Roman imprisonment produced the letters of Ephesians, Colossians, Philippians, and Philemon. They all certainly have a place in God's eternal plan.

i. In the same manner, each of us has a place in the service of God's eternal plan. Knowing this and working towards it is a great guard against losing heart in the midst of tribulation.

B. Paul prays in light of the mystery.

1. (14-15) Introduction to the prayer.

For this reason I bow my knees to the Father of our Lord Jesus Christ, from whom the whole family in heaven and earth is named,

a. **For this reason**: The basis of Paul's prayer was his knowledge of God's purpose. This means he confidently prayed according to God's will. We can't pray effectively if we do not have insight into God's purpose and will.

b. **I bow my knees**: Paul prayed in the posture of bowing his knees. This position of utmost humility was in contrast to the more normal posture of prayer in that culture, to pray standing with hands raised up.

i. The humility came when he considered God's great eternal plan, his place in that plan, and how God's work is unstoppable even when Paul was imprisoned.

ii. Solomon prayed on his knees (1 Kings 8:54). Ezra prayed on his knees (Ezra 9:5). The Psalmist called us to kneel (Psalm 95:6). Daniel prayed on his knees (Daniel 6:10). People came to Jesus kneeling (Matthew 17:14, Matthew 20:20, and Mark 1:40). Stephen prayed on his knees (Acts 7:60). Peter prayed on his knees (Acts 9:40). Paul prayed on his knees (Acts 20:36), and other early Christians prayed on their knees (Acts 21:5). Most importantly, Jesus prayed on His knees (Luke 22:41). The Bible has enough prayer *not* on the knees to show us that it isn't required, but it also has enough prayer *on* the knees to show us that it is good.

c. **To the Father of our Lord Jesus Christ**: Paul directed his prayer to the **Father**, who is presented as the "planner" among the members of the Trinity. In the Bible, prayer is usually directed to **the Father**, through the Son, by the empowering and direction of the Holy Spirit.

d. **From whom the whole family in heaven and earth is named**: In remembering that all God's family is called after His name, Paul showed that his mind was rather taken with this idea of the essential unity of the Body of Christ. God is Father of both Jew and Gentile.

i. Charles Spurgeon preached a touching sermon on this verse titled, *Saints in Heaven and Earth One Family*. In it he developed the idea that we are one with our brothers and sisters in heaven, and how this enriches our hope of heaven.

ii. Some commentators think Paul refers to heavenly families in the sense of families of angels. "May not the holy Angels be bound up in

spiritual *families*, though they marry not nor are given in marriage?"
(Alford)

2. (16-19) Paul prays again for the Ephesians.

That He would grant you, according to the riches of His glory, to be strengthened with might through His Spirit in the inner man, that Christ may dwell in your hearts through faith; that you, being rooted and grounded in love, may be able to comprehend with all the saints what *is* the width and length and depth and height; to know the love of Christ which passes knowledge; that you may be filled with all the fullness of God.

a. **To be strengthened with might through His Spirit in the inner man**: Paul asked that they would **be strengthened with might**, and that the strength would be **according to the riches of His glory** (a most generous measure). He also prayed that the strength would come **through the Holy Spirit** and that it would be put into their **inner man**.

i. There is an **inner man** just as real as our physical body. We all understand the importance of strength in our physical body, but many are exceedingly weak in the **inner man**.

ii. **According to the riches of His glory**: "It would be a disgrace to a *king* or a *nobleman* to give no more than a *tradesman* or a *peasant*. God acts up to the dignity of his infinite perfections; he gives *according* to the *riches* of his *glory*." (Clarke)

b. **That Christ may dwell in your hearts through faith**: Paul asked that Jesus would live in these believers, even as Jesus promised in John 14:23: *If anyone loves Me, he will keep My word; and My Father will love him, and We will come to him and make Our home with him.*

i. Two ancient Greek words convey the idea "to live in." One has the idea of living in a place as a stranger, and the other has the idea of settling down in a place to make it your permanent home. **Dwell** uses the ancient Greek word for a *permanent home*. Jesus wants to settle down in your heart, not just visit as a stranger.

ii. The glory of the indwelling Jesus is something for us to know, and to know by faith. It is there for us, but must be taken hold of **through faith**. "You have your Bible, and you have your knees; use them." (Carr John Glynn, godfather to H. C. G. Moule)

iii. We need spiritual strength to let Christ dwell within us because there is something in us that *resists* the influence of the indwelling Jesus. That something can be conquered as the Spirit of God gives us the victory of faith.

c. **Being rooted and grounded in love**: Paul asked that all this would take place as they were **rooted and grounded in love**. The meaning seems to be that they should be rooted and grounded in their love for one another, more than being rooted and grounded in their love for God and the knowledge of that love.

> i. "Two expressions are used: 'rooted,' like a living tree which lays hold upon the soil, twists itself round the rocks, and cannot be upturned: 'grounded,' like a building which has been settled, as a whole, and will never show any cracks or flaws in the future through failures in the foundation." (Spurgeon)

d. **May be able to comprehend with all the saints**: Paul asked that they might be able to understand together in community every dimension of the love of Jesus. Paul wanted them to know it by experience and not just in words.

> i. "In this measurement may you and I be skilled. If we know nothing of mathematics, may we be well-tutored scholars in this spiritual geometry, and be able to comprehend the breadths and lengths of Jesus's precious love." (Spurgeon)

e. **What is the width and length and depth and height**: This means that the love of Jesus has *dimensions* and that it can be *measured*.

> i. "Alas, to a great many religious people the love of Jesus is not a solid substantial thing at all – it is a beautiful fiction, a sentimental belief, a formal theory, but to Paul it was a real, substantial, measurable fact; he had considered it this way, and that way, and the other way, and it was evidently real to him, whatever it might be to others." (Spurgeon)

> ii. The love of Jesus has **width**. You can see how wide a river is by noticing how much it covers over. God's river of love is so wide that it covers over my sin, and it covers over every circumstance of my life, so that all things work together for good. When I doubt His forgiveness or His providence, I am narrowing the mighty river of God's love. His love is as wide as the world: *For God so loved the world* (John 3:16).

> iii. "Some of them seem to be so taken up with the height and length that they deny the breadth, and you would think from hearing them preach that Christ came into the world to save half-a-dozen, and that they were five of them... Out on their narrowness! There will be more in heaven than we expect to see there by a long way; and there will be some there with whom we had very little comfortable fellowship on earth who had fellowship with Christ, and who are therefore taken to dwell with him for ever." (Spurgeon)

iv. The love of Jesus has **length**. When considering the length of God's love, ask yourself, "When did the love of God start towards me? How long will it continue?" These truths measure the *length* of God's love. *Yes, I have loved you with an everlasting love* (Jeremiah 31:3).

v. The love of Jesus has **depth**. Philippians 2:7-8 tell us how deep the love of Jesus goes: *but made Himself of no reputation, taking the form of a bondservant, and coming in the likeness of men. And being found in appearance as a man, He humbled Himself and became obedient to the point of death, even the death of the cross.* You can't go lower than *the death of the cross*, and that is how deep the love of Jesus is for us.

vi. The love of Jesus has **height**. To see the height of God's love, ask yourself, "How high does it lift me?" It lifts me to heavenly places where I am seated with Christ. He has *raised us up together, and made us sit together in the heavenly places in Christ Jesus* (Ephesians 2:6).

vii. Can we really **comprehend** the **width and length and depth and height** of God's love? To come to any understanding of the dimensions of God's love, we must come to the cross. The cross pointed in four ways, essentially in every direction, because...

- God's love is wide enough to include every person.
- God's love is long enough to last through all eternity.
- God's love is deep enough to reach the worst sinner.
- God's love is high enough to take us to heaven.

f. **To know the love of Christ**: Paul wrote of something we can *know*. This isn't speculation, guesswork, emotions, or feelings. This is something to **know**.

i. "One of these philosophers kindly says that religion is a matter of belief; not of knowledge. This is clean in opposition to all the teaching of Scripture." (Spurgeon)

g. **That you may be filled with all the fullness of God**: Paul asked God to fill these Christians *unto* **all the fullness of God**. The word *unto* is a better translation than the word **with**. Paul wanted Christians to experience life in Jesus Christ, the fullness of God (Colossians 2:9), and to be filled to their capacity with Jesus, even as God is filled to His own capacity with His own character and attributes.

i. "Among all the great sayings in this prayer, this is the greatest. To be FILLED *with God* is a great thing; to be *filled with the* FULLNESS *of God* is still greater; but to be *filled with* ALL *the fullness of God* utterly bewilders the sense and confounds the understanding." (Clarke)

3. (20-21) A glorious doxology.

Now to Him who is able to do exceedingly abundantly above all that we ask or think, according to the power that works in us, to Him *be* glory in the church by Christ Jesus to all generations, forever and ever. Amen.

a. **Now to Him who is able to do exceeding abundantly above all that we ask or think**: As Paul came to this great height (what can there be higher than the *fullness of God*?), it is logical to ask how this can ever be. How can something so far above us ever become reality? It can only happen because God is able to do far beyond what **we ask or think**.

i. This doxology does not only belong to the prayer that precedes it, but also to every glorious privilege and blessing spoken of in the first three chapters. Who **is able to** bring such things to pass? Only God can do this because He can do far beyond our ability to think or ask.

ii. Paul says that God is able to do above all that *we* ask or think. The *we* included Paul and the other apostles and they certainly knew that Jesus could do great things.

- You can ask for every good thing you have ever experienced - God can do **above** that.

- You can think of or imagine things beyond your experience - God can do **above** that.

- You can imagine good things that are beyond your ability to name - God can do **above** that.

iii. Spurgeon on the phrase **exceedingly abundantly**: "He has constructed here in the Greek an expression which is altogether his own. No language was powerful enough for the apostle, - I mean for the Holy Ghost speaking through the apostle, - for very often Paul has to coin words and phrases to shadow forth his meaning, and here is one, 'He is able to do exceeding abundantly,' so abundantly that it exceeds measure and description." (Spurgeon)

iv. "Therefore he is able to do all things, and able to do *superabundantly above the greatest abundance*." (Clarke)

b. **According to the power that works in us**: God is able to do this in our life now, not beginning with heaven. This **power... works in us** now.

i. The things Paul prayed for in the previous verses (spiritual strength, the indwelling Jesus, experiential knowledge of God's love, and the fullness of God) belong to us as children of God. However, they must be received by believing prayer and can be furthered in the lives of others by our prayers for them.

c. **To Him be glory in the church by Christ Jesus:** The only fitting response to this great God is to give Him glory - especially in the church, the company of His redeemed, and that He receive that glory **throughout all ages, world without end** - Amen!

i. When the church understands and walks in God's eternal purpose, God will be glorified and the church will fulfill its important duty of simply glorifying God.

ii. "But the apostle felt that he must not say, 'Unto him be glory in my soul.' He wished that, but his one soul afforded far too little space, and so he cried 'unto him, be glory *in the church*.' He calls upon all the people of God to praise the divine name." (Spurgeon)

Ephesians 4 - Living to God's Glory

A. A call for unity among God's people.

1. (1) The foundation for all exhortation.

I, therefore, the prisoner of the Lord, beseech you to walk worthy of the calling with which you were called,

a. **Therefore**: Paul spent three chapters spelling out in glorious detail all that God did for us, freely by His grace. Now he brings a call to live rightly, but only *after* explaining what God did for us.

b. **Walk worthy of the calling with which you were called**: When we really understand how much God did for us, we will naturally want to serve and obey Him out of gratitude.

i. Understanding *who we are* is the foundation of this worthy walk. "Luther counsels men to answer all temptations of Satan with this only, *Christianus sum*, I am a Christian." (Trapp)

ii. The idea is clear. We don't walk worthy *so that* God will love us, but *because* He does love us. It is motivated out of gratitude, not out of a desire to earn merit.

iii. "Every believer is God's first-born; and so higher than the kings of the earth, Psalm 89:27. He must therefore carry himself accordingly, and not stain his high blood." (Trapp)

2. (2-3) The character of a worthy walk.

With all lowliness and gentleness, with longsuffering, bearing with one another in love, endeavoring to keep the unity of the Spirit in the bond of peace.

a. **With all lowliness and gentleness**: A worthy walk before God will be marked by **lowliness and gentleness**, not a pushy desire to defend our own rights and advance our own agenda.

i. Before Christianity, the word **lowliness** always had a bad association to it. In the minds of many it still does; but it is a glorious Christian virtue (Philippians 2:1-10). It means that we can be happy and content when we are not in control or steering things our way.

b. **Longsuffering, bearing with one another**: We need this so that the inevitable wrongs that occur between people in God's family will not work against God's purpose of bringing all things together in Jesus - illustrated through His current work in the church.

i. Chrysostom defined **longsuffering** as the spirit that has the power to take revenge, but never does. It is characteristic of a forgiving, generous heart.

c. **Endeavoring to keep the unity of the Spirit in the bond of peace**: This humble, forgiving attitude towards each other naturally fulfills this gift of the **unity of the Spirit**.

i. We must *endeavor to keep* this unity - we do not create it. God never commands us to create unity among believers. He has created it by His Spirit; our duty is to recognize it and keep it.

ii. This is a spiritual unity, not necessarily a structural or denominational unity. It is evident in the quick fellowship possible among Christians of different races, nationalities, languages, and economic classes.

iii. We can understand this **unity of the Spirit** by understanding what it *is not*. In a sermon on this text, Charles Spurgeon pointed out some of the things that the text does *not* say.

- It does not say, "To endeavor to maintain the unity of evil, the unity of superstition, or the unity of spiritual tyranny."

- It does not say, "Endeavoring to keep up your ecclesiastical arrangements for centralization."

- It does not say, "Endeavoring to keep the uniformity of the Spirit."

iv. Structural unity can even work *against* true **unity of the Spirit**. We can perhaps see a purpose God has in preventing a structural unity of the church right now, to keep misdirected efforts of the church (such as ambitions for political power) from fulfillment. "It is not a desirable thing that all Churches should melt into one another and become one; for the complete fusion of all Churches into one ecclesiastical corporation would inevitably produce another form of Popery, since history teaches us that large ecclesiastical bodies grow more or less corrupt as a matter of course. Huge spiritual corporations are, as a whole, the strongholds of tyranny and the refuges of abuse; and it is only a matter of time when they shall break to pieces." (Spurgeon)

v. "For the church fellowship in which the Gentile and Jewish believers were united was no mere enrollment on a register of membership; it involved their union with Christ by faith and therefore their union with each other as fellow-members of his body." (Bruce)

vi. We are confident that this unity is found in Jesus Christ, by the Spirit of God. "We want unity in the truth of God through the Spirit of God. This let us seek after; let us live near to Christ, for this is the best way of promoting unity. Divisions in Churches never begin with those full of love to the Savior." (Spurgeon)

3. (4-6) The description of the unity of the Church.

***There is* one body and one Spirit, just as you were called in one hope of your calling; one Lord, one faith, one baptism; one God and Father of all, who *is* above all, and through all, and in you all.**

a. **There is one body and one Spirit**: We have unity because of what we share in common. In Jesus we share one **body**, one **Spirit**, one **hope** of our **calling**, one **Lord**, one **faith**, one **baptism**, and one **Father**. Each of these common areas is greater than any potential difference.

b. **One baptism**: Some think that because Paul says there is **one baptism** that the idea of the baptism of the Holy Spirit as a subsequent experience is invalid. But Paul only spoke here of the baptism by water which is the visible token of God's common work in every believer, and thus a basis of unity. There aren't separate baptisms for Jew and Gentile.

i. The concept of the baptism in the Holy Spirit is spoken of clearly in Matthew 3:11, Acts 1:5 and 11:16. This may be considered an initial (and sometimes dramatic) experience one has with the fullness of the Holy Spirit, a filling God wants to continue through a person's Christian life.

B. The way God works unity: through spiritual gifts of leadership in the church.

1. (7-10) The giving of spiritual gifts to the church.

But to each one of us grace was given according to the measure of Christ's gift. Therefore He says:

**"When He ascended on high,
He led captivity captive,
And gave gifts to men."**

(Now this, "He ascended"; what does it mean but that He also first descended into the lower parts of the earth? He who descended is also the One who ascended far above all the heavens, that He might fill all things.)

a. **Grace was given**: We all have **grace** given to us **according to the measure** of Jesus' **gift**. This is basis for God's distribution of spiritual gifts through His church: **grace**, the free, unmerited giving of God. No one deserves or has earned spiritual gifts.

b. **When He ascended on high**: This giving happened (as described prophetically in Psalm 68:18) when Jesus **ascended** to heaven. This was evidence of His triumph over every foe (the leading of **captivity captive**).

   i. Bruce on the picture from Psalm 68: "One may picture a military leader returning to Jerusalem at the head of his followers, after routing an enemy army and taking many prisoners."

   ii. As Jesus said, *It is to your advantage that I go away; for if I do not go away, the Helper will not come to you; but if I depart, I will send Him to you* (John 16:7).

c. **When He ascended on high, He led captivity captive, and gave gifts to men**: Paul did not quote the passage exactly as it appears in Psalm 68. Either he altered it under the inspiration of the Holy Spirit or under similar inspiration he quoted from an ancient translation (called a Targum) that quotes the Psalm in this manner.

   i. Psalm 68:18 reads: *You have ascended on high, You have led captivity captive; You have received gifts among men.* There is certainly enough room in the language of the original Hebrew to *allow* Paul's reading, even though it is unusual.

   ii. "It is enough for me that the apostle, under the inspiration of God, applied the verse in this way; and whatever David might intend, and of whatever event he might have written, we see plainly that the sense in which the apostle uses it was the sense of the Spirit of God." (Clarke)

d. **Now this, "He ascended"; what does it mean**: In this, Paul demonstrated how the words **He ascended** in Psalm 68:18 had reference to the resurrection of Jesus, speaking first of His rising from **the lower parts of the earth**, and secondly of His ascension **far above all the heavens**.

   i. Some think that the phrase **lower parts of the earth** refers to Jesus' preaching *to the spirits in prison* described in 1 Peter 3:19 and 4:6. While this aspect of Jesus' ministry in Hades following His work on the cross is true (and prophesied in Isaiah 61:1-2 and Luke 4:18), Paul did not *necessarily* refer to it here.

2. (11-12) The offices of spiritual leadership in the church and their purpose.

And He Himself gave some *to be* apostles, some prophets, some evangelists, and some pastors and teachers, for the equipping of the saints for the work of ministry, for the edifying of the body of Christ,

a. **He Himself**: This means that Jesus established these offices. They are the work and appointment of Jesus, not men. Though pretenders may lay claim to them, the offices themselves are a Divine institution and not a human invention.

b. **Gave some to be apostles, some prophets, some evangelists, and some pastors and teachers**: Paul described four offices (not five, as in the commonly yet erroneously termed "five-fold ministry").

i. **Apostles**, who are special ambassadors of God's work, though not in the same authoritative sense of the first century apostles. Those first century apostles were used to provide a foundation (preserved as the New Testament) as described in Ephesians 2:20.

ii. **Prophets**, who speak forth words from God in complete consistency with the foundation of the Old and New Testaments. Sometimes they speak in a predictive sense, but not necessarily so, and they are always subject to the discernment and judgment of the church leadership (1 Corinthians 14:29). As with the **apostles**, modern **prophets** do not speak in the same authority as the first century prophets brought God's foundational word spoke (Ephesians 2:20).

iii. **Evangelists**, who are specifically gifted to preach the good news of salvation in Jesus Christ.

iv. **Pastors and teachers** (or, *pastor-teachers*; the ancient Greek clearly describes one office with two descriptive titles), who shepherds the flock of God primarily (though not exclusively) through teaching the Word of God. "Teaching is an essential part of the pastoral ministry; it is appropriate, therefore, that the two terms, *pastors and teachers*, should be joined together to denote one order of ministry." (Bruce)

v. These gifts are given at the discretion of Jesus, working through the Holy Spirit (1 Corinthians 12:11). The importance of having "all four in operation" in any church body is up to Jesus who appoints the offices. The job of responsible church leadership is to not hinder or prevent such ministry, but never to "promote it into existence."

c. **For the equipping of the saints for the work of ministry**: The purpose of these gifts of leadership is also clear. It is that **saints** (God's people) might be *equipped* **for the work of ministry** (service), so that the **body of Christ** would be built up (expanded and strengthened).

i. **Equipping** also has the idea of "to put right." This ancient Greek word was used to describe setting broken bones or mending nets. These ministries work together to produce strong, mended, fit Christians.

ii. God's people do the real **work of ministry**. Leaders in the church have the first responsibility to equip people to serve and to direct their service as God leads.

iii. "The primary purpose of the Church isn't to convert sinners to Christianity, but to *perfect* (complete and mature) the saints for the ministry and edification of the Body." (Smith)

3. (13-16) The desired goal of God's work through church leadership and equipped saints.

Till we all come to the unity of the faith and of the knowledge of the Son of God, to a perfect man, to the measure of the stature of the fullness of Christ; that we should no longer be children, tossed to and fro and carried about with every wind of doctrine, by the trickery of men, in the cunning craftiness of deceitful plotting, but, speaking the truth in love, may grow up in all things into Him who is the head; Christ; from whom the whole body, joined and knit together by what every joint supplies, according to the effective working by which every part does its share, causes growth of the body for the edifying of itself in love.

a. **Till we all come to the unity of the faith**: This is the first goal of God's work through the gifted offices and equipped saints. This is consistent with both the ultimate purpose of God (Ephesians 1:10) and the mystery of God revealed through Paul (Ephesians 3:6).

i. Again, by clearly stating that this is a **unity of the *faith***, Paul did not command a structural or organizational unity, but a spiritual unity around a common faith.

b. **And of the knowledge of the Son of God**: When the gifted offices work right and the saints are properly equipped, Christian maturity increases and there is greater intimacy in the experience of God.

c. **To a perfect man, to the measure of the stature of the fullness of Christ**: The gifted offices and equipped saints bring the saints to maturity, according to the **measure** of Jesus Himself. As years pass by, we should not only grow *old* in Jesus, but *more mature* in Him as well, as both individuals and as a corporate body.

d. **We should no longer be children, tossed to and fro and carried about with every wind of doctrine**: The gifted offices and equipped saints result in stability, being firmly planted on the foundation of the apostles and prophets (Ephesians 2:20).

i. Those who do not mature in this way are targets of deceivers, who are effective precisely because they operate with **trickery** and **cunning craftiness** – and they **lie in wait to deceive**. They are out there like land minds that the mature can avoid.

ii. The ancient Greek word for **tossed to and fro** is from the same words used to describe the stormy Sea of Galilee in Luke 8:24 (*raging of the water*). We can wrongly value *movement* over *growth*; mere movement is being tossed to and fro, but God wants us to **grow up in all things**.

iii. **By the trickery of men**: "The words... refer to the arts used by gamesters, who employ false *dice* that will always throw up one kind of number, which is that by which those who play with them cannot win." (Clarke) Running after spiritual fads always leaves one a loser.

e. **Speaking the truth in love**: This speaks to not only how we are to relate to one another in God's family, but also to how leaders and saints are to deal with deceivers. We should deal with them in **love**, but never budging from the **truth**.

f. **May grow up in all things into Him who is the head**: Another way maturity is described is as the growing up into Jesus, who is the head. Again, this defines the *direction* of maturity. We never grow "independent" of Jesus, we grow up **into Him**.

i. "A church that is only united in itself, but not united to Christ, is no living church at all. You may attain to the unity of the frost-bound earth in which men and women are frozen together with the cold proprieties of aristocracy, but it is not the unity of life." (Spurgeon)

ii. Adam Clarke on **grow up... into Him**: "This is a continuance of a metaphor taken from the members of a human body receiving nourishment equally and growing up, each in its due proportion to other parts, and to the body in general."

g. **According to the effective working by which every part does its share**: The evidence of maturity - that the leaders and the saints are all doing their job - is this **effective working**. This means every part and joint provides what it can supply in a coordinated effort. When this happens, it naturally causes the **growth of the body** (both in size and strength), but especially growth for building itself up **in love**.

i. Some people think of the church as a pyramid, with the pastor at the top. Others think of the church as a bus driven by the pastor, who takes his passive passengers where they should go. God wants us to see the church as a body, where **every part does its share**.

C. Putting off the old man, putting on the new man.

1. (17-19) The character of the old man.

This I say, therefore, and testify in the Lord, that you should no longer walk as the rest of the Gentiles walk, in the futility of their mind, having their understanding darkened, being alienated from the life of God, because of the ignorance that is in them, because of the blindness of their heart; who, being past feeling, have given themselves over to lewdness, to work all uncleanness with greediness.

a. **Therefore**: This makes the connection, not only with the glorious spiritual privileges laid out in Ephesians 1 through 3, but also with the high call of a unified, mature body as described in Ephesians 4:1-6. Because of this high calling, we should **walk** (live) in a different way than the world around us does.

   i. There is a constant tendency for Christians to display to the world that we really aren't so different after all. This is usually a misguided effort to gain the world's "respect" or approval. This must be resisted at all costs, because the goal in itself is both undesirable and unachievable.

   ii. This principle of compromise can be illustrated by the exchange between a liberal scholar theologian and a Christian professor. The liberal agreed, "I'll call you a scholar if you'll call me a Christian." The trade isn't worth it.

b. **No longer walk as the rest of the Gentiles walk**: The Gentile **walk** is characterized by **the futility of their mind**. In the end, their thinking is futile because their **understanding** is **darkened** - because they are **alienated from the life of God**.

   i. This is not to say that man, in his rebellion against God, is not capable of mighty intellectual achievements. Instead it is to say that all such achievements fall short of true wisdom, because *the fear of the LORD is the beginning of wisdom* (Proverbs 9:10).

   ii. **Futility**: "The thought is not that unregenerate minds are empty. It is that they are filled with things that lead to nothing." (Vaughan)

   iii. As Christians, we have a proper way and place to **walk**. It is as if Jesus turned us around and put us in the right direction, and now we have to **walk** and progress in that direction.

c. **Because of the blindness of their heart**: Fundamentally, the **ignorance** and lack of understanding of man is a **heart** problem. It is shown not only in a foolish denial of God, but also in his moral failures (**licentiousness, uncleanness, greediness**).

i. The **Gentiles** Paul speaks of were either atheists or they believed in gods who were themselves immoral. Therefore in their denial of the true God, they denied any standard of morality that they must answer to.

ii. **Past feeling** has the idea of one's skin becoming callous and no longer sensitive to pain. It is the logical result of **the blindness of their heart**. **Blindness** can also be understood here as *hardening*, and this ancient Greek word "is used medically to denote the callus formed when a bone has been fractured and reset. Such a callus is even harder than the bone itself." (Wood)

iii. **Licentiousness** is sin that flaunts itself, throwing off all restraint and having no sense of shame or fear; **uncleanness** is a broad word, mostly with reference to sexual impropriety.

iv. Barclay elaborates on the Greek word *aselgeia*, translated **licentiousness**: "The great characteristic of *aselgeia* is this - the bad man usually tries to hide his sin; but the man who has *aselgeia* in his soul does not care how much he shocks public opinion so long as he can gratify his desires." (Barclay)

2. (20-24) Putting on the new man.

But you have not so learned Christ, if indeed you have heard Him and have been taught by Him, as the truth is in Jesus: that you put off, concerning your former conduct, the old man which grows corrupt according to the deceitful lusts, and be renewed in the spirit of your mind, and that you put on the new man which was created according to God, in true righteousness and holiness.

a. **Put off... the old man... put on the new man**: This has the same idea of putting off or putting on a set of clothes. The idea is to "change into" a different kind of **conduct**.

i. Think of a prisoner who is released from prison, but still wears his prison clothes and acts like a prisoner and not as a free man. The first thing to tell that person is that they should put on some new clothes.

ii. Even as putting on different clothes will change the way you think about yourself and see yourself, even so putting on a different conduct will start to change your attitudes. This means that we shouldn't wait to *feel* like the **new man** before we **put on the new man**.

iii. Fundamentally, Paul says that for the Christian, there must be a break with the past. Jesus isn't merely *added* to our old life; the old life dies and He becomes our new life.

b. **You have not so learned Christ**: The repetition of this idea shows that putting on the new man has a strong aspect of *learning* and *education* to it. **You have *heard* Him and have been *taught* by Him, as the *truth* is in Jesus... and be renewed in the spirit of your *mind*.**

> i. Our Christian life must go beyond head knowledge, but it must absolutely include head knowledge and influence our whole manner of thinking. This is not just in the sense of knowing facts, but the ability to set our minds on the right things. This is so fundamental to the Christian life that Christian growth can even be described as *the renewing of your mind* (Romans 12:2).

> ii. The Ephesians **learned Christ**, not only learning *about* Jesus, but also learning *Him*. This means a living, abiding knowledge of Jesus will keep us from the kind of sinful conduct Paul speaks of. Just knowing *about* Jesus isn't enough to keep us pure.

> iii. "So, if you want to know the Lord Jesus Christ, you must live with him. First he must himself speak to you, and afterwards you must abide in him. He must be the choice Companion of your morning hours, he must be with you throughout the day, and with him you must also close the night; and as often as you may wake during the night, you must say, 'When I awake, I am still with thee.' " (Spurgeon)

c. **Put on the new man which was created according to God, in true righteousness and holiness**: The new man is the *new creation* (2 Corinthians 5:17) created in us at conversion. It is the person created according to the image of Jesus Christ and instinctively righteous and holy. It is in contrast to the old man, who is the person inherited from Adam and who instinctively rebels against God.

3. (25-32) The conduct of the new man.

Therefore, putting away lying, "Let each one *of you* speak truth with his neighbor," for we are members of one another. "Be angry, and do not sin": do not let the sun go down on your wrath, nor give place to the devil. Let him who stole steal no longer, but rather let him labor, working with *his* hands what is good, that he may have something to give him who has need. Let no corrupt word proceed out of your mouth, but what is good for necessary edification, that it may impart grace to the hearers. And do not grieve the Holy Spirit of God, by whom you were sealed for the day of redemption. Let all bitterness, wrath, anger, clamor, and evil speaking be put away from you, with all malice. And be kind to one another, tenderhearted, forgiving one another, just as God in Christ forgave you.

a. **Therefore, putting away lying**: The new man tells the truth. The motive for doing this is because we are **members of one another**, therefore there is no place for lying.

i. A body can only function properly if it tells itself the truth. If your hand touches something hot but your hand tells your brain that the thing is cool, your hand will be severely burned. That's why telling the truth is so important, because **we are members of one another**.

b. **Be angry, and do not sin**: The new man may get **angry**, but he does not sin. The new man knows how to let go of his **wrath**, thus giving no opportunity **to the devil**.

i. "Here it is suggested that anger can be prevented from degenerating into sin if a strict time limit is placed on it: *do not let the sun set on your anger*." (Bruce)

ii. The devil's work is to accuse and divide the family of God, and to sow discord among them. When we harbor anger in our heart, we do the devil's work for him.

c. **Let him who stole steal no longer**: The new man does not **steal**, but he works **with his hands**. He does this not only to provide for his own needs, but also to **have something to give him who has need**.

i. **Let him labor**: **Labor** is literally "to exert himself to the point of exhaustion." This is the kind of working heart God commands those who used to steal to have. Paul's idea is that we should work so that we can give. The purpose for getting becomes giving.

d. **Let no corrupt word proceed out of your mouth**: The new man knows how to watch his tongue, speaking only **what is good for necessary edification**, desiring to **impart grace** to all who hear him.

i. **Corrupt communication**: "Not only obscene vulgarity but slanderous and contemptuous talk." (Bruce)

e. **And do not grieve the Holy Spirit of God**: The new man will not **grieve the Holy Spirit**, knowing that He is our seal both in the sense of identification and protection.

i. There are many ways to grieve the Holy Spirit. We can neglect holiness and grieve the *Holy* Spirit. We can think in purely materialistic terms and grieve the Holy *Spirit*. The Spirit exalts Jesus (John 15:26); when we fail to do the same, we grieve the Spirit.

ii. "I think I now see the Spirit of God grieving, when you are sitting down to read a novel and there is your Bible unread.... You have no time for prayer, but the Spirit sees you very active about worldly things, and having many hours to spare for relaxation and amusement. And then he is grieved because he sees that you love worldly things better than you love him." (Spurgeon)

iii. The Holy Spirit's grief is not of a petty, oversensitive nature. "He is grieved with us mainly for our own sakes, for he knows what misery sin will cost us; he reads our sorrows in our sins... He grieves over us because he sees how much chastisement we incur, and how much communion we lose." (Spurgeon)

f. **Let all bitterness, wrath, anger, clamor, and evil speaking be put away from you**: The new man has control of his emotions (**bitterness, wrath, anger** and so forth). When such things do emerge, he is able to deal with them in a manner glorifying to God.

i. Aristotle defined **bitterness** as "the resentful spirit that refuses reconciliation."

ii. **Wrath** speaks of an outburst of the moment; **anger** speaks of a settled disposition. Both must be **put away**.

g. **And be kind to one another, tenderhearted, forgiving one another**: The new man seeks to show the same kindness, tender heartedness and forgiveness to others that God shows him. If we treat others as God treats us, we fulfill every thing Paul told us to do in this chapter.

h. **Just as God in Christ forgave you**: Our forgiveness to others is patterned after the forgiveness of Jesus towards us. When we think of the amazing way God forgives us, it is shameful for us to withhold forgiveness from those who have wronged us.

- God holds back His anger a long time until He forgives. He bears with us for a long time though we sorely provoke Him.

- God reaches out to bad people to woo them to Himself, and attempts reconciliation with bad people.

- God always makes the first move in forgiveness, trying to reconcile even though the guilty party is uninterested in forgiveness.

- God forgives our sin knowing that we will sin again, often in exactly the same way.

- God's forgiveness is so complete and glorious that He grants adoption to those former offenders.

- God, in His forgiveness, bore *all* of the penalty for the wrong we did against Him. He was innocent yet He bore the guilt.

- God keeps reaching out to man for reconciliation even when man rejects Him again and again.

- God requires no probationary period to receive His forgiveness.

- God's forgiveness offers complete restoration and honor. He loves, adopts, honors, and associates with those who once wronged Him.

- God puts His trust in us and invites us to work with Him as co-laborers when He forgives us.

  i. The older King James Version puts it like this: *even as God for Christ's sake hath forgiven you.* This gives us an assurance of forgiveness – that it is *for Christ's sake.* "God for Christ's sake hath forgiven thee. Get hold of that grand truth, and hold it, though all the devils in hell roar at thee. Grasp it as with a hand of steel; grip it as for life: 'God for Christ's sake hath forgiven me,' – may each one of us be able to say that. We shall not feel the divine sweetness and force of the text unless we can make a personal matter of it by the Holy Ghost." (Spurgeon)

  ii. "If anyone here who is a Christian finds a difficulty in forgiveness, I am going to give him three words which will help him wonderfully. I would put them into the good man's mouth. I gave them to you just now, and prayed you to get the sweetness of them; here they are again! 'For Christ's sake.' Cannot you forgive an offender on that ground?" (Spurgeon)

  iii. It isn't that we must forgive because Jesus *will* forgive us. We forgive because He *has* forgiven us. "It is the historical fact of Christ once for all putting away sin by the sacrifice of Himself, which is alluded to." (Moule)

Ephesians 5 - Life in the Spirit

A. Forsaking the darkness.

1. (1-2) Walking in love.

Therefore be imitators of God as dear children. And walk in love, as Christ also has loved us and given Himself for us, an offering and a sacrifice to God for a sweet-smelling aroma.

a. **Therefore**: Here, Paul concludes the thought from Ephesians 4, where he described how Christians should relate to one another.

b. **Be imitators of God**: The idea is simple – that we are to make *God* our example and model. We can't content ourselves comparing us among men. We must heed the idea of 1 Peter 1:15-16: *as He who called you is holy, you also be holy in all your conduct, because it is written, "Be holy, for I am holy."*

> i. It does not say, "Think about God" or "Admire God" or "Adore God," though those are all important Christian duties. This is a call to practical action, going beyond our inner life with God.

> ii. We could say this is a continuation of the same idea Paul mentioned in Ephesians 4:13 regarding the extent of Christian growth: *to a perfect man, to the measure of the stature of the fullness of Christ.* We could also say that this is a continuation of the idea from Ephesians 4:32, where we were commanded to be *forgiving one another, just as God in Christ also forgave you.* God's behavior towards us becomes our measure for our behavior towards one another.

> iii. It is important to see that God *is far more than our example.* Many errors come into the church when Jesus is presented *only* as an example of behavior. We are not *saved* by the example of Jesus, but *once saved* His example is meaningful to us. God is *more* than our example, but He is *also* our example.

c. **As dear children**: Children are natural imitators. They often do just what they see their parents or other adults do. When we act according to our nature as children of God, we will imitate Him.

i. As we do imitate God, we become representatives of God, especially before those who have shut God out of their life. "What are we sent into the world for? Is it not that we may keep men in mind of God, whom they are most anxious to forget? If we are imitators of God, as dear children, they will be compelled to recollect that there is a God, for they will see his character reflected in ours. I have heard of an atheist who said he could get over every argument except the example of his godly mother: he could never answer that." (Spurgeon)

d. **Walk in love, as Christ also has loved us**: As in all things, Jesus is our example. As He **has loved us and** has **given Himself for us**, we are to display the same kind of self-giving love.

e. **An offering and a sacrifice**: Jesus' giving of Himself was obviously a sacrifice pleasing to the Father. We can also offer a pleasing sacrifice (**a sweet-smelling aroma**) as we give ourselves in love to others.

i. We often think we could lay down our life in a dramatic way to show our love for others. But God often calls us to lay down our life little by little – in small coins (as it were) instead of one large payment – but it is laying down our lives nonetheless.

ii. Adam Clarke on **an offering**: "It means, any offering by which *gratitude* was expressed for temporal blessings received from the *bounty* of God."

iii. Adam Clarke on **a sacrifice**: "A *sin-offering*, a *victim for sin*; the same as *zebach*, which almost universally means that sacrificial act in which the blood of an *animal* was poured out as an atonement for sin. These terms may be justly considered as including every kind of *sacrifice*, *offering*, and *oblation* made to God on any account."

2. (3-4) A contrast to walking in love: conduct not fitting for the Christian.

But fornication and all uncleanness or covetousness, let it not even be named among you, as is fitting for saints; neither filthiness, nor foolish talking, nor coarse jesting, which are not fitting, but rather giving of thanks.

a. **Let it not even be named among you**: Paul groups together these ideas of sexual sin and impropriety, indicating that none of these are **fitting for saints** and should not even **be named among** God's people.

i. Paul used a comprehensive list of sexual sins:

- **Fornication** (*porneia*), a broad word describing sexual sin.

- **Uncleanness**, another broad word for "dirty" moral behavior, especially in a sexual sense.

- **Filthiness**, which has much the same idea as **uncleanness**.

- **Coarse jesting**, which has the idea of inappropriate, impure sexual humor.

ii. We must notice the theme of the moral appeal. It isn't "avoid these things so that you can be a saint." Rather, it is "you are a saint; now live in a manner fitting for a saint." The constant moral appeal of the New Testament is simply this: *be who you are in Jesus.*

b. **As is fitting for saints**: This emphasis on sexual sin was appropriate. The culture of Paul's day (and in the city of Ephesus especially) was given over to sexual immorality. The sort of behavior Paul says is not **fitting for saints** was pretty much completely approved by the culture of his day (and our own).

c. **Covetousness… foolish talking**: Paul also included **covetousness** and **foolish talking** in this list because of their close association with sexual sin. The desire to have something that doesn't belong to us and foolish speaking have both led many people into sexual sin. Yet **covetousness** and **foolish talking** also have relevance *beyond* their relation to sexual sin.

i. **Foolish talking** is literally "an easy turn of speech." In the context, the idea is of the one who can turn every conversation into a joking comment on sexual matters, usually with a double-entendre.

d. **But rather giving of thanks**: Positively, the Christian is to give **thanks** for sex. We receive it thankfully as a gift, and we enjoy sex in a way that glorifies the Giver.

i. God's purpose in giving sex is not primarily for the gratification of the individual, but for the bonding together of husband and wife in a one-flesh relationship. Certain expressions of sexuality are sin *not because* God wants to deprive some aspect of enjoyment, but because they work against His primary purpose for sex.

3. (5-7) The consequences of conduct not fitting for Christians.

For this you know, that no fornicator, unclean person, nor covetous man, who is an idolater, has any inheritance in the kingdom of Christ and God. Let no one deceive you with empty words, for because of these things the wrath of God comes upon the sons of disobedience. Therefore do not be partakers with them.

a. **Has any inheritance in the kingdom of Christ and God**: The people mentioned in Ephesians 5:3 (the **fornicator**, the **unclean person** and the **covetous man**) have no inheritance in God's kingdom. If God's kingdom is alive in them, a transformation has occurred so that they cannot rest in the habitual practice of these things.

i. Paul's idea in this passage can be applied out of context in a condemning way. One might say, "Well, I've thought about committing fornication, so that means that I have fornicated in my heart and that means that I am as guilty as someone who has actually committed the act of fornication. Since I am as guilty as that one, and they have no inheritance in the kingdom of God, neither do I, because of my thoughts about fornication." This deceptive thinking goes against the plain sense of God's word.

b. **Covetous man, who is an idolater**: Significantly, Paul says that the **covetous man** is an **idolater**. Idolatry happens in much more subtle (and powerful) ways than simply bowing down before a statue.

c. **Let no one deceive you with empty words**: We cannot allow **empty words** to excuse or minimize the judgment due to the practice of these sins. It is certain that **because of these things the wrath of God comes upon the sons of disobedience**.

d. **Therefore do not be partakers with them**: Paul assumes that Christians will not have their lives *habitually* marked by fornication, uncleanness or covetousness. Yet we should not even *occasionally* be **partakers with them** who are.

4. (8-12) The passing from darkness to light.

For you were once darkness, but now *you are* light in the Lord. Walk as children of light (for the fruit of the Spirit *is* in all goodness, righteousness, and truth), finding out what is acceptable to the Lord. And have no fellowship with the unfruitful works of darkness, but rather expose *them*. For it is shameful even to speak of those things which are done by them in secret.

a. **For you were once darkness**: As Paul condemned those who practiced fornication, uncleanness or covetousness as *the sons of disobedience* (Ephesians 5:6), he also recognized that this was the exact **darkness** Christians had emerged from. But now, having been enlightened, we are to **walk as children of the light**.

i. Again, the theme is repeated: you *are* **children of light**, so *live* like **children of light**.

ii. Paul doesn't only say that we were once *in* darkness. He says we **were once darkness** itself. Now, we are not only in the light, we **are light in the Lord**.

b. **For the fruit of the Spirit is in all goodness, righteousness, and truth**: In contrast to the walk in darkness and wrath is the **fruit of the Spirit**, more fully described in Galatians 5:22-23. **Goodness, righteousness, and truth** should mark us because we have the Holy Spirit in our life.

c. **And have no fellowship with the unfruitful works of darkness, but rather expose them**: Instead of associating with ungodliness, we expose the **unfruitful works of darkness**. However, we do not do this for the purpose of merely talking about them (which is **shameful**), but for the purpose of educating ourselves enough to avoid them.

i. Christians must guard against a prurient interest in **the works of darkness**, even in times of testimony or research.

ii. Paul was careful to say that we should avoid the **unfruitful *works* of darkness**, not the people who are in darkness.

B. Walking in the light.

1. (13-14) The fact of the light's presence.

But all things that are exposed are made manifest by the light, for whatever makes manifest is light. Therefore He says: "Awake, you who sleep, arise from the dead, and Christ will give you light."

a. **But all things that are exposed are made manifest by the light**: Even the things done **in secret** will be exposed. They will be made **manifest** by the light of God's searching judgment.

i. This is a *reason* for avoiding and exposing the unfruitful works of darkness as described in Ephesians 5:8-12. Since those unfruitful works are destined for exposure and their day will be over, it makes sense for Christians to avoid such unfruitful works.

b. **Awake, you who sleep, arise from the dead**: Our participation in the light is shown by our resurrection with Jesus (He *made us alive together with Christ*, Ephesians 2:5). Paul quoted what was probably a worship chorus from the early church to illustrate this truth.

i. Remember that this exhortation to **awake** comes to *Christians*. A Christian may be asleep and not know it. If you are asleep, you probably do not know it. As soon as you become aware of your sleep, it is evidence that you are now awake.

ii. "This sleepiness in the Christian is exceedingly dangerous, too, because he can do a great deal while he is asleep that will make him look as if he were quite awake." (Spurgeon)

- We can speak when we are asleep.
- We can hear when we are asleep.
- We can walk when we are asleep.
- We can sing when we are asleep.
- We can think when we are asleep.

2. (15-17) Walking in the light means walking in wisdom.

See then that you walk circumspectly, not as fools but as wise, redeeming the time, because the days are evil. Therefore do not be unwise, but understand what the will of the Lord *is*.

a. **See then that you walk circumspectly**: Because this light was given to us, we should walk **circumspectly** - carefully, wisely, **not as fools**.

i. Adam Clarke thought that the phrase **not as fools** was connected to the practices of devotion to the ancient god Bacchus, worship with drinking and partying. "*Do not become madmen*. Here is a most evident allusion to the *orgies of Bacchus*, in which his votaries acted like madmen; running about, tossing their heads from shoulder to shoulder, appearing to be in every sense completely frantic."

b. **Redeeming the time**: There were two ancient Greek words used for **time**. One had the idea simply of day upon day and hour upon hour. The other had the idea of a definite portion of time, a time where something should happen. It is the difference between *time* and **the time**. The idea here is of **the time**; it is a definite season of opportunity that Christians must redeem. This same word is translated *opportunity* in Galatians 6:10.

i. Paul isn't telling us to make the most of every moment, even though that is good advice. He tells us to seize opportunity for the glory of Jesus. It isn't to make the most of time, but to make the most of **the time**.

ii. The idea behind **redeeming the time** is that you buy up opportunities like a shrewd businessman. You make the most of every opportunity for Jesus Christ.

c. **Because the days are evil**: This is another reason why it is important to walk wisely. Jesus spoke of a time when, *many false prophets will rise up and deceive many. And because lawlessness will abound, the love of many will* *grow cold* (Matthew 24:11-12). Surely we are in those times, **because the days are evil**.

d. **Understand what the will of the Lord is**: This is what real wisdom is. It is the contrast to being **unwise**. Our main understanding of **the will of the Lord** comes from a good knowledge of His word.

3. (18) Walking in the light means constant filling with the Holy Spirit.

And do not be drunk with wine, in which is dissipation; but be filled with the Spirit,

a. **And do not be drunk with wine**: In contrast with the conduct of the world (being **drunk with wine**), we are to be **filled with the Spirit**. Paul's grammar here clearly says, "be *constantly being filled* with the Holy Spirit."

b. **Be filled with the Spirit**: The filling of the Holy Spirit is not a one-time event that we live off of the rest of our days. It is a constant filling, asking to be filled, and receiving the filling by faith.

i. There is a wonderful and significant *first* experience with the filling of the Holy Spirit, often thought of as the *Baptism of the Holy Spirit* (Matthew 3:11, Acts 1:5 and 11:16). This is an experience valid and important for every believer.

ii. Much of the weakness, defeat and lethargy in our spiritual life can be attributed to the fact that we are not constantly being filled with the Holy Spirit.

iii. The ancient Greek grammar for **be filled** also indicates two other important things. First, the verb is *passive*, so this is not a manufactured experience. Second, it is *imperative*, so this is not an optional experience.

c. **Do not be drunk with wine**: The carnal contrast to being filled with the Holy Spirit is being **drunk**. The Bible condemns drunkenness without reservation.

i. **In which is dissipation**: Paul says that drunkenness is **dissipation**. This means that drunkenness is a *waste* of resources that should be submitted to Jesus. John Trapp writes of drinking "all the three outs" – "That is, ale out of the pot, money out of the purse, and wit out of the head." (Trapp's commentary on Galatians 5:21)

ii. We should listen to what Proverbs tells us about drunkenness in passages such as Proverbs 20:1 and 23:29-33.

iii. We must not think that *only* the state of "falling down drunk" qualifies as sin. Being impaired in any way by drink is sin, as well as drinking with the *intention* of becoming impaired.

iv. "The danger of drunkenness lies not only in itself but in what it may induce" (Wood). Practically, the world pays a high price for the ruin of alcoholism and drug addiction. To speak of alcohol alone, according to the United States Center for Disease Control, in 2010 88,000 people died of alcohol related causes in the USA, and excessive drinking cost the USA economy $249 billion dollars – almost a quarter of a trillion dollars. It is fair to suppose that the figures are comparable if not worse in many other nations.

d. **But be filled with the Spirit**: Paul *contrasts* the effect of the Holy Spirit with the state of drunkenness. Alcohol is a depressant; it "loosens" people because it depresses their self-control, their wisdom, their balance and judgment. The Holy Spirit has an exactly opposite effect. He is a stimulant; He moves every aspect of our being to better and more perfect performance.

i. "We find it here imbedded amongst precepts laying down the great laws of self-control, and it comes just before the special directions which the Apostle gives for the quiet sanctities of the Christian home... But then, all the while, it is a thing supernatural. It is a state of man wholly unattainable by training, by reasoning, by human wish and will. It is nothing less than - God in command and control of man's whole life, flowing everywhere into it, that He may flow fully and freely out of it in effects around." (Moule)

4. (19-20) The Spirit-filled life is marked by worship and gratitude.

Speaking to one another in psalms and hymns and spiritual songs, singing and making melody in your heart to the Lord, giving thanks always for all things to God the Father in the name of our Lord Jesus Christ,

a. **Speaking to one another in psalms and hymns and spiritual songs, singing and making melody in your heart to the Lord**: When we are *filled with the Spirit*, we will have a desire to worship God and to encourage others in their worship of God.

i. The connection with being filled with the Spirit and praise is significant. Those who are filled with the Spirit will naturally praise, and praise is a way that we are filled with the Spirit.

b. **Psalms and hymns and spiritual songs**: This variety suggests that God delights in creative, spontaneous worship. The most important place for us to have a **melody** unto God is in our **heart**. Many who can't sing a beautiful melody with the voice can have beautiful melodies in their heart.

i. The emphasis is more on *variety* than on *strict categories.* "We can scarcely say what is the exact difference between these three expressions." (Clarke)

c. **Giving thanks always for all things to God**: The one who is filled with the Spirit will also be filled with thanksgiving. A complaining heart and the Holy Spirit just don't go together.

i. Paul recommends the same pattern for our thanksgiving as he practiced in prayer in Ephesians 3:14 - giving thanks **to God the Father in the name of our Lord Jesus Christ**.

ii. "Every hour, yea, every moment has brought a favor upon its wings. Look downward and give thanks, for you are saved from hell; look on the right hand and give thanks, for you are enriched with gracious gifts; look on the left hand and give thanks, for you are shielded from deadly ills; look above you and give thanks, for heaven awaits you." (Spurgeon)

5. (21) The Spirit-filled life is marked by mutual submission.

Submitting to one another in the fear of God.

a. **Submitting to one another in the fear of God**: When we are *filled with the Spirit*, it will show by our mutual submission to each other; and the submission will be done **in the fear of God**, not the fear of man.

b. **Submitting**: The word **submitting** here literally means, "to be under in rank." It is a military word. It speaks of the way that an army is organized among levels of rank. You have generals and colonels and majors and captains and sergeants and privates. There are levels of rank, and you are obligated to respect those in higher rank.

i. We know that as a person, a private can be smarter, more talented, and a better person than a general. But he is still *under rank* to the general. He isn't submitted to the general so much as a *person* as he is to the general as a *general.*

ii. The idea of submission doesn't have anything to do with someone being smarter or better or more talented. It has to do with a God-appointed order. "Anyone who has served in the armed forces knows that 'rank' has to do with order and authority, not with value or ability." (Wiersbe)

iii. We also see from this *how important* it is to be "under rank." In the military, they have a name for it when you no longer want to be "under rank." They call it "mutiny." "Just as an army would be in confusion if there were no levels of authority, so society would be in chaos without submission." (Wiersbe)

c. **Submitting to one another**: To understand what this means, we can first examine *what it does not mean*. It does not mean that there is no idea of "rank" in the body of Christ. We can see how someone might take that impression. "It says we should be **submitting to one another**. So I should be submitting to you and you should be submitting to me. No one has any more obligation to submit than anyone else."

i. We know this is what Paul *does not mean* because that would be a clear contradiction of other things that he wrote. For example, in 1 Corinthians 5:1-5, Paul clearly tells the Corinthian Christians to submit to his authority and to do something. Can you imagine the Corinthian Christians answering back, "Well Paul, you wrote that we should be **submitting to one another**. So we think you should submit to us here."

ii. Or, another example is Hebrews 13:17, which says *Obey those who rule over you and be submissive*. If Paul meant that there was no "rank" or "order of authority" among believers, then this command in Hebrews 13:17 is meaningless.

iii. The idea of this military word is more easily applied when one rank is above another. Yet here Paul didn't use it in that way. It is easily applied when you tell a bunch of privates, "Submit to the generals." It is a little more difficult to get a hold of the meaning when you say to a group of privates "Submit to one another." Paul isn't emphasizing the idea of *rank*, because he addresses all Christians. But there is something else important here.

iv. Paul means that we should take this "under rank" attitude of the military and apply it to our everyday dealing with each other. When a man joins the military, the first thing he does is strip away his individuality. He is now the member of a company or a battalion. He is no longer an individual. When you join the army, you essentially sign away your right to decide what you want to do with your life and your time. An army is filled with individuals, but they can never be individualistic. That is the first thing that a man is broken of when he joins the army.

v. "Let no man be so tenacious of his own will or his opinion in matters indifferent, as to disturb the peace of the Church; in all such matters *give way* to each other, and let *love* rule." (Clarke)

vi. In practical action **submitting to one another** implies the following, all in line with the idea of being a "team player":

- The Christian must not be thoughtless, but think of others.

- The Christian must not be individualistic, must not be self-assertive. "Self-assertion is the very antithesis of what the Apostle is saying." (Lloyd-Jones)

- The Christian must never be self-seeking.

- We must have a "team attitude."

- We must be happy when someone else succeeds or does well.

- We must bear our own discomforts and trials with courage.

d. **In the fear of God**: This is an important point, because Paul repeats the idea all through the extended section speaking about submission:

- *Wives, submit to your own husbands, as to the Lord.*

- *Children, obey your parents in the Lord, for this is right.*

- *Bondservants, be obedient to those who are your masters according to the flesh, with fear and trembling, in sincerity of heart, as to Christ.*

  i. The words **in the fear of God** describe what should be our *motive* for **submitting to one another**. We should submit to one other - see ourselves no longer in an individualistic way, but as a unit, as a company or a battalion - out of respect for God the Father respect for Jesus Christ.

  ii. The motive for submission is *not* social kindness. The motive for submission is *not* the law of God. The motive for submission is *respect for Jesus Christ*. If we respect Jesus, we then should submit to one another because we love Jesus. Paul uses the term **fear** in this passage, but it is a **fear** – a respect – that is *compatible* with love. It is a fear of disappointing Jesus, a fear of grieving Him. That is totally compatible with love. When you really respect someone, you care about pleasing him or her, and you are afraid to disappoint that one.

C. The Spirit-filled life, submission, and responsibility in marriage.

"The danger is that we should think of marriage amongst Christians as essentially the same as it is with everybody else, the only difference being that these two people happen to be Christians whereas the others are not. Now if that is still our conception of marriage then we have considered this great paragraph entirely in vain. Christian marriage, the Christian view of marriage, is something that is essentially different from all views." (D. Martyn Lloyd-Jones)

1. (22) Walking in the light means wives submit to their husbands.

Wives, submit to your own husbands, as to the Lord.

a. **Wives**: Paul addressed **wives** and their responsibility in the Christian marriage first. This isn't because they are the bigger problem or because they need special attention. The reason is that the apostle was particularly concerned about this question of submission. That was the principle that he introduced in Ephesians 5:21. This aspect of submission has a particular application to wives in a Christian marriage.

> i. The same logic continues on into Ephesians 6. Children are addressed before parents because Paul was primarily concerned about submission. Slaves are addressed before their masters because the apostle was primarily concerned about submission.

> ii. There is no question that the apostle is continuing the thought from Ephesians 5:21, *submitting to one another in the fear of God*. In many of the best ancient Greek manuscripts, Ephesians 5:22 doesn't even have the word *submit*. It simply reads *wives, to your own husbands*. The topic is submission and Paul focused on a particularly important realm of submission - the Christian marriage, from the wife unto the husband.

> iii. It is as if Paul said this: "I commanded you to submit to one another in a very general way. Now, if you do it in a general way, how much more so should **wives** do it to their own husbands in this special relationship of marriage."

b. **Wives, submit**: To **submit** means that you recognize someone has legitimate authority over you. It means you recognize that there is an order of authority, and that you are part of a unit, a team. You as an individual are not more important that the working of the unit or the team.

> i. When we **submit** to God, we recognize God's authority and act accordingly. When we **submit** to the police, we recognize the authority of the police and act accordingly. When we **submit** to our employer, we recognize the authority of our employer and act accordingly.

> ii. *Submission does not mean inferiority*. As well, *submission does not mean silence*. Submission means "sub-mission." There is a mission for the Christian marriage, and that mission is obeying and glorifying God. The wife says, "I'm going to put myself under that *mission*. That *mission* is more important than my individual desires. I'm not putting myself below my husband, I'm putting myself below the *mission* God has for our marriage, for my life."

c. **To your own husbands**: This defines the *sphere* of a wife's submission. The Bible never commands a *general* submission of women unto men in society. This order is commanded only in the spheres of the home and in the church. God has not commanded in His word that men have exclusive authority in the areas of politics, business, education, and so on.

d. **As to the Lord**: This is a crucial phrase. It colors everything else we understand about this passage. There have been two main wrong interpretations of this phrase, each favoring a certain position.

i. The wrong interpretation that the interpretation that favors the husband says that **as to the Lord** means that a wife should submit to her husband as if he were God himself. The idea is "you submit to God in absolutely everything without question, so you must submit to your husband in the same absolute way." This interpretation believes thatthe words "**as to the Lord**" defines the *extent* of submission.

ii. This is wrong. It is true that the wife owes the husband a great deal of respect. Peter sets this across when he praises Sarah, the wife of Abraham, as an example of a godly wife, when she called Abraham "Lord." That doesn't mean "Lord" in the sense of God, but "Lord" in the sense of "master." That is a lot of respect. Yet still, it doesn't go as far as to say, "You submit completely to God, so you must submit to your husband the same way." Simply put, *in no place* does the Scripture say that a person should submit to another in that way. There are limits to the submission your employer can expect of you. There are limits to the submission the government can expect of you. There are limits to the submission parents can expect of children. In no place does the Scripture teach an unqualified, without exception, submission – except to God and God alone. To violate this is to commit the sin of idolatry.

iii. The wrong interpretation that favors the wife says that **as to the Lord** means "I'll submit to him as long as he does what the Lord wants." Then the wife often thinks it is her job to decide what the Lord wants. This interpretation thinks that **as to the Lord** defines the *limit* of submission.

iv. This is wrong. It is true that there are limits to a wife's submission; but when the wife approaches **as to the Lord** in this way, it degenerates into a case of "I'll submit to my husband when I agree with him. I'll submit to him when he makes the right decisions and carries them out the right way. When he makes a wrong decision, he isn't in **the Lord**, so I shouldn't submit to him then." *That is not submission at all.* Except for those who are plainly cantankerous and argumentative, *everyone* submits to others when they are in agreement. It is only when there is a *disagreement* that submission is tested.

e. **As to the Lord** does not define the *extent* of a wife's submission or the *limit* of a wife's submission. It defines the *motive* of a wife's submission.

i. "It means: 'Wives, submit yourselves unto your own husbands because it is a part of your duty to the Lord, because it is an expression of your submission to the Lord.' Or, 'Wives, submit yourselves to your own husbands; do it in this way, do it as a part of your submission to the Lord.' In other words, you are not doing it only for the husband, you are doing it primarily for the Lord Himself... You are doing it for Christ's sake, you are doing it because you know that He exhorts you to do it, because it is well-pleasing in His sight that you should be doing it. It is part of your Christian behaviour, it is a part of your discipleship." (Lloyd-Jones)

ii. "For the Lord's sake who commanded it, so that ye cannot be subject to him without being subject to them." (Clarke)

iii. **As to the Lord** means...

- A wife's submission to her husband is part of her Christian life and obedience.

- When a wife doesn't obey this word to **submit to your own husband, as to the Lord**, she isn't only falling short as a wife. She is falling short as a follower of Jesus Christ.

- This is completely out of the realm of the wife's *nature* or *personality*.

- This has nothing to do with a husband's intelligence, giftedness, or capability. It has to do with honoring the Lord Jesus Christ.

- This has nothing to do with whether or not the husband is right on a particular issue. It has to do with Jesus being right.

- This means that a woman should take great care in how she *chooses* her husband. Instead of looking for an attractive man, instead of looking for a wealthy man, instead of looking for a romantic man, a woman should first look for a man she can *respect*. G. Campbell Morgan recalls the story of the older Christian woman who had never married, and she explained, "I never met a man who could master me." She had the right idea.

  - If you want to please Jesus, if you want to honor Him, then **submit to your own husband as to the Lord**.

iv. "There can be no more compelling motive for any action than this; and every Christian wife who is concerned above everything else to please the Lord Jesus Christ, will find no difficulty in this paragraph;

indeed it will be her greatest delight to do what the Apostle tells us here." (Lloyd-Jones)

2. (23-24) Reasons for a Christian wife's submission.

For the husband is head of the wife, as also Christ is head of the church; and He is the Savior of the body. Therefore, just as the church is subject to Christ, so *let* the wives *be* to their own husbands in everything.

a. **For**: The command given in Ephesians 5:22 is difficult. God knows this, so He also includes *reasons* for His command. He wants us to understand the principle behind the command.

i. The first reason for a Christian wife's submission to her husband is found in Ephesians 5:22, in the words *as to the Lord*. This means that the motive of her submission must be obedience and respect to Jesus, instead of obedience and respect to her husband.

b. **For the husband is the head of the wife**: Paul states here the second reason for a wife's submission. It is because the husband is **the head of the wife**. In its full sense **head** has the idea of *headship* and *authority*. It means to have the appropriate responsibility to lead and the matching accountability. It is right and appropriate to submit to someone who is our **head**.

i. When you look at the Biblical idea of headship in other passages such as 1 Corinthians 11 and 1 Timothy 3, the emphasis is put constantly upon the fact that the man was created first and not the woman. So there is a priority *by creation* for man. The Scriptures also emphasize the fact that that woman was made out of the man, taken out of the man to show a connection to him, and that she was meant to be a help for man, a help for man that was fitting for him.

ii. "Notice that the Apostles lay great stress upon it. Man was created first. But not only that; man was also made the lord of creation. It was to man that this authority was given over the brute animal creation; it was man who was called upon to give them names. Here are indications that man was put into a position of leadership, lordship, and authority and power. He takes the decisions, he gives the rulings. That is the fundamental teaching with regard to this whole matter." (Lloyd-Jones)

iii. Passages such as 1 Corinthians 11:7-10 make the point that God created Adam first, and gave him responsibility over Eve. This happened *before* the fall. Therefore, this passage makes it clear that before and after the fall, God ordained there be different roles between husband and wife. The difference in roles between husband and wife are not the result of the fall, and are not erased by our new life in Jesus.

iv. "What he is saying is that the woman is different, that she is the complement of the man. What he does prohibit is that woman should seek to be manly, that is, that a woman should seek to behave as a man, or that a woman should seek to usurp the place, the position, and the power which have been given to man by God Himself. That is all he is saying. It is not slavery; he is exhorting his readers to realize what God has ordained." (Lloyd-Jones)

v. "When a woman gets married she gives up her name, she takes the name of her husband. That is Biblical, and also the custom of the whole world. That teaches us the relationship between the husband and the wife. It is not the husband who changes his name, but the wife." (Lloyd-Jones)

c. **As also Christ is head of the church... Therefore, just as the church is subject to Christ, so let the wives be to their own husbands**: Paul presents here a third reason for a Christian wife's submission to her husband. She should submit because the relationship of the husband and wife is a model of the union between Jesus and the Church.

i. This point is simple and clear. We have a model for the marriage relationship: the relationship between Jesus and the church. In that relationship, the headship of Jesus Christ is unquestioned. So also is the husband the head of the "team" that is the one-flesh relationship of husband and wife.

ii. Perhaps the Christian wife doesn't want a "head" or a leader of the team between husband and wife. If that is the case, the wife does not understand a Biblical marriage, and will always work against it in one way or another. It is the same dynamic as a Christian saying he doesn't want Jesus to be his "head."

d. **And He is the Savior of the body**: We can understand how the **husband is head of the wife** in the same way that **Christ is head of the church**. Sometimes it is difficult to see how the husband is the *Savior of the body* in the way that Jesus is the **Savior of the body**, that is, of the Church.

i. Lloyd-Jones thinks Paul used the wider understanding of the word **Savior**, which can simply mean *preserver*. 1 Timothy 4:10 speaks of Jesus being *the Savior of all men, especially of those who believe*. How can Jesus be the *Savior of all men*? In the sense that He *preserves* all men and *blesses* all men with good things from heaven above. It is in this way that husbands are to be their wife's *savior*. Paul essentially repeats the same idea in Ephesians 5:28-29: *So husbands ought to love their own wives as their own bodies; he who loves his wife loves himself. For no one* *ever hated his own flesh, but nourishes and cherishes it, just as the Lord does the church.*

ii. "What, then, is the doctrine? It is clearly this. The wife is the one who is kept, preserved, guarded, shielded, provided for by the husband. That is the relationship – as Christ nourishes and cherishes the church, so the husband nourishes and cherishes the wife – and the wife should realize that that is her position in this relationship." (Lloyd-Jones)

e. **Of the body**: The picture of the **body** shows how essential a Christian wife's submission is. "The wife must not act before the husband. All the teaching indicates that he is the head, that he ultimately controls. So she not only does not act independently of him, she does not act before him... it is equally true to say that she must not delay action, she must not stall action, she must not refuse to act. Go back to the analogy of the body. Think of somebody who has had a 'stroke'... the arm is not healthy, it resists movement." (Lloyd-Jones)

i. "We can sum it up thus: The teaching is that the initiative and the leadership are ultimately the husband's, but the action must always be co-ordinated. That is the meaning of this picture – co-ordinated action but leadership in the head. There is no sense of inferiority suggested by this. The wife is not inferior to her husband; she is different." (Lloyd-Jones)

f. **Therefore**: We see in this passage three reasons for a wife's submission to her husband:

- It is part of her obedience to Jesus (*as to the Lord*).

- It is appropriate to the order of creation (**the husband is the head of the wife**).

- It is appropriate because of the model of the relationship between Jesus and the Church (**as also Christ is head of the church... as the church is subject to Christ**).

i. The first reason is compelling enough, but in itself it doesn't close the issue. If all we had was *as to the Lord*, it might be fair enough to ask, "Aren't men to live *as to the Lord* also? Shouldn't men submit to their wives in obedience to Jesus in the same way?" Then you wouldn't have a real "head" of the home. This is the goal in some marriages. "No one is really in charge. We're equal partners. I'll submit to you sometimes and you submit to me other times. We'll just let Jesus be our head and work out each situation as it comes along and see who will submit to whom."

ii. To say it simply, that isn't a Biblical marriage relationship. It ignores the essential order of creation, and it ignores the model of the relationship between Jesus and the Church. This leads us to carefully notice something in general about submission. The principle of submission is presented in many different ways in the New Testament.

- Jesus submitted to His parents (Luke 2:51).

- Demons submitted to the disciples (Luke 10:17).

- Citizens should submit to government authority (Romans 13:1 and 5, Titus 3:1, 1 Peter 2:13).

- The universe will submit to Jesus (1 Corinthians 15:27 and Ephesians 1:22).

- Unseen spiritual beings submit to Jesus (1 Peter 3:22).

- Christians should submit to church leaders (1 Corinthians 16:15-16 and Hebrews 13:17).

- Wives should submit to husbands (Colossians 3:18, Titus 2:5, 1 Peter 3:5, Ephesians 5:22-24).

- The church should submit to Jesus (Ephesians 5:24).

- Servants should submit to masters (Titus 2:9 and 1 Peter 2:18).

- Christians should submit to God (Hebrews 12:9 and James 4:7).

iii. We notice that none of these relations are reversed. For example, masters are never told to submit to servants, Jesus is never told to submit to the church, and so forth. The consistent use of the idea of submission in the Scriptures illustrates basically a "one-way" submission according to how God has arranged the order of authority.

iv. If Paul stopped at Ephesians 5:24, it would be easy for a Christian wife to feel that all the obligations were on her. Thankfully, he continues and shows what obligations the Christian husband has in marriage. But the Christian wife still has her obligations.

- Both husband and wife are called to die to self – submission is the way the wife does it.

- Both husband and wife are called to sacrifice – submission is the way the wife does it.

- Both husband and wife are called to see their marriage as a model of Jesus' relationship with the church – submission is how the wife honors that model.

- Both husband and wife are called to honor the order of creation – submission is the way the wife fulfills her place in that order.

g. **To their own husbands in everything**: Paul says that the wife should be subject to her husband **in everything**. Does he really mean **everything**? This needs to be understood in same way we understand submission in other spheres. For example, when Paul says in Romans 13 that the Christian must submit to the state, we understand there are exceptions. So, what are the exceptions to **everything**?

> i. *When the husband asks or expects the wife to sin*, she is free from her obligation to submit. This applies in a place of clearly Biblical sin – such as signing a fraudulent tax return. It also applies in matters of true Christian conscience. But we must be very careful to distinguish between true Christian conscience and mere opinion. Yet the wife does not have to submit to a request to commit sin.

> ii. *When the husband is medically incapacitated or insane*, she is free from her obligation to submit. A wife does not have to submit to the requests a husband makes when he is insane or medically incapacitated.

> iii. *When the husband is physically abusive and endangers the safety of the wife or children*, the wife is free from her obligation to submit. She does not have to submit to his violence.

> iv. *When the husband breaks the marriage bond by adultery*. Obviously, a wife does not have to submit to her husband's adultery, and just accept it. The Bible says she has the right to "come out from under his rank" in such cases. "If the husband has been guilty of adultery the wife is no longer bound to give him obedience in everything. She can divorce him, she is allowed to do so by the Scripture. She is entitled to do so because adultery breaks the unity, breaks the relationship. They are now separate and no longer one. He has broken the unity, he has gone out of it. So we must not interpret this Scripture as teaching that the wife is this irrevocably, inevitably bound to an adulterous husband for the rest of her life. She may choose to be – that is for her to decide. All I am saying is, that this Scripture does not command it." (Lloyd-Jones)

3. (25a) The simple command to Christian husbands: love your wife.

Husbands, love your wives,

> a. **Husbands, love your wives**: Paul's words to Christian husbands safeguards his previous words to wives. Though wives are to submit to their husbands, it never excuses husbands acting as tyrants over their wives.

> i. According to 2 Timothy 1:7, God has given us the spirit of power – but also of love. Power, in their Christian life, is always to be exercised

in love. "It is not naked power, it is not the power of a dictator or a little tyrant, it is not the idea of a man who arrogates to himself certain rights, and tramples upon his wife's feelings and so on, and sits in the home as a dictator... No husband is entitled to say that he is the head of the wife unless he loves his wife... So the reign of the husband is to be a reign and a rule of love; it is a leadership of love." (Lloyd-Jones)

b. **Love your wives**: Paul used the ancient Greek word *agape*. The ancient Greeks had four different words we translate **love**. It is important to understand the difference between the words, and why the apostle Paul chose the Greek word *agape* here.

i. *Eros* was one word for love. It described, as we might guess from the word itself, *erotic* love. It refers to love driven by *desire*.

ii. *Storge* was the second word for love. It refers to family love, the kind of love there is between a parent and child or between family members in general. It is love driven by *blood*.

iii. *Philia* is the third word for love. It speaks of a brotherly friendship and affection. It is the love of deep friendship and partnership. It might be described as the highest love of which man, without God's help, is capable of. It is *fondness*, or love driven by *common interests and affection*.

iv. *Agape* is the fourth word for love. *Eros*, *storge*, and *philia* each speak about love that is *felt*. These describe "instinctive" love, love that comes spontaneously from the heart. Paul *assumes* that *eros* (desire) and *phileo* (fondness) are present. Christians should not act as if these things do not matter in the marriage relationship. They do matter. But Paul's real point is to address a higher kind of love, *agape* love. *Agape* describes a different kind of love. It is a love more of *decision* than of the *spontaneous heart*. It is as much a matter of the *mind* as the *heart*, because it chooses to love the undeserving.

v. "*Agape* has to do with the *mind*: it is not simply an emotion which rises unbidden in our hearts; it is a principle by which we deliberately live." (Barclay) *Agape* really doesn't have much to do with *feelings* - it has to do with *decisions*.

vi. Strictly speaking, *agape* can't be defined as "God's love," because men are said to *agape* sin and the world (John 3:19 and 1 John 2:15). Yet it can be defined as a sacrificial, giving, absorbing, love. The word has little to do with emotion; it has much to do with self-denial for the sake of another.

- It is a love that loves without changing.

- It is a self-giving love that gives without demanding or expecting re-payment.

- It is love so great that it can be given to the unlovable or unappealing.

- It is love that loves even when it is rejected.

- *Agape* love gives and loves because it wants to; it does not demand or expect repayment from the love given. It gives because it loves, it does not love in order to receive.

vii. We can read this passage and think that Paul is saying, "Husbands, be kind to your wives." Or "husbands, be nice to your wives." There is no doubt that for many marriages this would be a huge improvement. But that isn't what Paul wrote about. What he really meant is, "Husbands, continually decide to practice self-denial for the sake of your wives."

4. (25b-27) The standard and example of a Christian husband's love.

Just as Christ also loved the church and gave Himself for her, that He might sanctify and cleanse her with the washing of water by the word, that He might present her to Himself a glorious church, not having spot or wrinkle or any such thing, but that she should be holy and without blemish.

a. **Just as Christ also loved the church**: Jesus' *attitude* towards the church is a pattern for the Christian husband's love to his wife. This shows that the loveless marriage doesn't please God and does not fulfill His purpose. This is love given to the undeserving. This is love given *first*. This is love that may be *rejected*, but still loves.

i. "It is possible that some husbands might say, 'How can I love such a wife as I have?' It might be a supposable case that some Christian was unequally yoked together with an unbeliever, and found himself for ever bound with a fetter to one possessed of a morose disposition, of a froward temper, of a bitter spirit. He might therefore say, 'Surely I am excused from loving in such a case as this. It cannot be expected that I should love that which is in itself so unlovely.' But mark, beloved, the wisdom of the apostle. He silences that excuse, which may possibly have occurred to his mind while writing the passage, by taking the example of the Savior, who loved, not because there was loveliness in his Church, but in order to make her lovely." (Spurgeon)

b. **Just as Christ also loved the church**: We might say that Paul taught two things at once here. He taught about the nature of the relationship between husband and wife, and he taught about the relationship between Christ and His Church. Each illustrates important principles about the other.

i. It demonstrates the Jesus loves his church with a *special* love. Jesus loves the world and died for the world; but just as a husband can have a general love for everyone, he must also have a *special* love for his bride.

ii. "I ask you to notice what is not always the case with regard to the husband and the wife, that *the Lord Jesus loves his church unselfishly*; that is to say, he never loved her for what she has, but what she is; nay, I must go further than that, and say that he loved her, not so much for what she is, but what he makes her as the object of his love. He loves her not for what comes to him from her, or with her, but for what he is able to bestow upon her. His is the strongest love that ever was." (Spurgeon)

iii. Using the love of an ideal husband as a pattern, we could say that Jesus has a *constant* love for His people, an *enduring* love for His people, and a *hearty* love for His people.

c. **And gave Himself for her**: Jesus' *action* towards the church is a pattern. This helps us define what *agape* love is all about: it is self-sacrificing love. How should a husband love his wife? **As Christ loved the church and gave Himself for it**. What did that involve? Perhaps the best statement concerning that matter is in Philippians 2:5-8, where it shows that the focus of Jesus was on the church. It was for the church that He did what He did, not for Himself.

i. *Let this mind be in you which was also in Christ Jesus, who, being in the form of God, did not consider it robbery to be equal with God, but made Himself of no reputation, taking the form of a bondservant, and coming in the likeness of men. And being found in appearance as a man, He humbled Himself and became obedient to the point of death, even the death of the cross* (Philippians 2:5-8).

ii. This word is especially needful for husbands who see headship in submission with worldly understanding instead of godly understanding. Some husbands think that because God said they are the head of the home and the wife is obligated to submit to them that they do not have to be humble, lay down their lives, and sacrifice for the benefit of their wife. They need to understand the difference in thinking between worldly headship and godly headship.

- Worldly headship says, "I am your head, so you take your orders from me and must do whatever I want."

- Godly headship says, "I am your head, so I must care for you and serve you."

- Worldly submission says, "You must submit to me, so here are the things I want you to do for me."

- Godly submission says, "You must submit to me, so I am accountable before God for you. I must care for you and serve you."

iii. This is not the height of romantic love as the world knows it. This isn't love based on looks, image, the ability to be suave and cutting-edge cool. This is love expressed through *sacrifice*.

d. **That He might sanctify and cleanse her with the washing of water by the word**: When Jesus **gave Himself** for the church on the cross, it also provided cleansing from every stain sin makes. Since the work of Jesus on the cross comes to us through the Word of God and the preached word, it can be said that we are washed **of water by the word**.

i. When Paul wrote **the washing of water by the word**, he used the ancient Greek word *rhema*. "It is true that *rhema* is not quite the same as *logos*, but carries with it the definite sense of the *spoken* word... it may have the sense of that truth as *proclaimed*, the *preached* Word or Gospel." (Salmond) There is something cleansing about being under the teaching of the Word.

ii. "I do not believe that baptism is intended here, nor even referred to. I know that the most of commentators say it is. I do not think it. It strikes me that one word explains the whole. Christ sanctifies and cleanses us by the washing of water, but what sort of water? By the Word. The water which washes away sin, which cleanses and purifies the soul, is the Word." (Charles Spurgeon, a confirmed Baptist)

iii. This speaks of Jesus' work for the church. Obviously, a husband cannot spiritually cleanse his wife the same way Jesus cleanses the church. Yet a husband can take an active, caring interest in his wife's spiritual health. As the priest of the home, he helps her keep "clean" before the Lord.

e. **That He might present her to Himself a glorious church**: This means that Jesus Himself shares His prospects, His future with His bride. A Christian husband should also share his prospects and future with his wife. Even as a wife will share in the husband's future, so we will share in the glorious future of our Lord.

i. "Since the Church is not fit for Christ by nature, he resolved to make her so by grace. He could not be in communion with sin. Therefore it must be purged away. Perfect holiness was absolutely necessary in one who was to be the bride of Christ. He purposes to work that in her, and to make her meet to be his spouse eternally. The great means by which he attempts to do this, is, 'he gave himself for her.' " (Spurgeon)

f. **Not having spot or wrinkle**: The idea isn't that the bride is in this state *before* the wedding day, but *on* the wedding day. We are made this pure in heaven when we are joined to Jesus Christ in a way beyond all previous experience.

> i. "The Holy Ghost seems to exhaust language to describe this purity. He says, 'Without spot, or wrinkle, or any such thing!' She shall have nothing like a spot, nothing that can he construed into a wrinkle; she shall be fair, and the world shall be compelled to acknowledge that she is." (Spurgeon)

> ii. "When He presents her to Himself, with all the principalities and powers and the serried ranks for all the potentates of heaven looking on at this marvelous thing, and scrutinizing and examining her, there will not be a single blemish, there will not be a spot upon her. The most careful examination will not be able to detect the slightest speck of unworthiness or of sin." (Lloyd-Jones)

5. (28-29) The application of the principles to the duty of a Christian husband.

So husbands ought to love their own wives as their own bodies; he who loves his wife loves himself. For no one ever hated his own flesh, but nourishes and cherishes it, just as the Lord *does* the church.

a. **So husbands**: In Ephesians 5:22-24, Paul gave three reasons for a Christian wife's submission to her husband. In addressing the Christian husbands, Paul also gave three reasons to love their wife:

> i. First, they should love their wife this way because *this is what love is.* Paul indicates this in Ephesians 5:25: *Husbands, love your wives.*

> ii. Second, they should love their wife this way because *the relationship between husband and wife has a pattern*: the relationship of Jesus and His church. Paul indicates this in Ephesians 5:25-29: *Just as Christ also loved the church... So husbands ought to love their own wives... just as the Lord does the church.*

> iii. The third reason is found in Ephesians 5:28-32. The Christian husband must love his wife this way *because you are one with her*, just as Jesus is one with the church.

b. **So husbands ought to love their own wives as their own bodies**: The single word **as** is important. Paul did not say, "So ought men to love their wives in the same way as they love their bodies." That would be an improvement in many cases, but that is not the meaning. The meaning is, "So ought men to love their wives because they *are* their own bodies."

i. A man must love his wife as he would his body, as a part of himself. As Eve was a part of Adam, taken out of his side, so the wife is to the man because she is a part of him. The reality of this union must dominate the husband's thinking and actions in marriage.

ii. "The Apostle puts it in this form in order that a husband may see that he cannot detach himself from his wife. You cannot detach yourself from your body, so you cannot detach yourself from your wife. She is a part of you, says the Apostle, so remember that always." (Lloyd-Jones)

iii. "The husband must realize that his wife is a part of himself. He will not feel this instinctively; he has to be taught it; and the Bible in all its parts teaches it. In other words, the husband must understand that he and his wife are not two: they are one." (Lloyd-Jones)

iv. This means for that success in the marriage relationship, we must *think* and *understand*. The world relies upon overly romantic ideas about love and upon feelings to make marriage work, and never really makes a person *think* and *understand* about marriage.

c. **He who loves his wife loves himself:** Simply said, when you love your wife, *you benefit yourself.* Perhaps it is better to put it in the negative: *when you neglect your wife, you neglect yourself, and it will come back to hurt you.*

i. We all know what it is like to neglect something – like a noise or a maintenance issue on an automobile – and it comes back to hurt us. Husbands, it is *even more true* regarding your wife, because *she is part of you*. Only a fool neglects his own broken arm or infected leg; yet there are many foolish husbands who hurt or neglect their wives and they do and will suffer from it.

ii. "On the practical level, therefore, the whole of the husband's thinking must include his wife also. He must never think of himself in isolation or detachment. The moment he does so he has broken the most fundamental principle of marriage. In a sense, the moment a man thinks of himself in isolation he has broken the marriage. And he has no right to do that! There is a sense in which he cannot do it, because the wife is a part of himself. But if it happens he is certain to inflict grievous damage on his wife; and it is damage in which he himself will be involved because she is a part of him." (Lloyd-Jones)

d. **For no one ever hated his own flesh, but nourishes and cherishes it**: Any man in his right mind is going to take care of **his own flesh**, even if it is just in the sense of feeding and clothing and caring for his own body. He knows that if he doesn't, *he* is going to suffer for it. In the same way, once we know the Biblical fact of this unity, if we are in our right minds we will *nourish and cherish* our wives because she is part of us.

e. **Just as the Lord does the church**: The principle of *oneness* also is dominant in the relationship between Jesus and His people.

- There is oneness of *life*: We share the same vital resurrection life that resides in Jesus Himself.

- There is oneness of *service*: We are privileged to be co-workers with our Lord.

- There is oneness of *feeling*: Jesus feels a unique sympathy with us, and we feel a unique sympathy with Him.

- There is oneness of mutual *necessity*: We cannot exist without Him and He cannot exist without us, in the sense that a redeemer is not a redeemer without any redeemed; a savior is not a savior without any saved

- There is oneness of *nature*: The same genetic code links us with our Savior, and we are partakers of the divine nature

- There is oneness of *possession*: We share in the riches of His glory both now and in the age to come

- There is oneness of present *condition*: When our Savior is lifted high, so are His people with Him.

- There is oneness of *future destiny*: We will be glorified with Him.

6. (30-32) The mystical union between Jesus and the church, and its relation to marriage.

For we are members of His body, of His flesh and of His bones. "For this reason a man shall leave his father and mother and be joined to his wife, and the two shall become one flesh." This is a great mystery, but I speak concerning Christ and the church.

a. **For we are members of His body, of His flesh and of His bones**: Paul here brings the analogy back in a circle. First, the relationship between Jesus and the church spoke to us about the husband-wife relationship. Now the marriage relationship speaks to us about the relationship between Jesus and His people.

b. **For this reason a man shall leave his father and mother and be joined to his wife, and the two shall become one flesh**: Paul quoted this essential passage from Genesis 2:24. Relevant to marriage, it shows that just as the first man and the first woman were one - she was taken from him, and then brought back to him - so it could be said of every married man today that he is **joined to his wife**. God did the joining. Husbands can resent it, they can resist it, they can ignore it, but it doesn't change the fact.

i. It shows a fundamental principle for promoting oneness in marriage: there must be a *leaving* (of former associations) and a *cleaving* (joining together as one).

c. **This is a great mystery, but I speak concerning Christ and the church**: It would be easy to think that the Genesis 2:24 passage (also quoted by Jesus in Matthew 19:5) *only* speaks about marriage. Paul wants us to know that it also speaks about the relationship between **Christ and the church**.

i. This is true in regard to the pattern of the first man and the first woman. "Woman was made at the beginning as the result of an operation which God performed upon man. How does the church come into being? As the result of an operation which God performed on the Second Man, His only begotten, beloved Son on Calvary's hill. A deep sleep fell upon Adam. A deep sleep fell upon the Son of God, He gave up the ghost, He expired, and there in that operation the church was taken out. As the woman was taken out of Adam, so the church is taken out of Christ. The woman was taken out of the side of Adam; and it is from the Lord's bleeding, wounded side that the church comes." (Lloyd-Jones)

ii. It is also true in regard to the pattern of marriage in general.

- It shows us that Jesus wants more than just an external, surface relationship.

- It shows us that Jesus wants us to be *one* with Him.

- It shows us that there is a sense in which Jesus is incomplete without us. Adam was incomplete without Eve; we can say that Eve makes up the "fullness" of Adam and makes up that which was lacking in him. And that is exactly what the church does for Jesus; Ephesians 1:23 says of the church, *which is His body, the fullness of Him who fills all in all.*

iii. It shows the common connection of *unity* and *oneness* in the two relationships. "Unity, mark you for that is the essence of the marriage-bond. We are one with Christ, who made himself one with his people." (Spurgeon)

7. (33) A summary comment to husbands and wives.

Nevertheless let each one of you in particular so love his own wife as himself, and let the wife *see* that she respects *her* husband.

a. **Nevertheless**: Paul really taught on two things at once. He teaches about marriage, but he also teaches about God's *pattern* for marriage – the relationship between Jesus and His people. So in Ephesians 5:31 and 32 he has focused on the relationship between Jesus and His people and is getting really excited about it. Then Paul seemed to remember that his original topic was marriage, so that is why he used the word **nevertheless** in Ephesians 5:33.

i. This was Paul's way of saying, "I know I got off the topic a little bit. So let's come back to the matter of marriage, and I'll sum it up for you. **Nevertheless let each one of you in particular so love his own wife as himself, and let the wife see that she respects her husband.**"

b. **Let each one of you**: This means that *everyone* is included. We can say this about all the teaching on marriage. It is easy to say, "Well, I'm just not that sort of person, so I'll never do very well." Husbands do it, saying, "I'm just not very loving." Wives do it, saying, "I'm just not the submissive sort." But no matter what our natural disposition is, we have a target to shoot for, and **let each one of you in particular** means we all should set our eyes on the target the Bible shows us.

c. **So love his own wife as himself**: Paul again stressed the *unity* that a husband must recognize and let shape his thinking and his actions.

i. "Unity is the central principle in marriage; and it is because so many people in this modern world have never had any conception of what is involved in marriage, from the standpoint of unity, that they are riding so loosely to it and breaking their vows and pledges, so much so that divorce has become one of the major problems in our age. They have never caught sight of this unity; they are still thinking in terms of their individuality, and so you have two people asserting their rights, and therefore you get clashes and discord and separation. The answer to all that, says Paul, is to understand this great principle of unity." (Lloyd-Jones)

ii. "He is given the position of dignity and of leadership and of headship; and if he understands what it means he will never abuse it, he will never misuse it, by being harsh or dictatorial or unkind or unfair. To be guilty of such behaviour is a denial of the marriage principle, and means that there is an absence of the Spirit." (Lloyd-Jones)

d. **Let the wife see**: Paul called the wife to pay special attention here. This may be a point where many wives might excuse themselves for one reason or another, but Paul emphasized, "**Let the wife see**."

e. **Let the wife see that she respects her husband**: This word **respects** is the same word often used of the reverential fear and awe the disciples had toward Jesus. It is a strong statement, but it indicates that the wife should respect the husband so highly that it points in this direction.

> i. "The Apostle used a very striking word here. It is rightly translated in the Authorized Version as 'reverence'; but the word really means 'fear'. 'And the wife see that she fears her husband'. But we must remember that there are different types of fear... he speaks of 'reverential' fear. What it really means is 'deference', 'with reverential obedience'." (Lloyd-Jones)

> ii. "The wife is to treat her husband with deference; in other words, she is to recognize this biblical and Christian view of marriage, she is to regard the husband as her head, the head of this new unit. They are both one, but there is a head to the unit, as there is a head to our body, as Christ is the Head of the church." (Lloyd-Jones)

f. **Let each one of you in particular so love his own wife as himself, and let the wife see that she respects her husband**: If Paul's message in this great passage could be boiled down to two principles which must govern our thinking and our actions as married people, those two are:

- Husbands: Understand that you and your wife are one, are a unity.
- Wives: Understand that your unity has a head - your husband.

> i. Wives are quick to embrace and understand the *husband's* principle, and they want *that* to be the governing principle of the marriage.

> ii. Husbands are quick to embrace and understand the *wife's* principle, and they want *that* to be the governing principle of the marriage.

> iii. But we must let *our* principle govern *us*. When you have a husband thinking, "I'm one with my wife, and I must think and act that way," and a wife thinking, "My husband is the head of our oneness, and I need to respect and defer to him as the head," then you will have a healthy, Biblical marriage.

> iv. "The supreme thing always is to consider our Lord Jesus Christ. If a husband and wife are together considering Him, you need have no worry about their relationship to each other." (Lloyd-Jones)

Ephesians 6 - Walking in the Light and Fighting the Darkness

A. The Spirit-filled life and two other special areas of submission.

1. (1-3) The Spirit-filled life and the parent-child relationship.

Children, obey your parents in the Lord, for this is right. "Honor your father and mother," which is the first commandment with promise: "that it may be well with you and you may live long on the earth."

a. **Children, obey your parents**: The command is simple. Children are to **obey** their **parents**. This not only means that children have the responsibility to obey, but parents have the responsibility to *teach* their children obedience - one of the most important jobs for a parent.

i. We don't need to teach our children how to disobey because they have each inherited an inclination to sin from Adam - but obedience must be taught.

ii. It is essential that a parent teach the child obedience, so that the child will grow up knowing how to obey God even when he doesn't understand everything or doesn't want to.

iii. This is what all a parent's discipline for a child must come to. Disobedience must be punished, so that obedience can be learned.

b. **In the Lord, for this is right**: The apostle gives us two reasons for the child to obey the parent. First, they are to obey **in the Lord**. This means that their obedience is part of their Christian obedience, in a similar way to the wife's command to submit to her husband *as to the Lord* (Ephesians 5:22). The second reason is because it is simply **right** for a child to obey their parent.

i. What it *means* to **honor our father and mother** may change as we grow into adulthood, but the principle always endures. The adult child does not owe the parent obedience, but they do owe the parent *honor*.

ii. "When the bonds of family life break up, when respect for parents fails, the community becomes decadent and will not *live long*." (Foulkes)

c. **The first commandment with a promise**: Paul reinforced this idea with a reference to Deuteronomy 5:16, where God promised to bless the obedient child.

i. Christians have normally divided the Ten Commandments into the first four (directed towards God) and the last six (directed towards their fellow man). But the Jews divided the commandments in two sets of five, seeing the law to **honor your father and mother** more as a duty towards God than a duty towards man.

2. (4) How parents walk in the light: not provoking their children to wrath.

And you, fathers, do not provoke your children to wrath, but bring them up in the training and admonition of the Lord.

a. **Do not provoke your children to wrath**: Parents certainly have the opportunity to **provoke** their **children to wrath**, through an unkind, over-critical attitude that torments the child instead of training them. But Christian parents should never be like this.

i. "The gospel introduced a fresh element into parental responsibility by insisting that the feelings of the child must be taken into consideration. In a society where the father's authority (*patria potestas*) was absolute, this represented a revolutionary concept." (Wood)

b. **Provoke your children to wrath**: This harsh kind of parenting Paul speaks against gives an unnecessary justification to a child's natural rebellion.

i. "When you are disciplining a child, you should have first controlled yourself... What right have you to say to your child that he needs discipline when you obviously need it yourself?" (Lloyd-Jones)

c. **Bring them up in the training and admonition of the Lord**: This does not mean merely scolding your children in the sense of **admonition**. It means to *train* and *admonish*. Encouragement and rebuke must be combined with training and teaching.

i. This is a responsibility for **fathers**. They must not neglect their responsibility to teach and be a spiritual example for their children. It is not a responsibility that should be left to the mother or the Sunday School.

ii. **Training** is the same word translated *chastening* in Hebrews 12:5-11. It has the idea of training through corrective discipline. **Admonition** has more of the idea of *teaching* – both are necessary, though it may be significant that **training** comes first.

iii. Significantly, both **training and admonition** are used to describe the purpose of the Scriptures (2 Timothy 3:16 and 1 Corinthians 10:11). Parents are to raise their children on the Word of God.

d. **Bring them up**: This ancient Greek word was originally used of bodily nourishment as in Ephesians 5:29. But the word came to be used for the nurture of body, mind, and soul. The form here suggests "development by care and pains" or as Calvin translated, "Let them be fondly cherished."

3. (5-8) How employees walk in the light: working as servants of Jesus.

Bondservants, be obedient to those who are your masters according to the flesh, with fear and trembling, in sincerity of heart, as to Christ; not with eyeservice, as men-pleasers, but as bondservants of Christ, doing the will of God from the heart, with goodwill doing service, as to the Lord, and not to men, knowing that whatever good anyone does, he will receive the same from the Lord, whether *he is* a slave or free.

a. **Bondservants, be obedient... as to Christ**: The words "**as to Christ**" change our entire perspective as workers. It reminds us that our work can and should be done as if we were working for Jesus - *because we are!*

i. "The Gospel found slavery in the world; and in many regions, particularly the Roman and the Greek, it was a very bad form of slavery. The Gospel began at once to undermine it, with its mighty principles of the equality of all souls in the mystery and dignity of manhood, and of the equal work of redeeming love wrought for all souls by the supreme Master. But its plan was – not to batter, but to undermine... So while the Gospel in one respect left slavery alone, it doomed it in another." (Moule)

b. **Not with eyeservice**: We are not to work with **eyeservice** (working only when the boss is looking) or as **men-pleasers** (those who only care about pleasing man), but with **good will** (a good attitude, not complaining) **doing service, as to the Lord, and not to men**.

i. **As to the Lord** means that all our work is really done unto the Lord, not unto man. "Grace makes us the servants of God while still we are the servants of men: it enables us to do the business of heaven while we are attending to the business of earth: it sanctifies the common duties

of life by showing us how to perform them in the light of heaven."
(Spurgeon)

c. **Doing the will of God**: In Greek culture manual work was despised and
the goal of being successful was getting to the point where you never had to
do any work. This isn't how it is in God's kingdom, where hard work and
manual labor are honorable.

i. It should be said of every Christian that he is a hard worker and gives
his employer a full day's work for his pay; to do anything less is to steal
from your employer.

d. **He will receive the same from the Lord, whether he is a slave or free**:
Paul relates a final reason for working hard for the Lord. God will return to
us in the measure that we have worked hard for others; He will not allow
our hard work to go without reward.

i. This connects to an interesting principle. When people are born
again, their life changes and they become harder workers and less
wasteful, and they are blessed thereby and become prosperous. But
after becoming prosperous, we often allow our hearts to grow far from
God, then God disciplines us with hard times, and then we repent -
and then the cycle starts again. This is not a *necessary* cycle, but it is a
common one.

4. (9) How employers walk in the light: treating their workers well.

**And you, masters, do the same things to them, giving up threatening,
knowing that your own Master also is in heaven, and there is no
partiality with Him.**

a. **You, masters, do the same things to them**: Masters are told to **do the
same things to them** (their employees). Even as servants are to work hard
and honestly for their masters, so masters are to do the **same** on behalf of
those who work for them.

i. "So the Gospel leaves its message of absolutely *equal obligation*, in
Jesus Christ, upon the slave and upon the slave owner. The principle
will do its work. There is no word of Revolution." (Moule)

b. **Giving up threatening**: Employers are also to give up **threatening**
and other forms of harsh treatment. They do this knowing that they are
employees of their Master in heaven, and He judges without regard to
wealth or position.

B. Fighting against the darkness.

1. (10) The call to stand against the devil.

Finally, my brethren, be strong in the Lord and in the power of His might.

a. **Finally**: This comes at the end of the letter – a letter in which Paul has carefully established our place in Jesus, and then the basics of the Christian walk. This is his last section dealing with that walk. For Paul to write **finally** here means that he speaks in light of all he has previously said.

- In light of all that God has done for you.

- In light of the glorious standing you have as a child of God.

- In light of His great plan of the ages that God has made you part of.

- In light of the plan for Christian maturity and growth He gives to you.

- In light of the conduct God calls every believer to live.

- In light of the filling of the Spirit and our walk in the Spirit.

- In light of all this, *there is a battle to fight in the Christian life.*

b. **Be strong in the Lord and in the power of His might**: Literally, Paul wrote *strengthen yourselves in the Lord*. He probably took the idea from 1 Samuel 30:6, where it is said that David *strengthened himself in the LORD his God*.

i. The detailed teaching of spiritual warfare in this passage presents two essential components. First, you must **be strong in the Lord and in the power of His might**. Then, you must **put on the whole armor of God**. The two are essential, and much teaching on Christian combat neglects the first. If you take a weak man who can barely stand, and put the best armor on him he will still be an ineffective soldier. He will be easily beaten. So equipping for Christian combat must *begin* with the principle, **be strong in the Lord and in the power of His might**.

ii. Before a soldier is given a gun or shown how to fire a missile, he goes through *basic training*. One great purpose for basic training is to build up the recruit's physical strength. It is as if the army says, "Soldier, we are going to give you the best weapons and armor possible. But first we have to make sure that you are strong and that you can use what we give you."

c. **And in the power of His might**: This shows how to get this strength. This does not happen just by saying the words. It is not an incantation or a spell. You can't just walk around saying, "**be strong in the Lord and in the power of His might**" over and over and it will happen. Those kind of mental games can accomplish something, but it certainly wasn't what Paul meant here.

i. **Might** is inherent power or force. A muscular man's big muscles display his might, even if he doesn't use them. It is the *reserve* of strength.

ii. **Power** is the exercise of might. When the muscular man uses his might to bend an iron bar, he uses his power. It means that the reserve of strength is actually in operation.

iii. God has vast reservoirs of **might** that can be realized as **power** in our Christian life. But His **might** does not work in me as I sit passively. His might works in me as I rely on it, and step out to do the work. I can rely on it and do no work. I can do work without relying on it. But both of these fall short. I must rely on His might *and then* do the work.

iv. It is not "I do everything and God does nothing." It is not "I do nothing and God does everything." It is not "I do all I can and God helps with what I can't." Each of those approaches falls short. The key is for me to by faith rely on His **might** – and rely on it more and more – and then do the work.

v. In his great series of sermons on this text, D. Martyn Lloyd-Jones listed many ways in which he believes Christians *wasted* their strength. It was as if they had received some of the available **might** of God, but it simply leaked away like water in a bucket that is full of holes. These are some of the things Lloyd-Jones thought sapped the strength of the Christian:

- Committing to too many spiritual works or things.
- Too much conversation.
- Arguments, debates, wrangling.
- Laziness.
- Too much time in the wrong company.
- Too much foolish talk and joking.
- Love of money and career.
- A desire for respectability and image.
- An unequal yoking with an unbeliever.
- Ungodly entertainment.
- A wrong attitude toward or doubting the Word of God.

vi. "We have to walk on a knife-edge in these matters; you must not become extreme on one side or the other. But you have to be watchful.

And, of course, you can always tell by examining yourself whether your strength is increasing or declining." (Lloyd-Jones)

2. (11) The command for the whole armor of God.

Put on the whole armor of God, that you may be able to stand against the wiles of the devil.

a. **Put on the whole armor of God**: The **armor of God** will be explained more fully in the next passage; but here the emphasis is on **the *whole* armor of God**. God gives the believer a full set of equipment, and He sends us out into battle with everything we need at our disposal.

i. This ancient Greek word for **armor** is used in only one other place in the New Testament. In Luke 11:21-22, Jesus speaks of the *strong man* who is *fully armed*, but is stripped of *all his armor* when a *stronger* one comes and defeats him. We know that Jesus disarmed all principalities and powers (Colossians 2:15).

ii. This armor is **of God** both is the sense that it is from Him, and in the sense that it *is His actual armor*. In the Old Testament, it is the LORD who wears the armor (Isaiah 59:17). He now shares that armor with us. Equipped with God's armor, no wonder we are *more than conquerors* (Romans 8:37).

b. **That you may be able to stand against the wiles of the devil**: We express the strength we have in God by standing **against the wiles of the devil**. Satan's schemes against us come to nothing when we stand against them in the power of God.

i. Stott quoting Simpson: "The tactics of intimidation and insinuation alternate in Satan's plan of campaign. He plays both the bully and the beguiler. Force and fraud form his chief offensive against the camp of the saints."

3. (12) The fact of spiritual warfare.

For we do not wrestle against flesh and blood, but against principalities, against powers, against the rulers of the darkness of this age, against spiritual *hosts* of wickedness in the heavenly *places*.

a. **For we do not wrestle against flesh and blood, but against principalities, against powers**: Paul did not call the believer to *enter into* spiritual warfare. He simply announced it as a fact: **we do not wrestle against flesh and blood, but** (we do wrestle) **against principalities** and so forth. You *are in* a spiritual battle. If you are ignorant or ignore that fact, you probably aren't winning the battle.

b. **For we do not wrestle against flesh and blood**: The fact that our real battle is not against **flesh and blood** is forgotten by many Christians, who put all their efforts in that direction. Paul's idea here is much the same as in 2 Corinthians 10:3-4: *For though we walk in the flesh, we do not war according to the flesh. For the weapons of our warfare are not carnal but mighty in God for pulling down strongholds.*

i. Foulkes says a more literal translation is, *Not for us is the wrestling against flesh and blood.*

c. **Principalities, against powers, against the rulers of the darkness of this age, against spiritual hosts of wickedness in the heavenly places**: Paul used a variety of terms to refer to our spiritual enemies. We should regard them as being on many different levels and of many different ranks, yet they all have one goal: to knock the Christian down from their place of standing.

i. Ephesians 6:11 tells us that all of our warfare is combating *the wiles of the devil*. At the end of the day it is completely irrelevant if the particular opponent we face is a principality, a power, or a ruler of the darkness of this age. Collectively, they are all members of **spiritual hosts of wickedness in the heavenly places**. They are all part of a spiritual army that is organized and established into ranks and is under the headship of Satan who comes against us.

ii. We learn more about these **principalities** and **powers** from other passages in the New Testament.

- Romans 8:38 tells us that **principalities** cannot keep us from God's love. Therefore, there is a *limit* to their power.
- Ephesians 1:20-21 tells us that Jesus is enthroned in heaven, far above all **principalities** and **powers**. Colossians 1:16 tells us that Jesus created **principalities** and **powers**. Colossians 2:10 tells us that Jesus is head over all principalities and power. Therefore, Jesus is not the *opposite* of Satan or principalities.
- Ephesians 3:10-11 tells us that the church makes known the wisdom of God to **principalities** and **powers**. 1 Corinthians 15:24 tells us that **principalities** and **powers** have an end; one day their purpose will be fulfilled and God will no longer let them work. Therefore, God has a *purpose* in allowing their work.
- Colossians 2:15 tells us that Jesus disarmed **principalities** and **powers** at the cross. Therefore, *our victory is rooted in what Jesus did*, not in what we do. It isn't that there is no doing on our part

- but our doing is the *appropriation* and *application* of what Jesus did.

iii. Some interpret the nature of **principalities** and **powers** in purely naturalistic terms. Markus Barth wrote, "We conclude that by principalities and powers Paul means the world of axioms and principles of politics and religion, of economics and society, of morals and biology, of history and culture." Yet this contradicts what Paul says about our battle *not* being against **flesh and blood**.

4. (13) The proper response to the fact of spiritual warfare.

Therefore take up the whole armor of God, that you may be able to withstand in the evil day, and having done all, to stand.

a. **Therefore take up the whole armor of God**: Paul introduced the idea of **the whole armor of God** back in Ephesians 6:11. In the following passage he details the specific items related to the armor of God. In this verse, he simply states what the main purpose of spiritual warfare and the armor of God is.

b. **That you may be able**: Without the strength of God and the protection of spiritual armor, it is impossible to stand against the attacks of spiritual enemies.

c. **That you may be able to withstand in the evil day, and having done all, to stand**: This describes the purpose for the strength of God and the armor of God; what we are to use them for.

i. God has given His people a call, a mission, a course to fulfill. Satan will do his best to stop it. When he attacks and intimidates, we are to **stand**. It is plain that this is Paul's emphasis in Ephesians 6:11 and 6:13. We do the Lord's work and stand against every hint of spiritual opposition.

ii. God gives the Christian a glorious standing to maintain by faith and spiritual warfare:

- We stand in **grace** (Romans 5:2).
- We stand in the **gospel** (1 Corinthians 15:1).
- We stand in **courage** and **strength** (1 Corinthians 16:13).
- We stand in **faith** (2 Corinthians 1:24).
- We stand in Christian **liberty** (Galatians 5:1).
- We stand in Christian **unity** (Philippians 1:27).
- We stand in the **Lord** (Philippians 4:1).

- We should stand **perfect** and **complete** in the will of God (Colossians 4:12).

iii. All in all, there is a lot indicated by that one word, **stand**.

- It means that we are going to be attacked.
- It means that we must not be frightened.
- It means that we must not droop or slouch; nor be uncertain or half-hearted in the fight (no self-pity is allowed).
- It means that we are at our position and alert.
- It means that we do not give even a thought to retreat.

5. (14-15) The spiritual armor to *have*.

Stand therefore, having girded your waist with truth, having put on the breastplate of righteousness, and having shod your feet with the preparation of the gospel of peace;

a. **Stand therefore**: We can only **stand** when we are equipped with the armor God has given us in Jesus Christ. Each aspect of this symbolic armor answers to a specific dynamic within the Christian life that enables us to stand against spiritual attack.

i. Paul wrote this while in the custody of Roman soldiers. It was easy for him to look at the equipment of his guards and see how God has equipped the believer.

ii. The order in which the pieces of armor are described is the order in which the soldier would normally put them on.

b. **Having girded your waist with truth**: **Truth** is symbolically represented as a belt which both protects our abdomen and gathers up our garments so that we can fight effectively.

i. Strictly, the belt is not part of the armor, but before the armor can be put on, the garments underneath must be gathered together.

ii. "The soldier might be furnished with every other part of his equipment, and yet, wanting the girdle, would neither be fully accoutered nor securely armed. His *belt*... was no mere adornment of the soldier, but an essential part of his equipment... it was of especial use in keeping other parts in place, and in securing the proper soldierly attitude and freedom of movement." (Salmond)

iii. When a man sat down and was relaxed, he took off his belt. Putting on the belt prepared for action, it freed one for movement, and it put a soldier in a battle frame of mind. The same idea was communicated by Jesus in Luke 12:35-36.

iv. The belt of truth puts on the Biblical beliefs of the Christians as a whole, what other passages call *the faith*. Many people believe that the church will never go forward until it takes off this belt of truth, but that is completely wrong. This is part of the armor to *have*, which is a foundation to live upon all the time, our understanding of and confidence in the basic doctrines of the faith.

c. **Having put on the breastplate of righteousness: Righteousness** is represented as a **breastplate** which provides essential protection for the most vital organs. We can no sooner battle against spiritual enemies in our *own* righteousness than a soldier can effectively fight without his breastplate.

i. This is not our own earned righteousness, not a feeling of righteousness, but a righteousness received by faith in Jesus. It gives us a general sense of confidence, an awareness of our standing and position.

ii. "Thank God for experiences, but do not rely on them. You do not put on the 'breastplate of experiences', you put on the breastplate of 'righteousness.' " (Lloyd-Jones)

iii. We are sometimes tempted to say to the devil, "Look at all I've done for the Lord." But that is shaky ground, though sometimes it feels good. It is shaky because feelings and experiences change quickly. God's righteousness isn't. The breastplate of righteousness is your best defense against the sense of spiritual depression and gloom that comes against us.

d. **Having shod your feet with the preparation of the gospel of peace**: The **preparation of the gospel** is represented as the protective shoes (or sandals) worn by Roman soldiers. No one can fight effectively or effectively go about his business without this equipment.

i. **Preparation** is a word meaning "a prepared foundation." The gospel provides the footing for everything we do. However powerful the rest of your body is, if you are wounded in your feet you are easy prey for the enemy.

ii. On the shoes: "Josephus described them as 'shoes thickly studded with sharp nails'... so as to ensure a good grip. The military successes both of Alexander the Great and of Julius Caesar were due in large measure to their armies' being well shod and thus able to undertake long marches at incredible speed over rough terrain." (Wood)

iii. Paul had Isaiah 52:7 in mind when he refered to **having shod your feet**: *How beautiful upon the mountains are the feet of him who brings*

good news, who proclaims peace, who brings glad tidings of good things,
who proclaims salvation, who says to Zion, "Your God reigns!"

iv. The idea of **preparation** is really *readiness*. We must be mobile,
flexible, and ready with the truth. This is a place to *have* in the Christian
life, to live in constant readiness and flexibility.

6. (16-18) The spiritual armor to *take*.

Above all, taking the shield of faith with which you will be able to
quench all the fiery darts of the wicked one. And take the helmet of
salvation, and the sword of the Spirit, which is the word of God;

a. **Above all**: This really has the idea of "in addition to the previous," and
it applies to each of the three pieces of armor that follow. It isn't the idea,
these parts of the armor are more important than the others.

b. **Taking the shield of faith**: Ephesians 6:13-14 tells us of armor *to*
have. Some of the armor we must wear all the time and have as a standing
foundation. Therefore *having* comes first. We must be rooted in the belt
of truth, the breastplate of righteousness, and the "combat boots" of the
gospel. Yet now Paul will deal with aspects of the armor we are to *take* at
the necessary moments of spiritual warfare and opportunity.

c. **Taking the shield of faith with which you will be able to quench**
all the fiery darts of the wicked one: **Faith** is represented as a **shield**,
protecting us from the **fiery darts of the wicked one**, those persistent
efforts of demonic foes to weaken us through fear and unbelief.

i. The **shield** Paul describes is not the small round one, but the large,
oblong shield that could protect the whole body. In ancient warfare,
these **fiery darts** were launched in great numbers at the beginning of
an attack. The idea was not only to injure the enemy, but to shoot at
him at all sides with a massive number of arrows, and thus to confuse
and panic the enemy.

ii. "Even when such a missile was caught by the shield and did not
penetrate to the body, says Livy, it caused panic, because it was thrown
when well alight and its motion through the air made it blaze most
fiercely, so that the soldier was tempted to get rid of his burning shield
and expose himself to the enemy's spear-thrusts. But the *shield of faith*
not only catches the incendiary devices but extinguishes them." (Bruce)

iii. Thoughts, feelings, imaginations, fears, and lies – all of these can be
hurled at us by Satan as **fiery darts**. **Faith** turns them back.

d. **And take the helmet of salvation**: In the ancient world this usually
was a leather cap studded with metal for extra strength. Often some kind
of plume or decoration was added, perhaps to identify the solider to his

regiment. **Salvation** is pictured as this kind of **helmet**, protecting an essential part of the body. A soldier would be foolish to go into battle without his **helmet**.

> i. 1 Thessalonians 5:8 speaks of the helmet of salvation in connection to *the hope of salvation*. The helmet of salvation protects us against discouragement, against the desire to give up, giving us hope not only in knowing that we *are* saved, but that we *will be* saved. It is the assurance that God will triumph.

> ii. One of Satan's most effective weapons against us is *discouragement*. When we are properly equipped with the helmet of salvation, it's hard to stay discouraged.

e. **The sword of the Spirit, which is the word of God**: The idea is that the *Spirit provides a sword* for you, and that *sword is the word of God*. To effectively use the sword of the Spirit, we can't regard the Bible as a book of magic charms or tie one around our neck the way that garlic is said to drive away vampires.

> i. To effectively use the sword, we must regard it **as the word of God - *which is the word of God*.** If we are not confident in the inspiration of Scripture, that the sword really came from the Spirit, then we will not use it effectively at all.

> ii. But we must also take the sword of the Spirit in the sense of depending that He helps us to use it. Not only did the Spirit *give* us the Scriptures, but also He makes them alive to us (or us alive to them), and He equips us with the right thrust of the sword at the right time.

> iii. Think of a soldier or a gladiator in training, practicing sword thrusts and moves and positions. Now, he must practice them ahead of time and if he is a superior fighter and has a great fighting instinct, at the time of battle he will instantly recall which thrust, which position suits the precise moment. He will never be able to use the thrust in the fight if he has not first practiced it; but he still needs to make the move at the moment.

> iv. Therefore, effectively using the sword takes practice. The great example of this was Jesus combating the temptation of Satan in the wilderness.

7. (18-20) How to use spiritual strength and the armor of God.

Praying always with all prayer and supplication in the Spirit, being watchful to this end with all perseverance and supplication for all the saints; and for me, that utterance may be given to me, that I may open my mouth boldly to make known the mystery of the gospel, for which

I am an ambassador in chains; that in it I may speak boldly, as I ought to speak.

a. **Praying always with all prayer**: The idea is *all kinds of prayer* or *prayer upon prayer*. We should use every kind of prayer we can think of. Group prayer, individual prayer, silent prayer, shouting prayer, walking prayer, kneeling prayer, eloquent prayer, groaning prayer, constant prayer, fervent prayer - *just pray*.

i. We can say that it is through prayer that spiritual strength and the armor of God go to work. In theory, the prayerless Christian can be strong and wearing all the armor; but never accomplishes anything because he fails to goes into battle through prayer.

ii. Often we just don't pray because we are simply overconfident in our own abilities. Winston Churchill said to Britain in the early days of the Second World War: "I must drop one word of caution, for next to cowardice and treachery, overconfidence leading to neglect and slothfulness, is the worst of wartime crimes."

b. **For all the saints**: We can battle spiritually not only on our own behalf, but also on the behalf of others. The soldier isn't only concerned for his or her own safety. He feels an instinct to protect and to battle on behalf of *others*.

c. **And for me, that utterance may be given to me**: After bringing up the idea that spiritual warfare can be waged on behalf of others, Paul asks his readers to pray for him.

d. **Boldly to make known the mystery of the gospel**: Paul could have asked prayer for many things, but he wanted his readers to pray for this. He probably had in mind his upcoming defense before Caesar.

i. We *could* imagine Paul asking for many things, such as relief from his imprisonment or for other comforts. But his heart and mind were fixed on his responsibility as an **ambassador** of the gospel.

e. **That utterance may be given to me**: The idea behind **utterance** is clear speaking. Added to **boldly**, Paul asked for prayer that he might proclaim the gospel both *clearly* and with a *fearless* power. It is easy to neglect one or the other.

f. **I am an ambassador in chains**: Of course, the ancient Greek word for **chains** meant a prisoner's shackles. But it could also be used for the gold adornment worn around the neck and wrists of the wealthy and powerful. On special occasions, ambassadors wore such chains to show the riches, power, and dignity of the government they represented. Paul considers his prisoner's chains to actually be the glorious adornment of an **ambassador** of Jesus Christ.

C. Conclusion to the letter.

1. (21-22) The sending of Tychicus.

But that you also may know my affairs *and* how I am doing, Tychicus, a beloved brother and faithful minister in the Lord, will make all things known to you; whom I have sent to you for this very purpose, that you may know our affairs, and *that* he may comfort your hearts.

a. **Tychicus, a beloved brother and faithful minister**: Tychicus was an associate of Paul's mentioned in other letters (Acts 20:4, Colossians 4:7, 2 Timothy 4:12, Titus 3:12). Tychicus seems to have been often used by Paul as a messenger (**that you may know our affairs**).

b. **That he may comfort your hearts**: Paul wanted Tychicus to comfort the Ephesians (and everyone else who read the letter) about Paul's condition during his imprisonment in Rome.

2. (23-24) Final words.

Peace to the brethren, and love with faith, from God the Father and the Lord Jesus Christ. Grace *be* with all those who love our Lord Jesus Christ in sincerity. Amen.

a. **Peace to the brethren... Grace be with all those who love our Lord Jesus**: Paul concluded the letter as he began it, with reference to **grace** and **peace**, these two essential cornerstones for the Christian life.

b. **All those who love our Lord Jesus Christ in sincerity**: In sincerity is literally "in uncorruptness." The idea may well be *with an undying love.* Our love for the Lord should be undying.

c. **Grace be with all those who love our Lord Jesus Christ in sincerity**: Paul ended by pronouncing a blessing, which was his way of helping the Ephesians to walk in every spiritual blessing in the heavenly places in Christ. (Ephesians 1:3)

Bibliography - Galatians & Ephesians

Alford, Henry *The New Testament for English Readers, Volume II, Part I* (London: Rivingtons, 1869)

Barclay, William *The Letters to the Galatians and the Ephesians* (Philadelphia: Westminster Press, 1975)

Boice, James Montgomery "Galatians," *The Expositor's Bible Commentary, Volume 10* (Grand Rapids, Michigan: Zondervan, 1976)

Bruce, Frederick Fyvie T*he Epistles to the Colossians, to Philemon, and to the Ephesians* (Grand Rapids, Michigan: Eerdmans, 1984)

Calvin, John *The Epistles of Paul the Apostle to the Galatians, Ephesians, Philippians and Colossians*, translated by T.H.L. Parker (Grand Rapids, Michigan: Eerdmans, 1965)

Clarke, Adam *The New Testament with A Commentary and Critical Notes, Volume II* (New York: Eaton & Mains, 1831)

Cole, R. Alan *The Epistle of Paul to the Galatians* (Grand Rapids, Michigan: Eerdmans, 1988)

Foulkes, Francis *The Epistle of Paul to the Ephesians* (Grand Rapids, Michigan: Eerdmans, 1988)

Fung, Ronald Y.K. *The Epistle to the Galatians* (Grand Rapids, Michigan: Eerdmans, 1988)

Gaebelein, Arno C. *God's Masterpiece* (Glasgow: Pickering and Inglis, 1913)

Lightfoot, J.B. *St. Paul's Epistle to the Galatians* (Lynn, Massachusetts: Hendrickson Publishers, 1982)

Lloyd Jones, D. Martyn *God's Ultimate Purpose* (Grand Rapids, Michigan: Baker Book House, 1980)

Lloyd Jones, D. Martyn: *Life in the Spirit, In Marriage, Home & Work* (Grand Rapids, Michigan: Baker Book House, 1975)

Lloyd Jones, D. Martyn *The Christian Warfare* (Grand Rapids, Michigan: Baker Book House, 1981)

Luther, Martin *A Commentary on St. Paul's Epistle to the Galatians*, translated by Theodore Graebner, D.D. (Grand Rapids, Michigan: Zondervan, ?)

Meyer, F.B. *Our Daily Homily* (Westwood, New Jersey: Revell, 1966)

Morgan, G. Campbell *An Exposition of the Whole Bible* (Old Tappan, New Jersey: Revell, 1959)

Morgan, G. Campbell *Searchlights from the Word* (New York: Revell, 1926)

Morris, Leon *Galatians: Paul's Charter of Christian Freedom* (Downers Grove, Illinois: InterVarsity Press, 1996)

Moule, Handley C. G. *Ephesian Studies* (London: Pickering and Inglis, ?)

Poole, Matthew *A Commentary on the Holy Bible, Volume III: Matthew-Revelation* (London: Banner of Truth Trust, 1969, first published in 1685)

Rendall, Frederic "The Epistle to the Galatians," *The Expositor's Greek New Testament, Volume III* (London: Hodder and Stoughton, ?)

Salmond, S.D.F. "The Epistle to the Ephesians," *The Expositor's Greek New Testament, Volume III* (London: Hodder and Stoughton, ?)

Smith, Chuck *New Testament Study Guide* (Costa Mesa, California: The Word for Today, 1982)

Spurgeon, Charles Haddon *The New Park Street Pulpit, Volumes 1-6* and *The Metropolitan Tabernacle Pulpit, Volumes 7-63* (Pasadena, Texas: Pilgrim Publications, 1990)

Stott, John R.W. *God's New Society, The Message of Ephesians* (Downer's Grove, Illinois: InterVarsity Press, 1979)

Stott, John R.W. *The Message of Galatians* (Leicester, England: Inter-Varsity Press, 1986)

Trapp, John *A Commentary on the Old and New Testaments, Volume Five* (Eureka, California: Tanski Publications, 1997)

Vaughan, W. Curtis *The Letter to the Ephesians* (Nashville, Tennessee: Convention Press, 1963)

Wiersbe, Warren W. *The Bible Exposition Commentary, Volume 1* (Wheaton, Illinois: Victor Books, 1989)

Wood, A. Skevington "Ephesians," *The Expositor's Bible Commentary, Volume 11* (Grand Rapids, Michigan: Zondervan, 1978)

Wuest, Kenneth S. *Wuest's Word Studies In the Greek New Testament, Volume One* (Grand Rapids, Michigan: Eerdmans, 1973)

As the years pass I love the work of studying, learning, and teaching the Bible more than ever. I'm so grateful that God is faithful to meet me in His Word.

With both pleasure and gratitude, this book is dedicated to my brother Randy Guzik, a wonderful example of a man saved by grace through faith.

This book marks another happy giving of thanks for the proofreading help of Martina Patrick. Tim and Martina remain faithful friends and partners in God's work, and we especially appreciate all their prayers and support over the years. Thanks also to Annie Johnson for her proofreading help in preparing this commentary. Thanks to Brian Procedo for the cover design and all the graphics work.

Most especially, thanks to my wife Inga-Lill. She is my loved and valued partner in life and in service to God and His people.

David Guzik

David Guzik's Bible commentary is regularly used and trusted by many thousands who want to know the Bible better. Pastors, teachers, class leaders, and everyday Christians find his commentary helpful for their own understanding and explanation of the Bible. David and his wife Inga-Lill live in Santa Barbara, California.

You can email David at
david@enduringword.com

For more resources by David Guzik,
go to www.enduringword.com

www.ingramcontent.com/pod-product-compliance
Lightning Source LLC
LaVergne TN
LVHW011154080426
835508LV00007B/402